Microsoft Teams

Mastering Microsoft Teams: A Comprehensive Guide

Kiet Huynh

Table of Contents

CHAPTER I
Introduction to Microsoft Teams

1.1 What is Microsoft Teams?

1.1.1 Overview of Microsoft Teams

Microsoft Teams is a unified communication and collaboration platform that combines persistent workplace chat, video meetings, file storage, and application integration. It is part of the Microsoft 365 suite of productivity tools and is designed to help teams stay organized, collaborate more efficiently, and communicate seamlessly. Since its launch in 2017, Microsoft Teams has rapidly evolved to become a cornerstone of modern digital workplaces, catering to various industries and team dynamics.

A Unified Platform for Collaboration

At its core, Microsoft Teams provides a centralized hub where team members can engage in conversations, share files, and work together on projects. This integration streamlines workflows by bringing all necessary tools and resources into one platform, reducing the need to switch between multiple applications. The unified nature of Teams enhances productivity by allowing users to focus on their tasks without the distraction of managing several different tools.

Persistent Chat and Conversation Threads

One of the standout features of Microsoft Teams is its persistent chat functionality. Unlike traditional email chains or ephemeral chat apps, Teams retains conversation history, allowing team members to revisit discussions, decisions, and shared content at any time. This persistent nature ensures that important information is always accessible and that new team members can quickly get up to speed by reviewing past conversations.

Teams supports both individual and group chats, providing flexibility in how communications are handled. Users can create dedicated channels within a team for specific topics, projects, or departments, ensuring that discussions are organized and easily navigable. This structure helps reduce information overload and makes it simple to locate relevant conversations and documents.

Integrated Video and Voice Communication

In addition to text-based chat, Microsoft Teams offers robust video and voice communication capabilities. Users can initiate video calls and voice calls directly from the platform, facilitating real-time collaboration regardless of geographical location. The integration of these communication methods into a single platform eliminates the need for separate video conferencing tools and ensures a seamless transition between different modes of communication.

Teams meetings support a wide range of features designed to enhance the virtual meeting experience. These include screen sharing, meeting recording, and live captions, which improve accessibility and make it easier to follow along with discussions. The ability to schedule and join meetings directly from the Teams interface further streamlines the process, making it convenient for users to manage their calendar and commitments.

File Storage and Collaboration

Microsoft Teams integrates tightly with OneDrive and SharePoint, providing robust file storage and collaboration capabilities. Users can upload, share, and collaborate on documents within the platform, with changes synchronized in real time. This integration ensures that everyone is working on the latest version of a document, reducing the risk of version control issues.

Files shared within a team or channel are automatically stored in a SharePoint site associated with that team, providing a structured and secure environment for document management. This seamless integration with SharePoint also means that users can leverage SharePoint's advanced document management features, such as version history, metadata, and workflow automation, directly within Teams.

App Integration and Customization

One of the most powerful aspects of Microsoft Teams is its ability to integrate with a wide range of third-party apps and services. The Teams app store offers a vast selection of integrations, from project management tools like Trello and Asana to customer relationship management (CRM) systems like Salesforce. These integrations allow users to customize their Teams environment to fit their specific workflows and needs.

In addition to third-party apps, Teams also supports custom app development. Organizations can create bespoke integrations and workflows using Microsoft's developer tools and APIs, tailoring the platform to meet unique business requirements. This flexibility ensures that Teams can adapt to the evolving needs of any organization, providing a scalable and future-proof solution.

Security and Compliance

Security and compliance are critical considerations for any collaboration platform, and Microsoft Teams excels in this area. As part of the Microsoft 365 suite, Teams benefits from the robust security infrastructure that underpins all Microsoft services. This includes data encryption in transit and at rest, multi-factor authentication (MFA), and advanced threat protection.

Teams also supports a wide range of compliance certifications and standards, such as GDPR, HIPAA, and ISO/IEC 27001, ensuring that organizations can meet their regulatory requirements. Features like data loss prevention (DLP), eDiscovery, and legal hold help organizations protect sensitive information and respond effectively to legal and compliance obligations.

Accessibility and Inclusivity

Microsoft Teams is designed with accessibility and inclusivity in mind, ensuring that it can be used by individuals with a wide range of abilities. Features like live captions, screen reader support, and keyboard shortcuts make the platform more accessible to users with disabilities. Microsoft's commitment to accessibility ensures that Teams can be used effectively by all members of an organization, promoting a more inclusive workplace.

Continuous Improvement and Innovation

Microsoft is committed to continuously improving and innovating within the Teams platform. Regular updates introduce new features, enhancements, and integrations, ensuring that Teams remains at the forefront of digital collaboration tools. Microsoft's engagement with its user community, through feedback mechanisms and user forums, helps guide the development roadmap and ensures that the platform evolves in line with user needs and industry trends.

In summary, Microsoft Teams is a powerful, flexible, and secure collaboration platform that brings together chat, video, file sharing, and app integration into a single, unified environment. Its robust feature set, combined with seamless integration with other Microsoft 365 tools, makes it an indispensable tool for modern teams looking to enhance their productivity and collaboration. Whether used for daily communication, project management, or remote work, Microsoft Teams provides the tools and capabilities needed to succeed in today's fast-paced digital workplace.

1.1.2 Key Features and Benefits

Microsoft Teams, a hub for teamwork in Microsoft 365, is designed to bring together people, conversations, and content. It integrates with the productivity apps of Microsoft 365 and offers a vast array of features that enhance communication, collaboration, and productivity. Understanding these features and their benefits is crucial for effectively leveraging Teams in any organization.

1. Chat Functionality

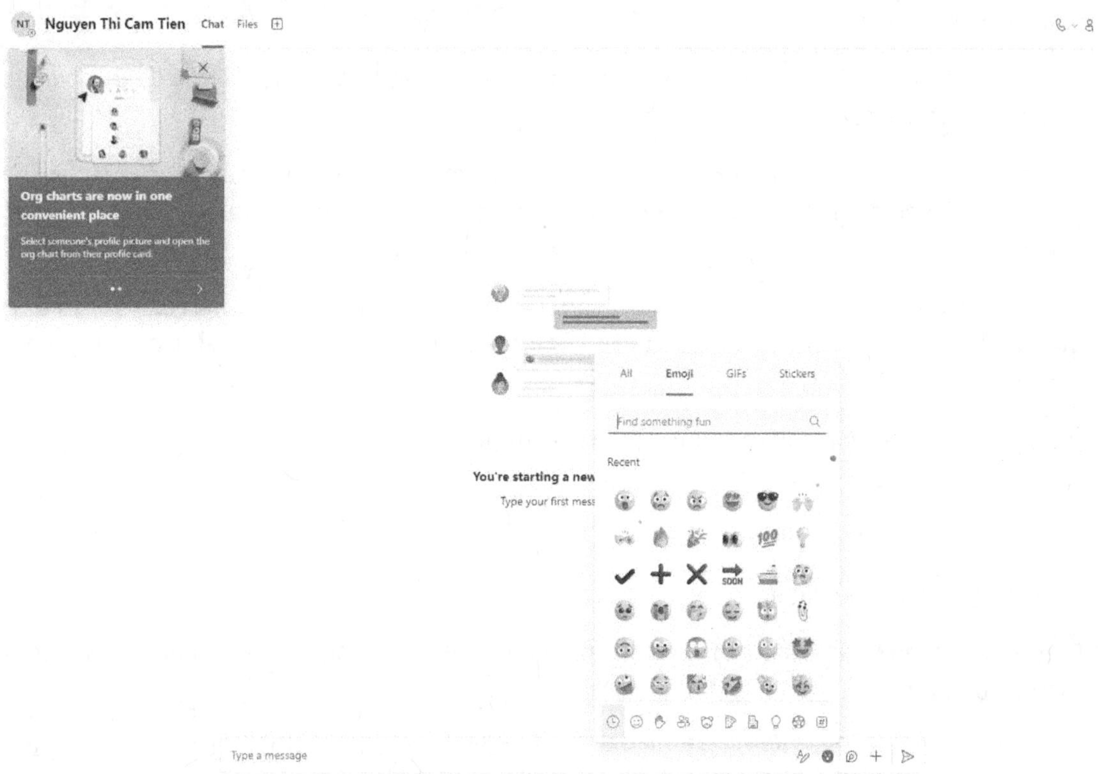

One of the core features of Microsoft Teams is its robust chat functionality, which supports both private one-on-one conversations and group chats.

- Real-time Messaging: Teams allows real-time text communication, which is essential for quick exchanges of information and instant decision-making. Users can send messages, files, and images seamlessly.

- Threaded Conversations: This feature helps in organizing chats by topic or conversation. Threaded conversations keep discussions focused and make it easier to follow the flow of communication.

- Rich Text Editing: Users can format their messages with bold, italics, bullet points, and more, ensuring clear and well-structured communication.

- Emojis, GIFs, and Stickers: These elements add a layer of personalization and fun to the communication, helping to build rapport and a sense of team culture.

2. Channels

Channels are dedicated sections within a team to keep conversations organized by specific topics, projects, or disciplines.

- Focused Discussions: Channels allow teams to create focused discussion spaces for different projects or topics, reducing clutter and making it easier to find relevant information.

- Channel Tabs: Each channel can have its own tabs for files, apps, and tools relevant to that channel. This customization helps in organizing resources efficiently and accessing them quickly.

- Pinned Posts: Important announcements or information can be pinned to the top of the channel, ensuring visibility and quick access.

3. Meetings and Video Conferencing

Teams offers a powerful suite of meeting and video conferencing tools that enable seamless virtual collaboration.

- Scheduling Meetings: Users can schedule meetings directly within Teams, integrating with Outlook calendars to streamline the process.

- Joining Meetings: With a single click, users can join meetings from various devices, ensuring flexibility and accessibility.

- Meeting Recording and Transcription: Meetings can be recorded and transcriptions generated automatically, making it easy to revisit and review discussions and decisions.

- Breakout Rooms: This feature allows participants to be split into smaller groups for focused discussions or workshops, enhancing engagement and collaboration.

- Live Events: Teams supports large-scale webinars and live events, enabling organizations to reach a wider audience.

4. File Sharing and Collaboration

The integration of Microsoft Teams with OneDrive and SharePoint provides robust file sharing and collaboration capabilities.

- Real-time Co-authoring: Multiple users can work on the same document simultaneously, making edits and seeing changes in real-time. This feature supports Word, Excel, PowerPoint, and other Office apps.

- File Versioning: Teams tracks the version history of files, allowing users to see previous versions and revert changes if necessary.

- Secure Sharing: Files can be shared securely within the team or with external partners, with control over permissions and access levels.

5. Integrations and Apps

Teams is highly extensible, supporting integrations with a wide array of third-party apps and services, as well as custom apps developed for specific needs.

- Office 365 Integration: Seamless integration with Office 365 apps like Outlook, OneNote, Planner, and Power BI enhances productivity by bringing all essential tools into one platform.

- Third-party Apps: Teams supports integration with hundreds of third-party apps like Trello, Asana, GitHub, and more, allowing teams to customize their workspace to fit their workflow.

- Custom Apps: Organizations can develop custom apps and bots to meet their unique requirements, integrating them into Teams to streamline processes and improve efficiency.

6. Security and Compliance

Microsoft Teams offers enterprise-grade security and compliance features, making it a reliable choice for organizations of all sizes.

- Data Encryption: Teams uses encryption in transit and at rest, ensuring that data is secure at all times.

- Compliance Standards: Teams meets various compliance standards such as GDPR, HIPAA, and more, making it suitable for use in highly regulated industries.

- Advanced Threat Protection: Built-in security features protect against malware, phishing, and other cyber threats, safeguarding sensitive information.

- Auditing and Reporting: Teams provides robust auditing and reporting capabilities, enabling administrators to monitor usage and ensure compliance with organizational policies.

7. Mobile Accessibility

The Teams mobile app ensures that team members can stay connected and productive even when they are on the go.

- Cross-Platform Support: The app is available on iOS and Android, providing a consistent experience across devices.

- Push Notifications: Users receive instant notifications for messages, meetings, and updates, ensuring they stay informed and responsive.

- Mobile Collaboration: The app supports all core features of Teams, including chat, meetings, and file collaboration, allowing users to work seamlessly from their mobile devices.

8. Customization and Extensibility

Teams can be tailored to meet the specific needs of different teams and departments within an organization.

- Custom Tabs and Bots: Custom tabs can be added to channels for quick access to frequently used files and apps. Bots can automate routine tasks and provide information or assistance to users.

- Personalized Settings: Users can personalize their Teams experience by customizing notifications, themes, and settings to match their preferences and workflow.

- App Templates: Microsoft provides app templates that can be customized and deployed within Teams, enabling organizations to quickly create and implement tailored solutions.

9. Task Management and Planning

Teams integrates with task management tools, enhancing productivity and project management capabilities.

- Microsoft Planner Integration: Planner integration allows teams to create, assign, and track tasks within Teams, providing visibility into project progress and deadlines.

- To-Do Lists: The Microsoft To-Do integration enables users to manage their personal tasks and to-do lists within Teams, ensuring nothing falls through the cracks.

- Task Notifications: Users receive notifications for task assignments, updates, and deadlines, helping them stay on top of their responsibilities.

10. Collaboration Beyond the Organization

Teams supports external collaboration, allowing organizations to work seamlessly with clients, partners, and vendors.

- Guest Access: External users can be added as guests in Teams, enabling them to participate in chats, meetings, and file collaboration while maintaining security controls.

- Federation with Other Organizations: Teams supports federation, allowing users to communicate and collaborate with users in other organizations that also use Teams.

- Shared Channels: Shared channels enable cross-organizational collaboration by allowing teams from different organizations to work together in a single channel, simplifying communication and coordination.

11. Analytics and Insights

Teams provides analytics and insights to help organizations understand usage patterns and improve productivity.

- Usage Reports: Teams administrators can access detailed reports on user activity, meeting participation, and app usage, helping them identify trends and areas for improvement.

- Productivity Insights: Microsoft Viva Insights integrates with Teams to provide personalized recommendations and insights to improve productivity and well-being.

- Advanced Analytics: Power BI integration allows organizations to create custom dashboards and reports, providing deep insights into team performance and project progress.

Benefits of Using Microsoft Teams

The features of Microsoft Teams collectively offer numerous benefits, making it a powerful tool for modern organizations.

1. Enhanced Communication

Teams brings together all forms of communication—chat, meetings, calls, and file sharing—into one platform, simplifying communication and reducing the need for multiple tools.

- Centralized Communication: Having a single platform for all communication reduces confusion and ensures that important information is easily accessible.

- Improved Responsiveness: Instant messaging and notifications help teams respond quickly to queries and issues, enhancing overall efficiency.

- Seamless Collaboration: Integrated communication tools support real-time collaboration, enabling teams to work together more effectively.

2. Increased Productivity

Teams' integration with Microsoft 365 apps and services streamlines workflows and enhances productivity.

- Time Savings: Features like real-time co-authoring, integrated task management, and automated workflows save time and reduce manual effort.

- Improved Focus: Customizable notifications and organized channels help users stay focused on their tasks and avoid distractions.

- Streamlined Processes: Integrations with third-party apps and custom bots automate routine tasks, freeing up time for more strategic work.

3. Flexibility and Accessibility

Teams supports flexible working arrangements and ensures that team members can stay connected from anywhere.

- Remote Work: With robust mobile and desktop apps, Teams enables remote work, supporting distributed teams and flexible working hours.

- Cross-Device Consistency: A consistent experience across devices ensures that users can seamlessly switch between their desktop, laptop, tablet, and smartphone.

- Accessibility Features: Teams includes features like screen readers, keyboard shortcuts, and live captions, making it accessible to all users, including those with disabilities.

4. Enhanced Security and Compliance

Teams provides enterprise-grade security and compliance features, giving organizations confidence in their data protection and regulatory adherence.

- Data Protection: Encryption, advanced threat protection, and secure sharing ensure that sensitive information is protected.

- Regulatory Compliance: Built-in compliance features help organizations meet regulatory requirements and maintain data governance.

- Control and Oversight: Administrators have granular control over permissions and access, ensuring that data is only accessible to authorized users.

5. Improved Collaboration and Teamwork

Teams fosters a collaborative environment, encouraging teamwork and improving organizational culture.

- Engagement: Features like emojis, GIFs, and stickers make communication fun and engaging, building a positive team culture.

- Transparency: Open channels and threaded conversations promote transparency and ensure that everyone is informed and involved in discussions.

- Support for Diverse Teams: Teams supports collaboration across different time zones and geographies, making it ideal for global organizations.

Conclusion

Microsoft Teams is a comprehensive collaboration platform that brings together communication, file sharing, task management, and more. Its robust feature set and integration with Microsoft 365 make it an essential tool for modern organizations, enhancing communication, productivity, and collaboration while ensuring security and compliance. By leveraging the key features and benefits of Teams, organizations can foster a more connected, productive, and engaged workforce.

1.1.3 Microsoft Teams vs. Other Collaboration Tools

In the modern workplace, collaboration tools are essential for enhancing productivity, fostering communication, and ensuring efficient project management. Microsoft Teams stands out among other collaboration tools for several reasons, but to fully appreciate its strengths, it is important to compare it with other leading tools in the market, such as Slack, Zoom, and Google Workspace. This section will explore how Microsoft Teams compares in terms of features, integrations, usability, security, and overall value.

Features

Microsoft Teams offers a comprehensive set of features designed to facilitate communication and collaboration within organizations. It includes chat functionalities, video conferencing, file sharing, and integration with a wide range of Microsoft Office 365 applications. Teams also support threaded conversations, which help keep discussions organized. The ability to create different channels within a team for specific topics or projects is another key feature that enhances organization and focus.

Slack, one of the most popular collaboration tools, also provides robust chat functionalities with support for threaded conversations, file sharing, and app integrations. However, Slack's primary strength lies in its messaging capabilities and its extensive library of third-party app integrations, which exceeds that of Microsoft Teams. Slack's interface is highly customizable, allowing users to tailor their workspace to their needs.

Zoom is renowned for its video conferencing capabilities. While it also supports chat and file sharing, its primary focus is on providing high-quality video meetings, webinars, and virtual events. Zoom offers features like breakout rooms, virtual backgrounds, and comprehensive host controls, which make it ideal for virtual meetings and online events.

Google Workspace (formerly G Suite) integrates Google Meet for video conferencing, Google Chat for messaging, and Google Drive for file sharing and collaboration. Google Workspace excels in its seamless integration with other Google services, such as Gmail, Calendar, and Docs, providing a unified experience across its suite of tools.

Integrations

Microsoft Teams integrates deeply with Office 365 applications such as Word, Excel, PowerPoint, SharePoint, OneDrive, and Outlook. This tight integration allows users to collaborate on documents in real-time, schedule meetings directly from Outlook, and manage files efficiently through SharePoint and OneDrive. Additionally, Teams supports integration with various third-party apps and services, including project management tools, CRM systems, and social media platforms.

Slack offers a vast ecosystem of integrations with over 2,000 third-party apps, including popular tools like Trello, Asana, Salesforce, and Google Drive. Slack's open API allows developers to create custom integrations tailored to specific business needs, making it a flexible choice for organizations that rely on a diverse set of tools.

Zoom integrates with a variety of productivity and collaboration tools, including Microsoft Teams, Slack, Google Calendar, and Outlook. These integrations enhance scheduling, meeting management, and collaboration, although Zoom's primary focus remains on video communication.

Google Workspace benefits from seamless integration with Google's extensive ecosystem. Google Meet, Chat, and Drive are natively integrated with Gmail, Calendar, Docs, Sheets, and Slides, allowing for efficient collaboration and communication. The integration with Google AI also adds value by providing features such as smart scheduling and predictive text.

Usability

Microsoft Teams is designed with a user-friendly interface that emphasizes ease of navigation. The layout is intuitive, with clear tabs for chats, teams, meetings, and files. The ability to create dedicated channels for different projects or topics helps keep discussions organized and accessible. The learning curve for Teams is relatively short, especially for users already familiar with Microsoft Office products.

Slack is also known for its user-friendly interface, which is clean, modern, and highly customizable. Slack's interface focuses on ease of communication, with channels and direct messages prominently featured. Users can easily customize their notifications, themes, and sidebar layout to suit their preferences, making Slack a favorite for many teams.

Zoom prioritizes simplicity in its design, with a straightforward interface that makes it easy to schedule, join, and manage meetings. The controls for video and audio settings are easily accessible, and the platform offers extensive in-meeting features such as screen sharing, recording, and chat.

Google Workspace provides a consistent and familiar user experience across its suite of applications. The interfaces of Google Meet, Chat, and Drive are straightforward and designed for ease of use. The integration with other Google services further simplifies navigation and enhances productivity.

Security

Microsoft Teams places a strong emphasis on security and compliance, leveraging Microsoft's enterprise-grade security infrastructure. Teams data is encrypted both in transit and at rest, and the platform supports multi-factor authentication (MFA) to enhance security. Additionally, Teams complies with a wide range of industry standards and regulations, including GDPR, HIPAA, and ISO 27001.

Slack also prioritizes security, offering features such as data encryption, MFA, and single sign-on (SSO). Slack complies with various industry standards and regulations, including GDPR and ISO/IEC 27001. The platform provides enterprise-grade security controls to protect user data and ensure compliance.

Zoom has made significant improvements in its security features following earlier concerns. The platform now includes end-to-end encryption for meetings, MFA, and advanced host controls to manage participant permissions. Zoom complies with standards such as GDPR and SOC 2, ensuring robust security for users.

Google Workspace leverages Google's advanced security infrastructure, providing encryption for data in transit and at rest, MFA, and SSO. Google Workspace complies with numerous industry standards and regulations, including GDPR, HIPAA, and ISO 27001, ensuring comprehensive security and compliance for users.

Overall Value

Microsoft Teams offers exceptional value, particularly for organizations already using Office 365. The deep integration with Office applications, combined with comprehensive communication and collaboration features, makes Teams a powerful tool for enhancing productivity and teamwork. The platform's security and compliance capabilities further add to its value for enterprises.

Slack provides excellent value for teams that prioritize messaging and app integrations. Its extensive library of third-party integrations and highly customizable interface make it a versatile tool for a wide range of organizations. Slack's focus on enhancing communication and collaboration through a user-friendly platform is a key strength.

Zoom delivers strong value for organizations that require reliable and high-quality video conferencing. Its extensive meeting features and user-friendly interface make it an ideal choice for virtual meetings, webinars, and online events. Zoom's focus on providing a seamless video communication experience sets it apart.

Google Workspace offers great value through its seamless integration of communication and productivity tools. The unified experience across Gmail, Calendar, Meet, Chat, and Drive enhances efficiency and collaboration. Google Workspace's AI-powered features and robust security further contribute to its overall value.

Conclusion

In conclusion, while each collaboration tool has its unique strengths, Microsoft Teams stands out for its comprehensive feature set, deep integration with Office 365, robust security, and overall usability. Teams is particularly well-suited for organizations that rely heavily on Microsoft products and seek a unified platform for communication, collaboration, and productivity. Whether you are a small business, a large enterprise, or an educational institution, Microsoft Teams offers a versatile and powerful solution for enhancing team collaboration and achieving business goals.

1.2 Getting Started with Microsoft Teams

1.2.1 Setting Up Your Account

Setting up your Microsoft Teams account is the first and crucial step towards utilizing this powerful collaboration tool. Whether you're an individual looking to organize your projects or a business aiming to streamline communication and teamwork, Microsoft Teams offers a comprehensive platform to meet your needs. This section will guide you through the process of setting up your account, ensuring you can start using Teams effectively.

Step 1: Accessing Microsoft Teams

To begin, you need to access Microsoft Teams. If your organization uses Office 365, Teams is likely included in your subscription. You can access Teams through the following methods:

- Web Application: Visit teams.microsoft.com to use the web version of Teams.

- Desktop Application: Download and install the Teams desktop app for Windows or macOS from the [Microsoft Teams download page](https://www.microsoft.com/en-us/microsoft-teams/download-app).

- Mobile Application: Download the Teams app from the App Store (iOS) or Google Play Store (Android).

Step 2: Signing In

Once you've accessed Teams through your preferred method, you'll need to sign in with your Microsoft account. If you're part of an organization, use your work or school account. For personal use, you can sign in with a personal Microsoft account or create one if you don't already have it.

Step 3: Setting Up Your Profile

After signing in, it's important to set up your profile. A well-completed profile helps your colleagues identify and connect with you more easily. Follow these steps to set up your profile:

- Profile Picture: Click on your profile picture icon at the top right corner and select "Change picture" to upload a profile photo.

- Status Message: Set a status message to let your team know your current availability or share important information. Click on your profile picture, select "Set status message," and type your message.

- Contact Information: Ensure your contact details are up-to-date. You can usually update your contact information through your Office 365 account settings.

Step 4: Navigating the Teams Interface

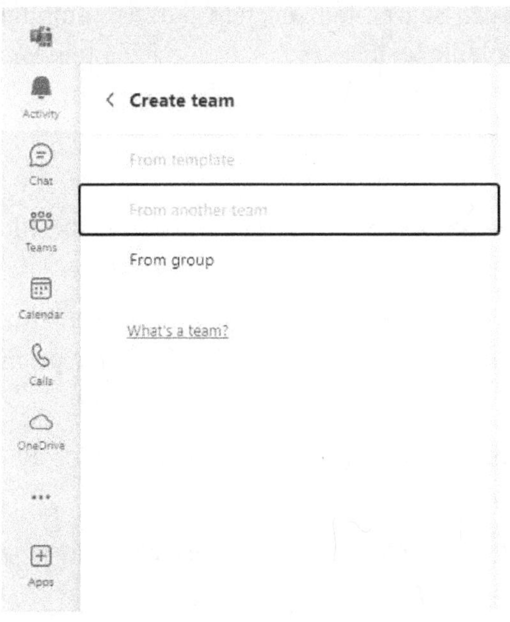

Familiarizing yourself with the Teams interface will help you navigate the platform more efficiently. The main components of the Teams interface include:

- Activity Feed: This is where you see notifications and updates related to your activities in Teams.

- Chat: The Chat tab allows you to have private conversations with individuals or groups.

- Teams: The Teams tab is where you can access different teams you are a part of and the channels within those teams.

- Calendar: This integrates with your Outlook calendar, allowing you to schedule and join meetings directly from Teams.

- Calls: If your organization uses Teams for calling, you can make and receive calls here.

- Files: Access and manage your files within Teams and across your integrated Office 365 applications.

Step 5: Creating or Joining a Team

Teams are the core of Microsoft Teams, providing a collaborative space for various groups within your organization. Here's how to create or join a team:

- Creating a Team: Click on the "Teams" tab, then select "Join or create a team" at the bottom of the sidebar. Choose "Create team" and follow the prompts to set up your new team. You can create a team from scratch, use an existing Office 365 group, or use a template.

  - Name and Description: Give your team a meaningful name and description.

  - Privacy Settings: Choose whether your team will be private (invitation only) or public (anyone in your organization can join).

- Joining a Team: If you've been invited to a team, you will receive an invitation link. Click on the link to join the team. Alternatively, you can search for and join public teams by clicking "Join or create a team" and browsing available teams.

Step 6: Setting Up Channels

Within each team, you can create channels to organize conversations and work on specific topics or projects. Here's how to set up channels:

- Creating a Channel: Navigate to the team where you want to create a channel, click on the three dots next to the team name, and select "Add channel." Provide a name and description for the channel.

- Channel Types: Choose between standard channels, accessible to all team members, and private channels, restricted to selected members.

- Channel Settings: Customize channel settings such as moderation preferences and who can post messages.

Step 7: Customizing Your Team and Channel Settings

Customization allows you to tailor Teams to your specific needs and preferences. Here are some ways to customize your team and channel settings:

- Team Settings: Click on the three dots next to the team name, select "Manage team," and explore the settings options. You can customize member permissions, team picture, fun settings (emojis, memes, etc.), and more.

- Channel Notifications: Manage channel notifications by clicking on the three dots next to the channel name and selecting "Channel notifications." Choose your notification preferences for new posts and replies.

Step 8: Integrating Applications

Microsoft Teams integrates seamlessly with various applications, enhancing its functionality. Here's how to integrate apps:

- Adding Apps: Click on the three dots in the left-hand sidebar and select "Apps." Browse through the available applications and click "Add" to integrate them with Teams.

- Using Tabs: Add tabs to your channels for quick access to frequently used apps and files. Click the "+" icon at the top of the channel and select the app you want to add as a tab.

- Custom Bots and Connectors: Enhance productivity by integrating bots and connectors. Bots can automate tasks and provide information, while connectors bring content and updates from external services into Teams.

Step 9: Setting Up Teams for Collaboration

Microsoft Teams is designed to facilitate collaboration. Here are some tips to set up effective collaboration:

- Organize Channels by Project or Topic: Structure your channels based on specific projects, departments, or topics to keep conversations focused and organized.

- Utilize Team Meetings: Schedule regular team meetings to discuss progress, share updates, and address any issues. Use the Calendar tab to schedule and manage meetings.

- Collaborative Document Editing: Use Office 365 integration to collaborate on documents in real-time. Upload files to channels, and team members can edit them simultaneously.

- Utilize Tags: Create and use tags to categorize members based on their roles or expertise. This makes it easier to @mention and notify specific groups within the team.

Step 10: Managing Permissions and Access

Properly managing permissions and access ensures that your team remains secure and organized. Here's how to manage permissions:

- Team Owner and Member Roles: Assign roles within your team. Owners have higher privileges, including adding or removing members and managing settings. Members can participate in conversations and access shared resources.

- Private Channels: Use private channels for sensitive discussions. Only selected members can access these channels.

- Guest Access: Allow external users to join your team by enabling guest access. Go to the Teams settings and enable guest access, then invite guests using their email addresses.

- Setting Up Policies: If you're an admin, configure policies to control how Teams is used within your organization. This includes messaging policies, meeting policies, and app policies.

Step 11: Exploring Help and Support Resources

As you set up your Teams account, you may encounter questions or need assistance. Microsoft provides extensive help and support resources:

- Help Center: Access the Microsoft Teams Help Center by clicking on your profile picture and selecting "Help." Here, you can find guides, tutorials, and FAQs.

- Training: Microsoft offers free training courses and webinars for Teams users. Visit the Microsoft Teams Training page for more information.

- Community Forums: Engage with other Teams users in the Microsoft Tech Community forums. Share experiences, ask questions, and learn from others.

- Support: For technical issues, you can contact Microsoft Support directly through the Help Center.

By following these steps, you'll have your Microsoft Teams account set up and ready for efficient collaboration and communication. Whether you're new to Teams or transitioning from another platform, this guide ensures a smooth start, enabling you to harness the full potential of Microsoft Teams.

1.2.2 Navigating the User Interface

Navigating the user interface of Microsoft Teams is crucial for leveraging the platform's full potential. This section will guide you through the various components of the Teams interface, ensuring you become proficient in using the tool effectively for collaboration and communication.

The Teams Home Screen

Upon logging into Microsoft Teams, you will be greeted by the home screen, which serves as the central hub for your activities. The layout is designed to be intuitive, with primary navigation elements on the left-hand side and the main workspace occupying the center and right parts of the screen.

1. The App Bar

The app bar, located on the left side of the interface, is the primary navigation tool in Microsoft Teams. It contains several key icons, each representing different functionalities:

- Activity: This section aggregates notifications and recent activities from all your teams and channels. It's the first place to check for updates and new messages.

- Chat: Direct access to one-on-one and group chats. Here, you can start new conversations or continue existing ones.

- Teams: This icon provides a list of all the teams you are a member of, including the channels within each team. It's the gateway to collaborative workspaces.

- Calendar: Integrated with your Outlook calendar, this feature allows you to schedule, join, and manage meetings directly within Teams.

- Calls: Access your call history, voicemail, and contacts. This is also where you can make voice and video calls.

- Files: A centralized location for accessing all the files shared within your teams and chats, as well as your OneDrive storage.

2. The Command Box

At the top of the app bar is the command box, a versatile tool that allows for quick navigation and actions. You can use it to search for specific items, people, or messages by typing keywords. Additionally, you can execute commands by typing "/" followed by the command you wish to use, such as /call to make a call or /files to view recent files.

3. The Teams and Channels List

When you click on the Teams icon in the app bar, the main panel displays a list of all your teams. Each team can be expanded to show its channels. Channels are sub-sections within a team, usually dedicated to specific topics or projects. They can be standard (visible to all team members) or private (restricted to a subset of members).

4. The Channel Tabs

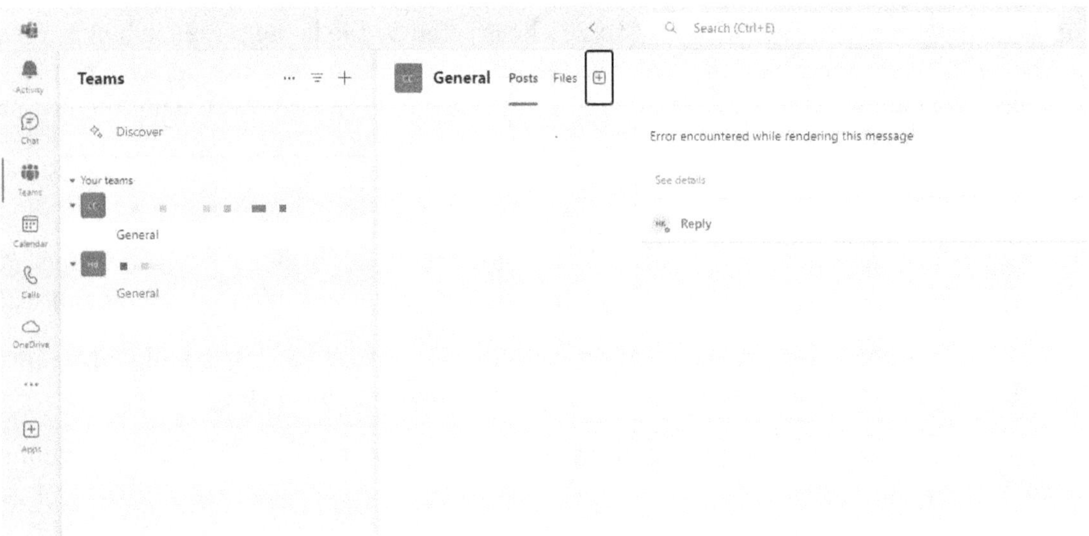

Each channel has tabs at the top, which organize different types of content and tools. By default, every channel includes the following tabs:

- Posts: The conversation space where team members can post messages, reply, and engage in discussions.

- Files: A dedicated area for storing and managing files related to the channel. You can upload, share, and collaborate on documents here.

- Wiki: A simple yet powerful tool for creating and organizing documentation, notes, and other reference materials.

You can add more tabs to enhance your workflow, integrating various apps and services like OneNote, Planner, or third-party tools.

5. The Main Workspace

The main workspace occupies the central part of the screen, displaying the content of the selected tab. For instance, if you're in the Posts tab of a channel, the main workspace shows the conversation thread. If you switch to the Files tab, it will display the file repository for that channel.

6. The Messaging Toolbar

Within the Posts tab, at the bottom of the main workspace, you'll find the messaging toolbar. This is where you compose and send messages. The toolbar includes several useful features:

- Format: Access text formatting options such as bold, italic, underline, font size, and lists.

- Attach: Attach files from your computer, OneDrive, or other cloud storage services.

- Emoji, GIFs, and Stickers: Enhance your messages with emojis, GIFs, and stickers for a touch of personality and fun.

- Meet Now: Start an instant meeting with the members of the channel.

- Stream: Share videos directly from Microsoft Stream.

- Praise: Send recognition and kudos to team members.

7. The Right-Side Pane

In certain views, such as during a chat or a meeting, a right-side pane may appear. This pane provides additional context or tools related to the ongoing activity. For example, during a meeting, it might show participant information, chat messages, and meeting notes.

Navigating Meetings and Calls

Meetings and calls are integral parts of Microsoft Teams, offering robust features for real-time collaboration. Here's how to navigate these functionalities:

1. Scheduling and Joining Meetings

The Calendar icon in the app bar opens your integrated Outlook calendar. From here, you can schedule new meetings by clicking the "New meeting" button. You can specify details such as the title, participants, date, time, and whether it's a recurring event.

To join a meeting, you can click on the event in your calendar and select the "Join" button. You can also join meetings directly from the invitation link sent via email or chat.

2. Meeting Interface

Once in a meeting, the interface provides several controls and options:

- Meeting Toolbar: Located at the bottom, it includes controls for muting/unmuting your microphone, turning your camera on/off, sharing your screen, opening the chat, and viewing participants.

- Participants Panel: Shows a list of attendees, with options to invite more people, mute participants, and manage roles.

- Chat Panel: A space for text-based communication during the meeting, allowing participants to share links, files, and comments.

- Share Tray: Accessed from the toolbar, this allows you to share your entire screen, a specific window, or a PowerPoint presentation.

- More Actions: The ellipsis (...) button on the toolbar provides additional options like recording the meeting, changing device settings, and applying background effects.

3. Making and Receiving Calls

The Calls icon in the app bar brings up the call interface. Here, you can:

- Dial a Number: Use the dial pad to make a call to a phone number.

- Call a Contact: Search for a contact and initiate a voice or video call.

- View Call History: See a log of your recent calls and return missed calls.

- Access Voicemail: Listen to and manage your voicemail messages.

Customization and Personalization

Microsoft Teams allows users to customize their experience to better suit their preferences and workflow:

1. Changing Themes and Layouts

Under the profile icon in the top right corner, you can access the settings menu. In the "General" section, you can choose between different themes (Default, Dark, High Contrast) to personalize the appearance of Teams. You can also toggle the layout settings, such as grid view for teams and compact mode for chats.

2. Notification Settings

The settings menu also contains a "Notifications" section, where you can customize how and when you receive alerts for messages, mentions, replies, and more. This ensures you stay informed without being overwhelmed by notifications.

3. Managing Devices

In the "Devices" section of the settings menu, you can configure audio and video devices for meetings and calls. This includes selecting the default microphone, speaker, and camera, as well as adjusting related settings.

4. Keyboard Shortcuts

For power users, Microsoft Teams offers a variety of keyboard shortcuts that can streamline navigation and actions. You can view the list of shortcuts by pressing Ctrl + . (Ctrl and period) or accessing it through the settings menu.

5. Personal Status and Availability

Your availability status can be set manually or automatically based on your activity. Options include Available, Busy, Do Not Disturb, and Away. Setting your status helps manage expectations for communication and lets your colleagues know when you're reachable.

Conclusion

Mastering the navigation of Microsoft Teams' user interface is a foundational step in becoming proficient with the platform. Understanding the layout, features, and customization options allows you to optimize your workflow and enhance collaboration within your teams. With this knowledge, you're well-equipped to explore the more advanced functionalities and integrations that Microsoft Teams offers.

1.2.3 Basic Functionality and Features

Microsoft Teams is a robust collaboration platform that integrates various functionalities to facilitate effective communication and teamwork. Understanding the basic functionalities and features is crucial for leveraging the full potential of Teams. In this section, we will explore these key features and functionalities in detail.

1. Chat and Messaging

One of the core features of Microsoft Teams is its chat and messaging capabilities. Users can engage in one-on-one or group conversations, making it easier to communicate instantly with colleagues. The chat functionality includes several features to enhance the user experience:

- Rich Text Formatting: Users can format their messages with bold, italic, underline, and highlight options, ensuring that important information stands out.

- Emojis, GIFs, and Stickers: Teams supports the use of emojis, GIFs, and stickers, adding a fun and personal touch to communications.

- Threaded Conversations: In group chats, users can create threaded conversations to keep discussions organized and contextually relevant.

- Mentions (@): Users can mention individuals or entire teams using the @ symbol, which sends a notification to the mentioned parties, drawing their attention to specific messages.

2. Teams and Channels

Teams and Channels form the structural backbone of Microsoft Teams, enabling organized collaboration:

- Teams: A Team is a collection of people, content, and tools that come together for a specific project, department, or interest group. Teams can be public (open to everyone in the organization) or private (restricted to invited members only).

- Channels: Within a Team, Channels are used to organize conversations and content by topic, project, or department. Channels can be standard (accessible to all Team members) or private (restricted to specific members within the Team). Each Channel includes tabs for conversations, files, and other apps.

3. Meetings and Calls

Microsoft Teams excels in its ability to facilitate virtual meetings and calls:

- Scheduling Meetings: Users can schedule meetings directly from Teams or integrate with Outlook. Meeting invitations include options for setting the date, time, and recurrence, as well as inviting participants.

- Joining Meetings: Joining a meeting is straightforward; users can join through a link in the calendar invite, from within the Teams app, or via a web browser. Teams supports both video and audio conferencing, providing flexibility in how users connect.

- Meeting Tools: During meetings, users have access to a range of tools, including screen sharing, whiteboard collaboration, and meeting recording. The "Together Mode" creates a virtual auditorium view, making participants feel more connected.

- Calls: Teams includes robust calling features, supporting both internal and external calls. Users can make one-on-one or group calls, and leverage call features such as call forwarding, voicemail, and call recording.

4. File Sharing and Collaboration

Collaboration in Microsoft Teams is enhanced through its file sharing and co-authoring capabilities:

- File Sharing: Users can upload and share files directly in conversations or channels. Files are stored in SharePoint for Teams channels or OneDrive for personal chats, ensuring secure and organized storage.

- Co-Authoring: Teams supports real-time co-authoring, allowing multiple users to work on the same document simultaneously. Changes are synchronized instantly, and users can see who is editing the document at any time.

- Version History: Version history is available for files stored in SharePoint or OneDrive, enabling users to track changes and revert to previous versions if needed.

5. Integrations and Apps

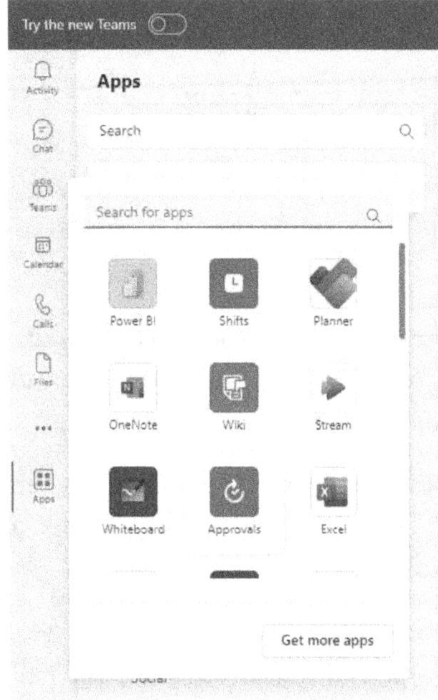

Microsoft Teams integrates seamlessly with other Microsoft 365 applications and third-party apps:

- Office 365 Integration: Teams integrates with Office 365 applications such as Word, Excel, PowerPoint, and OneNote. Users can create, edit, and collaborate on documents without leaving the Teams interface.

- Third-Party Apps: Teams supports a wide range of third-party applications, which can be added as tabs within channels. Popular integrations include Trello, Asana, GitHub, and Adobe Creative Cloud.

- Bots and Connectors: Bots can automate tasks and provide information within Teams. Connectors allow Teams to receive updates and notifications from external services like Twitter, GitHub, and RSS feeds.

6. Tabs and Customization

Customization in Teams helps tailor the workspace to specific needs:

- Tabs: Tabs are customizable sections within a channel, allowing users to add apps, files, or websites that are frequently used. This helps centralize resources and streamline workflows.

- Custom Tabs: Users and developers can create custom tabs to integrate internal tools or services, further enhancing the Teams experience.

7. Activity Feed

The Activity Feed is the central hub for notifications and updates:

- Notifications: Users receive notifications for mentions, replies, likes, and other activities. Notifications can be customized to ensure users stay informed about important updates.

- Activity: The feed displays a chronological list of activities, allowing users to quickly catch up on recent interactions and developments.

8. Search and Command Box

The search and command box is a powerful tool for finding information and executing commands within Teams:

- Search: Users can search for messages, files, people, and other content using keywords. Advanced search filters help narrow down results.

- Commands: The command box supports quick actions and commands, such as setting status, starting chats, or accessing specific features. Commands are initiated with a slash (/) followed by the action.

9. Mobile Accessibility

Microsoft Teams offers mobile applications for iOS and Android, ensuring users can stay connected on the go:

- Mobile App Features: The mobile app provides most of the core functionalities of the desktop version, including chat, meetings, file sharing, and app integrations.

- Notifications: Push notifications keep users informed about messages, calls, and meetings, ensuring they don't miss important updates.

10. Security and Compliance

Security is a top priority in Microsoft Teams, ensuring that data and communications are protected:

- Data Encryption: Teams encrypts data both in transit and at rest, safeguarding sensitive information.

- Compliance: Teams adheres to various compliance standards, including GDPR, HIPAA, and ISO 27001, ensuring that organizations meet regulatory requirements.

- Access Controls: Teams provides granular access controls, allowing administrators to manage permissions and ensure that only authorized users can access sensitive information.

11. Analytics and Reporting

Teams offers analytics and reporting tools to monitor usage and performance:

- Usage Reports: Administrators can access reports on user activity, meeting participation, and app usage, helping them understand how Teams is being utilized.

- Insights: Insights provide detailed information on user engagement and collaboration patterns, enabling organizations to optimize their Teams environment.

In conclusion, Microsoft Teams is a versatile platform that brings together various functionalities to enhance communication and collaboration. By understanding and utilizing these basic features, users can significantly improve their productivity and work more efficiently as a team. As we continue exploring Microsoft Teams, we will delve deeper into its advanced features and customization options, empowering users to make the most of this powerful tool.

1.3 Understanding Teams and Channels

1.3.1 Creating and Managing Teams

Microsoft Teams is a powerful platform designed to foster collaboration and communication within organizations. Understanding how to create and manage teams is crucial for leveraging the full potential of this tool. This section will guide you through the detailed steps of setting up and managing teams in Microsoft Teams.

Creating Teams

Step 1: Accessing the Teams Application

To create a team, first, open the Microsoft Teams application. You can do this through the desktop app, web app, or mobile app. Sign in with your organizational account if you are not already logged in.

Step 2: Navigating to the Teams Section

Once logged in, navigate to the "Teams" section. This is typically found on the left sidebar of the application. Click on "Teams" to open the main teams interface.

Step 3: Creating a New Team

To create a new team, click on the "Join or create a team" link located at the bottom of the teams list. This will take you to a new screen where you will see options to join existing teams or create a new one. Click on the "Create a team" button.

Step 4: Choosing a Team Type

Microsoft Teams offers several types of teams, each designed for different purposes:

- Class: Ideal for educational environments where teachers and students collaborate.

- PLC (Professional Learning Community): For educators to collaborate and share resources.

- Staff: Designed for school administration and staff collaboration.

- Other: Suitable for general collaboration within organizations.

For most business scenarios, you will choose the "Other" option. Click on "Other" to proceed.

Step 5: Setting Up Team Details

You will now be prompted to enter the details of your new team:

- Team Name: Choose a descriptive name that reflects the purpose of the team.

- Description: Provide a brief description of the team's objectives.

- Privacy Settings: Choose between "Private" (only invited users can join) and "Public" (anyone in your organization can join).

After filling out the necessary details, click "Next" to create your team.

Step 6: Adding Team Members

Once your team is created, you can start adding members. You can add individuals by typing their names or email addresses. Microsoft Teams will suggest users from your organization as you type. Select the desired members and click "Add". You can also skip this step and add members later.

Managing Teams

Creating a team is just the beginning. Effective team management is essential to ensure smooth collaboration and communication. Here are the key aspects of managing teams in Microsoft Teams:

1. Team Settings

To manage your team, click on the ellipsis (three dots) next to the team name and select "Manage team". This will open the team management interface, where you can configure various settings.

2. Member Roles and Permissions

Microsoft Teams allows you to assign different roles to team members:

- Owners: Team owners have full control over the team settings, including adding and removing members, and managing channels.

- Members: Team members can participate in conversations, access shared files, and collaborate on projects.

To assign roles, go to the "Members" tab in the team management interface. Here, you can change the role of any member by clicking on the drop-down menu next to their name and selecting "Owner" or "Member".

3. Adding and Removing Members

You can add new members to your team at any time. In the team management interface, click on "Add member" and enter the names or email addresses of the individuals you want to add. To remove a member, click on the ellipsis next to their name and select "Remove from team".

4. Channels

Channels are sub-sections within a team that help organize conversations and content. Each team starts with a "General" channel by default. To create a new channel, click on the ellipsis next to the team name, select "Add channel", and fill in the details:

- Channel Name: Choose a name that reflects the purpose of the channel.

- Description: Provide a brief description of what the channel is for.

- Privacy Settings: Choose between "Standard" (visible to everyone in the team) and "Private" (only accessible to specific team members).

5. Channel Management

Channels can be managed similarly to teams. Click on the ellipsis next to a channel name to access options such as "Manage channel", "Get email address", "Connectors", and "Delete this channel". These options allow you to configure channel-specific settings and integrations.

6. Team Settings

In the team management interface, go to the "Settings" tab to configure team-wide settings:

- Team Picture: Upload a custom picture to represent your team.

- Member Permissions: Control what members can do, such as creating channels, adding apps, and deleting messages.

- Guest Permissions: If your team includes external users, you can set specific permissions for guests.

- @mentions: Configure settings for @mentions to control notifications and mentions within the team.

- Team Code: Generate a team code that can be shared with others to join the team without an invitation.

7. Analytics and Reporting

Microsoft Teams provides analytics to help you understand team activity. In the team management interface, go to the "Analytics" tab to view metrics such as the number of active users, messages, and files shared. This information can help you monitor engagement and identify areas for improvement.

8. Apps and Integrations

Enhance your team's functionality by integrating apps and services. In the team management interface, go to the "Apps" tab to explore available apps. You can add apps to your team to streamline workflows, integrate third-party services, and enhance collaboration. Popular integrations include Microsoft Planner, OneNote, and third-party apps like Trello and Asana.

9. Compliance and Security

Ensure your team complies with organizational policies and security standards. Microsoft Teams provides various compliance and security features, including data encryption, multi-factor authentication, and eDiscovery. In the team management interface, go to the "Settings" tab and explore options under "Compliance" and "Security" to configure these features.

10. Team Notifications

Managing notifications is crucial for staying updated without being overwhelmed. In the team management interface, go to the "Settings" tab and configure notification settings to control how team members receive alerts for messages, mentions, and other activities.

Best Practices for Creating and Managing Teams

To ensure your teams are effective and productive, consider the following best practices:

1. Define Clear Objectives: Establish clear objectives for each team and channel to ensure everyone understands their purpose.

2. Organize Channels Effectively: Use channels to organize conversations and content by topics, projects, or departments.

3. Promote Engagement: Encourage team members to actively participate in conversations and share updates regularly.

4. Regularly Review and Update: Periodically review team settings, member roles, and permissions to ensure they align with your organization's needs.

5. Leverage Integrations: Utilize integrations with other tools and services to enhance productivity and streamline workflows.

6. Provide Training and Support: Offer training sessions and resources to help team members effectively use Microsoft Teams.

By following these steps and best practices, you can create and manage teams in Microsoft Teams effectively, fostering a collaborative and productive environment within your organization.

1.3.2 Understanding Channels

Channels are the fundamental units within a Team in Microsoft Teams where work gets done. Each Team can have multiple channels, which helps in organizing conversations, files, and tasks around specific topics or projects. Understanding channels is crucial for leveraging Microsoft Teams effectively.

1.3.2.1 Types of Channels

Microsoft Teams offers two main types of channels: Standard and Private.

- Standard Channels: These are accessible to everyone on the team. They are ideal for general topics, updates, and collaboration that involves the entire team.

- Private Channels: These are only accessible to a subset of team members. Private channels are useful for sensitive discussions, focused projects, or confidential information that shouldn't be shared with the entire team.

1.3.2.2 Creating Channels

Creating a channel is a straightforward process, but it's important to follow best practices to ensure they serve their intended purpose. Here's how to create both Standard and Private channels:

- *Standard Channels:*

1. Navigate to the team where you want to add the channel.

2. Click on the three dots (ellipsis) next to the team name and select "Add channel."

3. Enter a name and description for the channel. Make sure the name is descriptive enough for team members to understand its purpose.

4. Set the privacy setting to "Standard - Accessible to everyone on the team."

5. Click "Add" to create the channel.

- *Private Channels:*

1. Follow steps 1-3 as above.

2. Set the privacy setting to "Private - Accessible only to a specific group of people within the team."

3. Click "Next," then add the members who should have access to this channel.

4. Click "Done" to create the private channel.

1.3.2.3 Naming Conventions and Best Practices

Having a clear naming convention helps in organizing channels efficiently and making it easier for team members to find relevant information. Here are some tips:

- Consistency: Use a consistent naming format for all channels. For example, if your team uses projects, you might name channels as "Project Alpha - Design" or "Project Alpha - Development."

- Clarity: Names should be clear and descriptive. Avoid using abbreviations that might not be universally understood.

- Purpose-Oriented: Channel names should reflect their purpose. For example, "General" for general updates, "Marketing" for marketing discussions, or "Q3 Planning" for quarterly planning.

1.3.2.4 Managing Channel Settings

Each channel in Microsoft Teams has settings that can be customized to fit your needs. Here's how you can manage them:

- Channel Moderation: For Standard channels, you can set up moderation to control who can start new posts and reply to existing ones. This is particularly useful in channels where you need to manage the flow of information.

1. Go to the channel settings by clicking on the three dots next to the channel name.
2. Select "Manage channel."
3. Turn on "Channel moderation" and configure the settings as needed.

- Channel Notifications: Customize how you receive notifications for activity in the channel. You can adjust settings for all activity, mentions, or only direct replies.

1. Click on the three dots next to the channel name.
2. Select "Channel notifications" and choose your preferences.

- Channel Tabs: Add tabs for apps, files, and other tools that your team frequently uses. For example, you can add a Planner tab for task management, a OneNote tab for collaborative notes, or a Power BI tab for analytics.

1. Click the "+" icon at the top of the channel.
2. Select the app you want to add and follow the on-screen instructions.

1.3.2.5 Organizing Content within Channels

Effective use of channels involves organizing content to keep the workspace tidy and functional. Here are some strategies:

- Posts and Replies: Use posts for announcements and new topics, and replies for continuing discussions. This keeps conversations organized and easy to follow.

- Pinned Posts: Pin important messages to the top of the channel for easy reference.

1. Hover over the message you want to pin.

2. Click on the three dots and select "Pin."

- Files Tab: Use the Files tab to store and manage documents related to the channel. Create folders within the Files tab to keep documents organized by topic or project phase.

- Wiki Tab: Use the Wiki tab for shared knowledge and quick reference guides. It's ideal for storing standard operating procedures, FAQs, and team guidelines.

1.3.2.6 Channel Meetings

Channels provide a centralized space for team meetings. You can schedule or start ad-hoc meetings directly from a channel, ensuring all discussions and notes are accessible to the team.

- Scheduled Meetings:

1. Click on the "Meetings" tab in the channel.

2. Select "Schedule a meeting" and fill out the details.

3. The meeting will appear in the channel's conversation tab, where team members can join and discuss.

- Ad-hoc Meetings:

1. Click on the video icon in the channel's conversation tab.

2. Select "Meet now" to start an immediate meeting.

3. Notify team members via the channel conversation to join.

1.3.2.7 Archiving and Deleting Channels

Channels can be archived or deleted when they are no longer needed. Archiving retains the content for future reference, while deleting removes it permanently.

- Archiving Channels: Archiving is not a built-in feature for channels, but you can achieve a similar effect by limiting access and hiding the channel.

1. Move content to other channels if needed.

2. Remove members and limit permissions.

3. Use "Manage team" settings to hide the channel from view.

- Deleting Channels:

1. Click on the three dots next to the channel name.

2. Select "Delete this channel." Note that this action is irreversible, and all content will be lost.

1.3.2.8 Best Practices for Channel Management

To ensure that channels remain effective tools for collaboration, consider the following best practices:

- Regular Reviews: Periodically review and clean up channels. Archive or delete channels that are no longer in use.

- Clear Guidelines: Establish and communicate guidelines for creating and using channels. This helps team members understand when and how to create new channels and use existing ones.

- Engagement: Encourage team members to actively participate in channel discussions. Regular engagement helps keep channels relevant and useful.

- Training: Provide training and resources to help team members use channels effectively. This can include how-to guides, video tutorials, and regular Q&A sessions.

Understanding and utilizing channels effectively can significantly enhance your team's productivity and collaboration. By following best practices and leveraging the features of Microsoft Teams, you can create a well-organized and efficient workspace that meets the needs of your team.

1.3.3 Customizing Team and Channel Settings

Customizing team and channel settings in Microsoft Teams is essential for creating an environment that meets your organization's needs and ensures effective collaboration. This section will guide you through the various customization options available for teams and channels, helping you tailor your workspace to enhance productivity and communication.

Overview of Customization Options

Customizing team and channel settings involves several aspects:

- Team Settings: Including permissions, member roles, and team-wide settings.

- Channel Settings: Including channel moderation, notifications, and tabs.

We'll cover each aspect in detail to ensure you can leverage all the customization features available in Microsoft Teams.

Customizing Team Settings

Team settings allow you to define how members interact within the team, manage permissions, and set team-wide configurations. Here's how you can customize these settings:

Managing Team Roles

Microsoft Teams offers two primary roles:

- Owners: Team owners have full control over the team and can manage settings, add or remove members, and change team roles.

- Members: Members can participate in conversations, access shared files, and use apps but have limited control over settings.

*Steps to Manage Team Roles:*1. Access Team Settings: Go to the team you want to manage, click on the three dots (...) next to the team name, and select "Manage team."

2. Change Roles: Under the "Members" tab, you'll see a list of all team members. Next to each member's name, there's a dropdown where you can change their role to either "Owner" or "Member."

Best Practices for Managing Roles:

- Limit the Number of Owners: Having too many owners can lead to conflicting changes. Ideally, designate a few responsible individuals as owners.

- Clear Role Definitions: Ensure all members understand their roles and the associated permissions to avoid confusion.

Setting Team-Wide Permissions

Team-wide permissions allow you to control what members can do within the team, such as creating channels, adding apps, or mentioning the entire team.

Steps to Set Permissions:

1. Access Permissions: In the "Manage team" settings, navigate to the "Settings" tab and click on "Member permissions."

2. Configure Permissions: You'll find various options to enable or disable specific actions, such as:

  - Allow members to create, update, and delete channels.

  - Allow members to add and remove apps.

  - Allow members to upload custom apps.

  - Enable team mentions.

Best Practices for Setting Permissions:

- Restrict Channel Creation: To maintain a clean and organized workspace, consider restricting channel creation to owners.

- Control App Access: Limit the ability to add or remove apps to prevent unauthorized or unnecessary integrations.

Customizing Team Appearance

Customizing the appearance of your team can help with branding and make it easily recognizable.

Steps to Customize Team Appearance:

1. Change Team Picture: In the "Manage team" settings, go to the "Settings" tab and click on "Team picture." Upload an image that represents your team.

2. Set Team Description: Provide a brief description of your team in the "Description" field under the "General" tab to help new members understand the team's purpose.

Best Practices for Customizing Appearance:

- Use Clear and Recognizable Images: Choose images that are relevant to your team and easily identifiable.

- Provide Informative Descriptions: Ensure the team description clearly outlines the team's objectives and scope.

Customizing Channel Settings

Channels within a team can be customized to suit the specific needs of different projects or departments. Customizing channel settings involves setting up moderation, notifications, and tabs.

Channel Moderation

Channel moderation allows you to control who can start new posts and manage the flow of communication within the channel.

Steps to Enable Channel Moderation:

1. Access Channel Settings: Go to the desired channel, click on the three dots (...) next to the channel name, and select "Manage channel."

2. Enable Moderation: In the "Settings" tab, turn on "Channel moderation."

3. Assign Moderators: Add moderators who will have the authority to start new posts and manage messages within the channel.

Best Practices for Channel Moderation:

- Select Responsible Moderators: Choose individuals who can effectively manage discussions and ensure they stay on topic.

- Communicate Moderation Policies: Inform all channel members about the moderation rules and the role of moderators.

Configuring Channel Notifications

Channel notifications help keep members informed about important updates without overwhelming them with alerts.

Steps to Configure Notifications:

1. Access Notification Settings: In the channel settings, navigate to the "Notifications" tab.

2. Customize Notification Preferences: Set preferences for all members or allow individuals to customize their own notification settings. Options include:

   - All activity

   - Mentions and replies

   - Custom notifications

Best Practices for Notifications:

- Balance Notification Frequency: Set notifications to ensure important updates are seen without causing notification fatigue.

- Encourage Personalization: Allow members to adjust their notification settings based on their preferences and roles.

Adding and Customizing Tabs

Tabs in channels provide quick access to tools, files, and apps relevant to the channel's purpose.

Steps to Add and Customize Tabs:

1. Add a Tab: Click the plus (+) icon at the top of the channel to add a new tab.

2. Select a Tab Type: Choose from a variety of options, including Office 365 apps (e.g., Excel, OneNote), third-party apps, and custom URLs.

3. Configure Tab Settings: Customize the tab's settings to meet the channel's needs. For example, you can link directly to a specific file or set up a tab to display a project management tool.

Best Practices for Tabs:

- Use Relevant Tabs: Only add tabs that provide value and are frequently used by the channel members.

- Organize Tabs Logically: Arrange tabs in a way that makes sense for the workflow of the channel, with the most important tabs easily accessible.

Customizing Messaging and Permissions

In addition to team and channel settings, you can also customize messaging and permissions to streamline communication and maintain control over information sharing.

Managing Messaging Policies

Messaging policies determine how members can communicate within the team and channels.

Steps to Manage Messaging Policies:

1. Access Messaging Policies: In the Teams admin center, navigate to "Messaging policies."

2. Configure Policies: Adjust settings such as:

   - Allowing owners to delete sent messages.

   - Enabling read receipts.

   - Permitting the use of @mentions.

Best Practices for Messaging Policies:

- Enable Read Receipts: This helps ensure messages are seen and acknowledged, enhancing communication transparency.

- Control Mentions: Limit the use of @mentions to prevent unnecessary disruptions.

Setting Up Compliance and Information Protection

Ensuring compliance and protecting sensitive information is critical in any collaborative environment.

Steps to Set Up Compliance and Information Protection:

1. Configure Data Loss Prevention (DLP): In the Microsoft 365 compliance center, set up DLP policies to prevent sensitive information from being shared inappropriately.

2. Set Retention Policies: Define how long messages and files should be retained to comply with legal and regulatory requirements.

3. Implement Sensitivity Labels: Use sensitivity labels to classify and protect documents within Teams.

Best Practices for Compliance and Information Protection:

- Regularly Review Policies: Ensure compliance and protection policies are up-to-date with the latest regulations and organizational needs.

- Educate Members: Train team members on the importance of compliance and how to handle sensitive information.

Enhancing User Experience with Customization

Customization is not just about setting permissions and policies; it's also about enhancing the overall user experience. Here are some additional tips:

Using Themes and Backgrounds

Microsoft Teams allows you to personalize the visual appearance of your workspace.

Steps to Change Themes and Backgrounds:

1. Change Theme: Go to "Settings" and select "General." Choose from the available themes, such as default, dark, or high contrast.

2. Set Meeting Backgrounds: During a video call, click on the three dots (...) and select "Show background effects" to choose or upload a custom background.

Best Practices for Themes and Backgrounds:

- Choose Readable Themes: Ensure the selected theme does not compromise readability and usability.

- Use Professional Backgrounds: Select backgrounds that are appropriate for the work environment and avoid distractions.

Creating Custom Bots and Workflows

Automating tasks with custom bots and workflows can significantly enhance productivity.

Steps to Create Bots and Workflows:

1. Use Power Automate: Access Power Automate to create workflows that integrate with Teams, such as automated notifications or approvals.

2. Develop Custom Bots: Utilize the Microsoft Bot Framework to develop custom bots that can assist with routine tasks and provide information.

Best Practices for Bots and Workflows:

- Automate Repetitive Tasks: Identify tasks that can be automated to save time and reduce manual effort.

- Test Thoroughly: Ensure bots and workflows are thoroughly tested before deployment to avoid disruptions.

Conclusion

Customizing team and channel settings in Microsoft Teams is crucial for creating an effective and user-friendly collaborative environment. By managing team roles, setting permissions, configuring channels, and enhancing the user experience, you can ensure that Microsoft Teams meets the specific needs of your organization. Proper customization not only streamlines workflows but also fosters better communication and collaboration, ultimately leading to increased productivity and satisfaction among team members.

CHAPTER II
Communication in Microsoft Teams

2.1 Chatting in Teams

2.1.1 Starting a Chat

Introduction to Chatting in Microsoft Teams

Microsoft Teams provides a versatile chat feature that allows users to communicate directly and efficiently within their organization. Whether you are discussing a project, seeking quick clarification, or simply catching up with a colleague, the chat functionality in Teams is designed to streamline these interactions. This section will guide you through the process of starting a chat in Teams, including the different methods available and best practices for effective communication.

1. Understanding the Chat Interface

Before you begin a chat, it's important to familiarize yourself with the chat interface in Microsoft Teams:

- Activity Feed: Displays notifications related to your chats, mentions, and other updates.

- Chat Tab: Located on the left-hand side of the Teams application, it provides access to all your ongoing and past conversations.

- Search Bar: Allows you to search for people, chats, and messages.

- Compose Box: Where you type your messages.

- Options Menu: Provides additional actions such as formatting messages, attaching files, or using emojis.

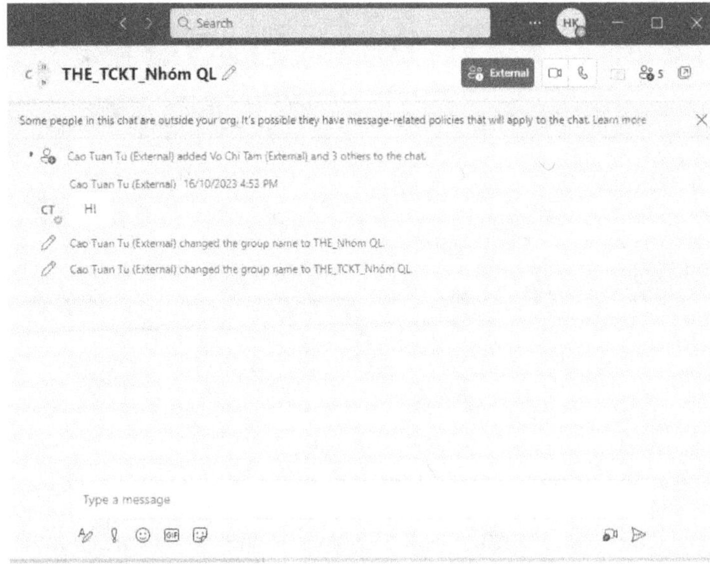

2. Starting a New Chat

To initiate a new chat in Microsoft Teams, follow these steps:

- Open Microsoft Teams: Launch the application on your desktop or mobile device.

- Navigate to the Chat Tab: Click on the "Chat" icon on the left side of the Teams interface. This will bring you to your chat history and a list of your recent conversations.

- Click on the New Chat Button: Located at the top of the chat list, represented by a pencil icon or "New Chat" button. This opens a new chat window.

- Enter the Recipient's Name: In the "To" field, type the name of the person you want to chat with. Microsoft Teams will auto-suggest names based on your organization's directory. You can select the person from the dropdown list.

- Compose Your Message: Type your message in the compose box at the bottom of the chat window. You can format your text, add bullets, or use other text formatting options by clicking on the format button (represented by an "A" icon with a paintbrush).

- Send the Message: Press the "Enter" key or click the send button (represented by an arrow) to deliver your message.

3. Starting a Group Chat

If you need to communicate with multiple people at once, you can start a group chat:

- Click on the New Chat Button: As described earlier.

- Add Multiple Recipients: In the "To" field, start typing the names of the people you want to include in the group chat. Select each person from the suggestions.

- Name the Group Chat: After adding recipients, you can name the group chat for easier reference. Click on the pencil icon next to the chat name at the top of the window and enter a new name.

- Compose and Send Your Message: Type your message and hit "Enter" to send it to all participants in the group chat.

4. Using the Chat Features

Microsoft Teams offers several features to enhance your chat experience:

- Formatting Options: Use the formatting toolbar to make your messages more readable. Options include bold, italic, underline, text color, and highlighting.

- Attaching Files: To share files, click on the attachment icon (represented by a paperclip) in the compose box. You can upload files from your computer, OneDrive, or other cloud storage services.

- Adding Emojis, GIFs, and Stickers: Enhance your messages with emojis, GIFs, and stickers. Click on the emoji icon (smiley face) to browse and insert emojis. For GIFs and stickers, use the respective icons available in the chat compose box.

- Using @Mentions: To get someone's attention in a group chat, use the @mention feature. Type @ followed by the person's name, and they will receive a notification.

- Pinning Important Chats: To keep track of important conversations, you can pin chats to the top of your chat list. Right-click on the chat and select "Pin."

5. Managing Chats

Efficiently managing your chats ensures you stay organized:

- Marking Messages as Unread: If you want to revisit a message later, mark it as unread. Right-click on the message and select "Mark as unread."

- Managing Notifications: Customize your notification settings for different chats by clicking on the three dots next to the chat and selecting "Notification settings."

- Archiving or Deleting Chats: To clean up your chat list, you can archive or delete conversations. Right-click on the chat and select the appropriate option.

6. Best Practices for Effective Chat Communication

- Be Clear and Concise: Keep your messages brief and to the point to avoid confusion and ensure quick responses.

- Use Professional Language: Maintain a professional tone, especially in work-related chats, to uphold a respectful and productive environment.

- Respond Promptly: Aim to respond to messages in a timely manner to facilitate smooth communication and collaboration.

- Respect Privacy: Be mindful of the information you share in chats and ensure you have permission before sharing sensitive or confidential details.

7. Troubleshooting Common Chat Issues

- Messages Not Sending: Check your internet connection and ensure that Microsoft Teams is up to date. Restart the application if necessary.

- Inability to Find Contacts: Verify that the person you're trying to chat with is part of your organization and ensure their name is correctly spelled.

- Notification Issues: Adjust your notification settings and check if Do Not Disturb mode is enabled.

8. Conclusion

Starting a chat in Microsoft Teams is a straightforward process that can significantly enhance your communication and collaboration with colleagues. By understanding the chat interface, utilizing features, and following best practices, you can effectively manage conversations and contribute to a productive work environment. Whether you're sending a quick message or engaging in group discussions, Microsoft Teams provides the tools you need to stay connected and informed.

2.1.2 Using Emojis, GIFs, and Stickers

Effective communication within Microsoft Teams goes beyond plain text messages. Emojis, GIFs, and stickers add a layer of expressiveness and engagement, making conversations more vibrant and engaging. These tools can help convey emotions, emphasize points, and even inject some fun into professional interactions. Here, we will delve into how to effectively use these features in Microsoft Teams.

Introduction to Emojis, GIFs, and Stickers

Emojis, GIFs, and stickers are visual elements that enhance digital communication. Emojis are small icons that represent emotions, objects, or symbols. GIFs (Graphics Interchange Format) are short, looping animations that can depict a wide range of reactions or actions. Stickers are larger, often cartoon-like images or animations that can add personality to your messages.

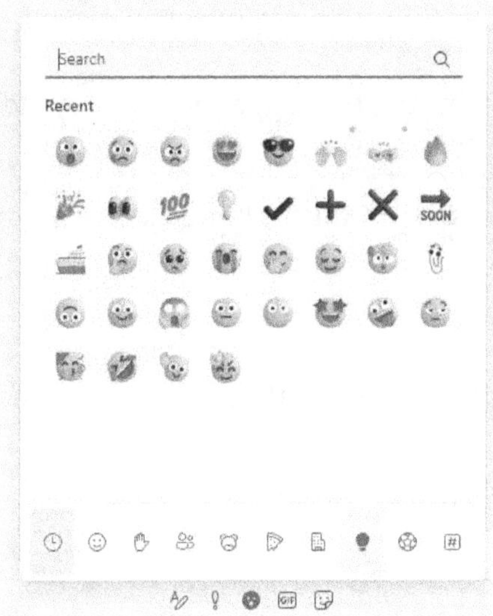

These elements are integrated into Microsoft Teams to enrich the user experience, promote creativity, and facilitate more nuanced communication. Let's explore how to access and use each of these features.

Accessing Emojis, GIFs, and Stickers in Microsoft Teams

To access emojis, GIFs, and stickers in Microsoft Teams, follow these steps:

1. Open the Chat or Channel: Start by opening the chat window or the channel where you want to send the message.

2. Locate the Emoji, GIF, and Sticker Buttons:

- Emojis: Click on the smiley face icon located at the bottom of the message box.

- GIFs: Click on the GIF icon (represented by a small animation icon) next to the emoji icon.

- Stickers: Click on the sticker icon (a square smiley face) next to the GIF icon.

Using Emojis in Microsoft Teams

1. Selecting and Inserting Emojis:

   - Click on the emoji icon to open the emoji menu.

   - Browse through the categories (smileys, people, animals, food, etc.) or use the search bar to find a specific emoji.

   - Click on the desired emoji to insert it into your message.

2. Emoji Shortcuts:

   - Type a colon (:) followed by the name of the emoji to quickly insert it. For example, typing `:smile:` will bring up the smile emoji.

   - As you type, Teams will suggest emojis matching your input.

3. Reacting with Emojis:

   - Hover over a message and click on the emoji reaction button that appears (a smiley face with a plus sign).

   - Choose an emoji reaction (like, love, laugh, surprise, sad, or angry) to quickly respond to a message.

4. Emoji Etiquette:

   - Use emojis to convey emotions and tone, but avoid overusing them in professional communication.

   - Ensure the emoji aligns with the context and message content.

Using GIFs in Microsoft Teams

1. Selecting and Inserting GIFs:

   - Click on the GIF icon to open the GIF search menu.

   - Use the search bar to find a relevant GIF or browse through the trending or categorized GIFs.

- Click on the desired GIF to insert it into your message.

2. GIF Reactions:

- Use GIFs to react to messages in a lively and animated way.

- Make sure the GIF is appropriate for the conversation context and the audience.

3. Custom GIFs:

- Upload custom GIFs by dragging and dropping them into the message box or using the "Attach" paperclip icon to upload from your device.

- Ensure custom GIFs adhere to company policies and professional standards.

4. GIF Etiquette:

- Use GIFs to add humor or emphasize a point, but avoid using them excessively in formal communication.

- Be mindful of cultural differences and avoid GIFs that could be misinterpreted.

Using Stickers in Microsoft Team

1. Selecting and Inserting Stickers:

- Click on the sticker icon to open the sticker menu.

- Browse through the available sticker packs or use the search bar to find a specific sticker.

- Click on the desired sticker to insert it into your message.

2. Customizing Stickers:

- Some stickers allow for customization, such as adding text. Click on the sticker and follow the prompts to customize it before sending.

- Customized stickers can add a personal touch to your messages.

3. Sticker Packs:

- Microsoft Teams offers a variety of sticker packs, including popular themes and characters.

- Explore different packs to find stickers that suit your style and the conversation context.

4. Sticker Etiquette:

- Use stickers to add personality and flair to your messages, but avoid overusing them in professional or formal contexts.

- Ensure the stickers are appropriate for the conversation and the audience.

Practical Applications of Emojis, GIFs, and Stickers

1. Enhancing Team Morale:

- Use emojis, GIFs, and stickers to celebrate achievements and milestones. For example, a "thumbs up" emoji or a celebratory GIF can recognize a team member's success.

- Share motivational stickers or GIFs to boost team morale and foster a positive work environment.

2. Facilitating Clear Communication:

- Emojis can help clarify the tone of a message, reducing the risk of misunderstandings. For example, a smiley face can indicate friendliness, while a winking face can show humor.

- GIFs can visually explain complex concepts or processes, making information easier to understand.

3. Building Rapport and Engagement:

- Use emojis, GIFs, and stickers to build rapport with colleagues, especially in remote or distributed teams. These elements can create a sense of connection and camaraderie.

- Engage participants in meetings and discussions by using visual elements to make interactions more lively and interactive.

4. Personalizing Communication:

- Customize your communication style by incorporating emojis, GIFs, and stickers that reflect your personality.

- Tailor your use of these elements to match the preferences and culture of your team or organization.

Managing Emoji, GIF, and Sticker Settings

1. Admin Controls:

- Administrators can control the availability and usage of emojis, GIFs, and stickers within Microsoft Teams.

- Access the Teams admin center to manage settings, such as enabling or disabling specific features or content types.

2. User Preferences:

- Users can customize their preferences for receiving and displaying emojis, GIFs, and stickers.

- Adjust notification settings to control how you are alerted to reactions and visual content in Teams.

Best Practices for Using Emojis, GIFs, and Stickers

1. Know Your Audience:

- Tailor your use of visual elements to the preferences and expectations of your audience. For example, a team of designers might appreciate creative and playful use of GIFs, while a finance team might prefer more restrained use.

2. Balance Professionalism and Personality:

- Strike a balance between professionalism and personality in your communication. Use visual elements to add flavor, but ensure they are appropriate for the context.

3. Avoid Miscommunication:

- Be aware of the potential for miscommunication with emojis, GIFs, and stickers. Ensure that your visual content clearly conveys the intended message and tone.

4. Stay Updated:

- Keep up with new emojis, GIFs, and stickers added to Microsoft Teams. Staying updated ensures you have the latest tools to enhance your communication.

5. Respect Company Policies:

- Adhere to company policies regarding the use of visual elements in communication. Ensure that your use of emojis, GIFs, and stickers aligns with organizational guidelines and values.

Conclusion

Emojis, GIFs, and stickers are powerful tools in Microsoft Teams that enhance communication by adding expressiveness, engagement, and clarity. When used appropriately, they can foster a positive team culture, facilitate clear communication, and build rapport among team members. By understanding how to effectively use these features and adhering to best practices, you can leverage them to create a more dynamic and enjoyable communication experience in Microsoft Teams.

2.1.3 Managing Chat Settings

Managing chat settings in Microsoft Teams is crucial for optimizing communication, ensuring privacy, and customizing the user experience. This section will provide a comprehensive guide on how to manage chat settings effectively.

Overview of Chat Settings

Microsoft Teams offers a variety of chat settings that users can adjust to meet their communication needs. These settings include notifications, privacy options, formatting tools, and more. By customizing these settings, users can enhance their productivity, ensure privacy, and make their interactions more efficient and enjoyable.

Accessing Chat Settings

To access chat settings in Microsoft Teams, follow these steps:

1. Open Teams: Launch Microsoft Teams on your device.

2. Navigate to Settings: Click on your profile picture or initials in the upper-right corner of the Teams interface.

3. Select Settings: From the dropdown menu, choose 'Settings'.

4. Choose Notifications or Privacy: Depending on the specific settings you want to manage, select either 'Notifications' or 'Privacy'.

Notification Settings

Notifications are vital for staying informed about new messages, mentions, and updates. However, too many notifications can be overwhelming. Microsoft Teams allows users to customize their notification preferences to balance between staying informed and avoiding distractions.

1. Banner and Email Notifications: Users can choose how they want to be notified for different types of messages (e.g., banner, email, or both). Banners appear as pop-ups on the screen, while email notifications are sent to the user's inbox.

 - Mentions: Customize notifications for when someone mentions you in a chat.

 - Messages: Set preferences for notifications for new messages in chats and channels.

 - Other Notifications: Adjust settings for notifications related to likes, reactions, and other activities.

2. Sound Notifications: Enable or disable sound notifications for incoming messages. This can be useful for maintaining focus during work hours.

3. Notification Frequency: Choose how often you want to receive notifications for different activities. For instance, you can opt for immediate, daily, or weekly summaries.

Privacy Settings

Privacy settings are essential for controlling who can contact you and how your information is shared within Microsoft Teams. These settings help maintain a secure and private communication environment.

1. Blocked Contacts: Manage your blocked contacts list to prevent unwanted communication. To block a contact, go to the chat with that person, click on their name, and select 'Block'.

2. Read Receipts: Enable or disable read receipts to control whether others can see when you have read their messages. This feature can be found under the 'Privacy' tab in settings.

3. Status Messages: Set a status message to inform others of your availability or provide context for your status (e.g., "In a meeting, will respond later"). This can be accessed by clicking on your profile picture and selecting 'Set status message'.

Formatting and Personalization

Microsoft Teams provides various formatting options to personalize your chats and make them more engaging.

1. Rich Text Formatting: Use the formatting toolbar in the chat window to apply bold, italic, underline, and strikethrough to your text. You can also change the font size and color.

2. Bullet Points and Numbering: Organize information clearly by using bullet points or numbered lists. These options are available in the formatting toolbar.

3. Code Snippets: For technical discussions, insert code snippets using the code formatting option. This feature maintains the formatting of the code, making it easier to read and understand.

4. Hyperlinks: Insert hyperlinks into your messages by selecting the text you want to hyperlink and clicking the link icon in the formatting toolbar.

5. Images and Attachments: Enhance your messages by attaching images or files. Click the paperclip icon in the chat window to upload attachments from your device or OneDrive.

Chat History and Search

Managing chat history and using the search feature efficiently can save time and improve productivity.

1. Viewing Chat History: Scroll through your chat window to view previous messages. You can also use the 'Activity' tab to see a summary of recent interactions.

2. Searching Chats: Use the search bar at the top of the Teams interface to find specific messages or files. Enter keywords or phrases to locate relevant conversations. Advanced search filters allow you to narrow down results by date, person, or team.

3. Pinning Chats: Pin important chats to the top of your chat list for quick access. To pin a chat, hover over the chat, click the three dots (more options), and select 'Pin'.

4. Saving Messages: Save important messages for future reference by clicking the three dots next to the message and selecting 'Save this message'. Access saved messages from your profile menu under 'Saved'.

Managing Chat Settings on Mobile Devices

Microsoft Teams mobile app also provides options to manage chat settings. Here's how to do it:

1. Open Teams App: Launch the Microsoft Teams app on your mobile device.

2. Access Settings: Tap on your profile picture or initials at the top left corner.

3. Select Notifications or Privacy: Choose the respective options to customize your notifications and privacy settings.

Mobile Notification Settings

1. Push Notifications: Enable or disable push notifications for chats, mentions, and other activities.

2. Quiet Hours and Quiet Days: Set quiet hours and days to mute notifications during non-working hours or weekends.

Mobile Privacy Settings

1. Read Receipts: Toggle read receipts on or off for mobile chats.

2. Blocked Contacts: Manage your blocked contacts directly from the mobile app.

Tips for Effective Chat Management

1. Regularly Review Settings: Periodically review and update your chat settings to ensure they align with your current communication needs.

2. Utilize Do Not Disturb: Use the 'Do Not Disturb' status during focused work periods to minimize interruptions.

3. Stay Organized: Use pins, saved messages, and search features to keep your chats organized and easily accessible.

4. Set Expectations: Communicate your availability and response times with your team to manage expectations and reduce stress.

Conclusion

Managing chat settings in Microsoft Teams is essential for effective communication and productivity. By customizing notifications, privacy options, and formatting tools, users can create a personalized and efficient communication environment. Regularly reviewing and adjusting these settings ensures that they continue to meet your needs as they evolve. With these tools and tips, you can make the most out of Microsoft Teams and enhance your team's collaboration experience.

2.2 Meetings and Calls

Effective communication within an organization relies heavily on well-coordinated meetings and calls. Microsoft Teams provides a robust platform to facilitate these interactions, whether they are quick catch-ups, detailed project discussions, or large-scale webinars. This section will guide you through the essentials of scheduling and joining meetings in Microsoft Teams, ensuring that you and your team can collaborate seamlessly.

2.2.1 Scheduling and Joining Meetings

Scheduling Meetings

Scheduling a meeting in Microsoft Teams can be done in several ways, each tailored to fit different needs and preferences. Here's a step-by-step guide on how to schedule meetings using various methods:

1. Scheduling via the Calendar:

The Calendar feature in Microsoft Teams is a central hub for managing all your meetings. Here's how to schedule a meeting using the Calendar:

1. Access the Calendar:

- Open Microsoft Teams.

- Click on the "Calendar" icon on the left-hand side menu.

2. Create a New Meeting:

- Click on the "New Meeting" button at the top right corner of the Calendar view.

- A new window will pop up, prompting you to fill in the meeting details.

3. Fill in Meeting Details:

- Title: Enter a descriptive title for the meeting.

- Required Attendees: Add the email addresses of the people you want to invite. You can also select attendees from your organization's directory.

- Date and Time: Set the date and time for the meeting. You can also specify if this will be a recurring meeting by clicking on the "Does not repeat" dropdown and selecting the appropriate recurrence pattern.

- Location: Specify if the meeting will have a physical location or if it will be a Teams meeting.

- Description: Add a detailed description or agenda for the meeting to provide context to the attendees.

4. Send the Invitation:

- Once all details are filled in, click "Save." The meeting invitation will be sent to all specified attendees, and the meeting will appear on their Calendars.

2. Scheduling via the Outlook Integration:

If you are using Microsoft Outlook, you can schedule Teams meetings directly from your Outlook calendar. Here's how:

1. Open Outlook Calendar:

- Launch Microsoft Outlook.

- Navigate to the "Calendar" view.

2. Create a New Meeting:

- Click on "New Teams Meeting" in the Calendar ribbon.

3. Fill in Meeting Details:

- The "New Meeting" window will open, pre-populated with a Teams meeting link.

- Fill in the meeting title, required attendees, date, time, and location as needed.

- Add any additional details or agenda in the body of the meeting invitation.

4. Send the Invitation:

- Click "Send" to distribute the meeting invitation to the attendees.

3. Scheduling via the Teams Chat:

You can also schedule a meeting directly from a chat with your team or individual members:

1. Open Chat:

- Go to the "Chat" tab in Microsoft Teams.

- Select the chat with the person or group you want to schedule a meeting with.

2. Schedule a Meeting:

- Click on the "Schedule a meeting" icon below the message box.

- Fill in the meeting details such as title, date, time, and attendees.

3. Send the Invitation:

- Click "Send" to schedule the meeting. The invitation will appear in the chat and on the attendees' Calendars.

4. Scheduling via the Channel:

If you want to schedule a meeting for an entire team or channel:

1. Navigate to the Channel:

- Go to the "Teams" tab.

- Select the team and channel where you want to schedule the meeting.

2. Schedule a Meeting:

- Click on the "Meet" button at the top right corner of the channel.

- Select "Schedule a meeting."

3. Fill in Meeting Details:

- Enter the meeting title, date, time, and other necessary details.

- You can add specific team members or leave it open for all channel members.

4. Send the Invitation:

- Click "Send" to schedule the meeting. The invitation will be posted in the channel and added to the Calendars of the team members.

Joining Meetings

Joining a meeting in Microsoft Teams is straightforward and can be done through various methods, ensuring that you can always connect with your team regardless of your location or device. Here's how to join meetings using different methods:

1. Joining via the Teams App:

1. Open Teams:

- Launch Microsoft Teams on your desktop or mobile device.

2. Navigate to the Calendar:

- Click on the "Calendar" icon on the left-hand side.

3. Join the Meeting:

- Locate the meeting you want to join.

- Click on the meeting and then select "Join."

4. Adjust Meeting Settings:

- Before joining, you can configure your audio and video settings. You can choose to enable or disable your camera and microphone, and select the audio source (computer audio, phone call, or room system).

5. Join Now:

- Click "Join Now" to enter the meeting.

2. Joining via the Meeting Link:

1. Locate the Meeting Invitation:

- Find the meeting invitation in your email, Teams chat, or Calendar.

2. Click the Meeting Link:

- Click on the "Join Microsoft Teams Meeting" link.

3. Open Teams:

- The link will open Microsoft Teams or your web browser if you don't have the app installed.

4. Join the Meeting:

- Follow the prompts to join the meeting. You may need to allow permissions for your microphone and camera if using the web version.

3. Joining via Phone:

1. Dial the Conference Number:

- If your meeting invitation includes a phone number and conference ID, you can join the meeting via phone.

2. Enter the Conference ID:

- Dial the provided phone number.

- When prompted, enter the conference ID followed by the pound () sign.

4. Joining via the Outlook Calendar:

1. Open Outlook:

- Launch Microsoft Outlook.

2. Navigate to the Calendar:

- Go to the "Calendar" view.

3. Join the Meeting:

- Locate the meeting in your Calendar.

- Click on the meeting and select "Join Teams Meeting."

Best Practices for Scheduling and Joining Meetings

To ensure that your meetings are productive and efficient, consider the following best practices:

1. Schedule Meetings with a Clear Purpose:

 - Ensure that each meeting has a clear agenda and objectives. This helps attendees prepare and contributes to a more focused and productive meeting.

2. Use Recurring Meetings for Regular Check-ins:

 - For regular team updates or recurring discussions, schedule recurring meetings to save time and ensure consistency.

3. Send Reminders:

 - Use the reminder feature in Teams or Outlook to send reminders to attendees about upcoming meetings.

4. Join Meetings Early:

 - Aim to join meetings a few minutes early to test your audio and video settings and ensure everything is working correctly.

5. Utilize Meeting Tools:

 - Make use of Teams' meeting tools such as screen sharing, whiteboards, and meeting notes to enhance collaboration and engagement during the meeting.

6. Follow-Up:

 - After the meeting, send out meeting notes, action items, and follow-up tasks to ensure everyone is aligned and aware of their responsibilities.

By mastering the scheduling and joining of meetings in Microsoft Teams, you can ensure that your team remains connected, engaged, and productive. Whether you are coordinating a small team discussion or a large-scale webinar, Microsoft Teams provides the tools and features needed to facilitate effective communication and collaboration.

2.2.2 Meeting Features and Tools

Microsoft Teams provides a robust set of features and tools to facilitate effective and interactive meetings. Whether you're hosting a quick check-in, a comprehensive project discussion, or a large webinar, Teams has you covered with a variety of functionalities designed to enhance collaboration and communication. This section will delve into the essential meeting features and tools available in Microsoft Teams, providing detailed guidance on how to leverage them for productive meetings.

1. Meeting Controls and Layouts

During a Teams meeting, the control bar at the bottom of the screen provides quick access to various functionalities:

- Mute/Unmute: Click the microphone icon to mute or unmute your audio. This is crucial for maintaining clear communication and reducing background noise.

- Camera On/Off: Toggle the camera icon to enable or disable your video feed. Enabling video helps with engagement and non-verbal communication.

- Share Screen: The screen share icon allows you to share your entire screen, a specific window, or a PowerPoint presentation. This is essential for presentations, demonstrations, and collaborative work on documents.

- More Actions: The three-dot menu provides access to additional options such as recording the meeting, changing your device settings, and applying background effects.

- Participants: Click the participants icon to view the list of attendees. From here, you can manage participants, including muting them or assigning roles.

- Chat: The chat icon opens the meeting chat panel, where participants can exchange messages, links, and files.

- Reactions: Use emojis to provide real-time feedback without interrupting the speaker. Reactions include raising your hand, thumbs up, applause, and more.

- Leave: Click the red phone icon to leave the meeting when it concludes.

2. Screen Sharing and Presentation Modes

Screen sharing in Microsoft Teams is versatile and supports various presentation modes:

- Entire Screen: Share everything on your screen, ideal for demonstrating workflows or software.

- Window: Share a specific application window, which helps focus the audience's attention on a single task or document.

- PowerPoint Live: Upload and present PowerPoint slides directly within Teams. This mode allows participants to navigate through the slides independently while you present.

- Whiteboard: Launch the Microsoft Whiteboard to collaborate visually. Participants can draw, write, and brainstorm together in real-time.

3. Meeting Chat and File Sharing

The meeting chat is a persistent feature that remains available before, during, and after the meeting. Use the chat to:

- Send Messages: Share text messages, links, and updates during the meeting.

- Share Files: Upload documents, spreadsheets, and other files directly to the chat. These files are stored in the associated Teams channel, making them accessible for future reference.

- Inline Replies: Respond directly to specific messages within the chat, helping to keep conversations organized.

4. Reactions and Raise Hand

Teams includes real-time reactions that participants can use without disrupting the flow of the meeting:

- Reactions: Click the reactions button to send emojis like thumbs up, heart, applause, laughing, or surprise. These reactions appear temporarily on the participant's video feed.

- Raise Hand: Use the raise hand feature to signal that you have a question or comment. This is especially useful in larger meetings to manage participation and ensure everyone gets a chance to speak.

5. Breakout Rooms

Breakout rooms enable you to split a larger meeting into smaller groups for focused discussions or activities:

- Creating Breakout Rooms: The meeting organizer can create breakout rooms and assign participants to them manually or automatically.

- Managing Breakout Rooms: Organizers can move between rooms to facilitate discussions and bring everyone back to the main meeting room when needed.

- Timers and Announcements: Set a timer for breakout sessions and send announcements to all rooms to keep participants informed.

6. Live Captions and Transcription

Accessibility is a key feature in Microsoft Teams:

- Live Captions: Enable live captions to display real-time text of what participants are saying. This feature supports inclusivity for those with hearing impairments or non-native speakers.

- Transcription: Record and transcribe meetings to capture a written record of the conversation. Transcripts are useful for reviewing discussions, sharing meeting notes, and ensuring that no details are missed.

7. Meeting Recording

Recording meetings allows you to capture the entire session for future reference:

- Starting a Recording: Click the more actions button and select "Start recording." All participants are notified when recording begins.

- Storing Recordings: Recordings are stored in Microsoft Stream or OneDrive for Business, depending on your organization's settings. You can access and share the recording link with participants.

- Playback and Sharing: Recordings can be played back directly within Teams, shared with team members, or downloaded for offline use.

8. Polls and Q&A

Engage participants with interactive polls and Q&A sessions:

- Creating Polls: Use the Forms app to create polls before or during the meeting. Polls can be used for quick feedback, decision-making, or gauging opinions.

- Q&A: Host Q&A sessions where participants can submit questions. This is particularly useful for webinars and large meetings to manage inquiries and provide structured responses.

9. Together Mode and Large Gallery View

Enhance the visual experience of your meetings with unique viewing options:

- Together Mode: This feature places participants in a virtual auditorium, making it feel like everyone is in the same room. It fosters a sense of unity and is particularly engaging for team-building sessions.

- Large Gallery View: Display up to 49 video feeds simultaneously, ideal for large meetings where you want to see more participants on screen.

10. Custom Backgrounds and Background Effects

Maintain professionalism or add a personal touch with custom backgrounds:

- Applying Background Effects: Blur your background or choose from a selection of preloaded images. This helps to reduce distractions and maintain focus on the speaker.

- Custom Backgrounds: Upload your own images to use as virtual backgrounds. This can be useful for branding, creating a themed meeting environment, or simply adding a bit of fun.

11. Attendee Roles and Permissions

Control the flow of the meeting by managing attendee roles:

- Organizer: The person who schedules the meeting has full control over settings and permissions.

- Presenter: Presenters can share content, manage breakout rooms, and mute participants.

- Attendee: Attendees can participate in the meeting but have restricted permissions to ensure the meeting runs smoothly.

12. Meeting Analytics and Reporting

Track the effectiveness and engagement of your meetings:

- Attendance Reports: After the meeting, download attendance reports to see who joined and how long they stayed.

- Engagement Metrics: Analyze chat activity, raised hands, and poll responses to gauge participant engagement.

- Follow-Up Actions: Use the insights from analytics to plan follow-up actions, address any concerns, and improve future meetings.

By mastering these features and tools, you can conduct efficient, engaging, and productive meetings in Microsoft Teams. Each tool is designed to enhance communication, foster collaboration, and ensure that your team stays connected and informed. Whether you're hosting a small team huddle or a large-scale webinar, Microsoft Teams provides the capabilities to meet your needs and drive successful outcomes.

2.2.3 Recording and Transcribing Meetings

Recording and transcribing meetings in Microsoft Teams is a powerful feature that can enhance productivity, ensure accountability, and provide a valuable resource for those who could not attend the meeting. This section will guide you through the process of recording and transcribing meetings in Microsoft Teams, highlighting best practices and tips to make the most of these features.

1. Why Record Meetings?

Recording meetings in Microsoft Teams offers numerous benefits:

- Reference Material: Recorded meetings serve as a valuable reference for reviewing discussions and decisions made during the meeting.

- Accountability: Having a recording ensures that everyone is aware of the meeting's content, fostering accountability.

- Inclusivity: Recordings can be shared with those who were unable to attend, ensuring that everyone stays informed.

- Training and Documentation: Recorded meetings can be used for training new employees or documenting procedures.

2. How to Record a Meeting

Recording a meeting in Microsoft Teams is straightforward. Here's a step-by-step guide:

- Step 1: Start or Join a Meeting

Begin by starting a new meeting or joining an existing one. You can start a meeting by clicking on the "Meet now" button in a channel, scheduling a meeting through the calendar, or joining a scheduled meeting.

- Step 2: Access the Recording Feature

Once in the meeting, click on the "More actions" button (represented by three dots) in the meeting controls. From the dropdown menu, select "Start recording."

- Step 3: Recording Notification

All participants will receive a notification that the meeting is being recorded. This notification ensures transparency and consent.

- Step 4: Stopping the Recording

To stop recording, click on the "More actions" button again and select "Stop recording." The recording will automatically stop when all participants leave the meeting.

- Step 5: Accessing the Recording

After the meeting, the recording will be processed and saved to Microsoft Stream (or OneDrive/SharePoint, depending on your organization's settings). A link to the recording will be shared in the meeting chat.

3. Managing Recordings

After recording a meeting, you can manage the recording in several ways:

- Sharing: Share the recording with team members or external parties by sharing the link.

- Permissions: Adjust permissions to control who can view or edit the recording.

- Download: Download the recording for offline viewing or backup purposes.

- Delete: If the recording is no longer needed, you can delete it to free up storage space.

4. Transcribing Meetings

Transcribing meetings provides a written record of everything said during the meeting. This can be particularly useful for creating minutes, searching for specific information, and ensuring clarity.

5. How to Transcribe a Meeting

To transcribe a meeting in Microsoft Teams:

- Step 1: Enable Transcription

Before you can transcribe meetings, you need to ensure that transcription is enabled for your organization. This setting can be configured by your IT administrator in the Teams admin center.

- Step 2: Start Transcription

During the meeting, click on the "More actions" button (three dots) and select "Start transcription." Like recording, participants will be notified that transcription has started.

- Step 3: Viewing the Transcript

The transcript will appear on the right side of the meeting window. As participants speak, their words will be transcribed in real-time.

- Step 4: Saving the Transcript

After the meeting, the transcript will be saved along with the recording (if enabled) and can be accessed from the meeting chat or the recording's storage location.

6. Best Practices for Recording and Transcribing Meetings

To make the most of recording and transcribing meetings, consider the following best practices:

- Notify Participants: Always inform participants before starting a recording or transcription. This ensures transparency and compliance with privacy regulations.

- Clear Audio: Ensure that all participants use good quality microphones and avoid background noise for accurate transcription and clear recordings.

- Use Transcripts for Minutes: Use the transcript as a basis for meeting minutes, making it easier to capture all key points and decisions.

- Review and Edit Transcripts: After the meeting, review the transcript for accuracy and make any necessary corrections.

- Storage and Organization: Organize your recordings and transcripts in a logical manner, using folders and naming conventions to make them easy to find later.

- Compliance: Ensure that your recording and transcription practices comply with your organization's policies and any applicable laws or regulations.

7. Advanced Features and Integrations

Microsoft Teams offers several advanced features and integrations that can enhance your recording and transcription experience:

- Integration with Microsoft Stream: Microsoft Stream provides additional tools for managing, sharing, and editing recordings. You can add captions, trim videos, and create channels for organized video storage.

- Automated Transcription Services: Consider using third-party transcription services or tools that integrate with Microsoft Teams for enhanced transcription accuracy and additional features.

- Analytics and Insights: Use analytics tools to gain insights from your recorded meetings, such as participation metrics and engagement levels.

8. Common Challenges and Solutions

While recording and transcribing meetings in Microsoft Teams is generally straightforward, you may encounter some challenges. Here are a few common issues and their solutions:

- Recording Not Starting: If the recording feature is not available, check with your IT administrator to ensure it is enabled for your organization.

- Poor Audio Quality: Encourage participants to use high-quality microphones and minimize background noise. If audio quality issues persist, consider using external recording devices.

- Transcript Inaccuracies: Transcription accuracy can vary based on audio quality and participants' accents. Review and edit transcripts for critical meetings to ensure accuracy.

9. Legal and Ethical Considerations

Recording and transcribing meetings involve capturing sensitive information, so it's important to be mindful of legal and ethical considerations:

- Consent: Always obtain consent from participants before recording or transcribing meetings. This can be done verbally at the start of the meeting or through written agreements.

- Privacy: Protect the privacy of meeting participants by securely storing recordings and transcripts and limiting access to authorized individuals.

- Compliance: Ensure that your recording and transcription practices comply with relevant laws and regulations, such as data protection and privacy laws.

10. Conclusion

Recording and transcribing meetings in Microsoft Teams can significantly enhance team communication, collaboration, and productivity. By following the steps and best practices outlined in this section, you can make the most of these features and ensure that your meetings are well-documented and accessible to all participants.

As you continue to explore Microsoft Teams, you'll discover even more ways to leverage its powerful communication tools to streamline your workflows and improve team efficiency. Whether you're conducting virtual meetings, collaborating on projects, or simply staying connected with your team, Microsoft Teams provides the tools you need to succeed.

2.3 Collaboration and File Sharing

2.3.1 Sharing Files in Teams

File sharing is a cornerstone of collaboration in Microsoft Teams. It allows team members to access, edit, and comment on documents in real-time, ensuring that everyone is on the same page. This section will guide you through the various aspects of sharing files in Teams, from basic file sharing to advanced collaboration features.

Understanding File Sharing in Teams

Microsoft Teams integrates seamlessly with OneDrive and SharePoint, providing robust file management capabilities. When you share a file in a Teams chat or channel, it is automatically stored in a specific location in SharePoint or OneDrive, depending on the context of the share.

- In a Channel: Files shared in a channel are stored in the corresponding SharePoint site for the team.

- In a Chat: Files shared in private or group chats are stored in the sender's OneDrive for Business account.

Basic File Sharing in Teams

1. Sharing Files in a Channel

To share a file in a channel, follow these steps:

1. Navigate to the desired channel where you want to share the file.

2. Click on the paperclip icon in the message compose box.

3. Select the source of your file: You can choose from your computer, OneDrive, or the Teams and Channels within your organization.

4. Select the file you want to share and click "Open."

5. Add a message if necessary and click "Send."

The file will appear in the channel's conversation thread, and a copy will be saved in the channel's "Files" tab. Team members can now view, edit, or download the file directly from the conversation thread or the Files tab.

2. Sharing Files in a Chat

To share a file in a private or group chat, the process is similar:

1. Open the chat where you want to share the file.

2. Click on the paperclip icon in the message compose box.

3. Choose the file source (Your computer, OneDrive, etc.).

4. Select the file and click "Open."

5. Add a message if desired and click "Send."

The file will appear in the chat thread, and a copy will be stored in your OneDrive for Business, under the "Microsoft Teams Chat Files" folder. Recipients can view, edit, or download the file from the chat.

Advanced File Sharing Features

1. Co-Authoring Documents

One of the most powerful features of Microsoft Teams is the ability to co-author documents. Co-authoring allows multiple team members to work on a document simultaneously, with changes being updated in real-time.

To co-author a document:

1. Share the document in a channel or chat as described above.

2. Click on the file to open it in Teams.

3. Team members can now edit the document simultaneously. Changes made by one person are immediately visible to others.

Teams supports co-authoring for Word, Excel, PowerPoint, and OneNote files. This feature eliminates the need for sending multiple versions of a document back and forth, significantly enhancing productivity and collaboration.

2. File Permissions and Sharing Links

Microsoft Teams allows you to manage file permissions and create sharing links to control who can access and edit your files. This is particularly useful when you need to share a file with someone outside your team or organization.

To manage file permissions:

1. Right-click on the file in the Files tab or chat.

2. Select "Manage access" or "Share".

3. Choose the level of access (Can view, Can edit, etc.).

4. If creating a sharing link, set the link permissions (Anyone, People in your organization, Specific people, etc.).

5. Click "Copy link" and share it as needed.

3. Integrating with OneDrive and SharePoint

Files shared in Teams are seamlessly integrated with OneDrive and SharePoint, providing a unified file storage and management experience.

- OneDrive Integration: When sharing files in private chats, they are stored in OneDrive, allowing you to manage permissions and access from within your OneDrive account.

- SharePoint Integration: Files shared in channels are stored in the corresponding SharePoint site, ensuring they are accessible to all team members. SharePoint also provides advanced document management features, such as version history, metadata, and workflows.

Best Practices for File Sharing in Teams

1. Organizing Files Effectively

To keep your files organized and easy to find, consider the following best practices:

- Use Folders: Create folders within the Files tab to categorize documents by project, topic, or department.

- Consistent Naming Conventions: Adopt a consistent naming convention for your files to make them easier to search and identify.

- Tags and Metadata: Utilize tags and metadata in SharePoint to add descriptive information to your files, making them easier to sort and filter.

2. Ensuring Security and Compliance

Security is a top priority when sharing files in Teams. Here are some tips to ensure your files remain secure:

- Set Appropriate Permissions: Always set the correct permissions when sharing files to control who can view or edit them.

- Use Sensitivity Labels: Apply sensitivity labels to classify and protect sensitive information.

- Regular Audits: Conduct regular audits of your file permissions and access logs to ensure compliance with your organization's policies.

3. Enhancing Collaboration

To enhance collaboration, leverage the integrated tools and features provided by Teams:

- Comments and Conversations: Use the comments and conversations feature within Office documents to discuss changes and provide feedback.

- Version History: Utilize the version history feature in SharePoint to track changes and revert to previous versions if needed.

- Integration with Other Apps: Integrate third-party apps like Trello, Asana, or Jira to manage tasks and projects directly from Teams.

Troubleshooting Common File Sharing Issues

Despite its robust features, you may encounter some common issues when sharing files in Teams. Here are solutions to a few common problems:

1. File Upload Errors

If you experience errors when uploading files:

- Check File Size and Type: Ensure the file size and type are supported by Teams. The maximum file size for uploads is typically 15 GB.

- Network Connection: Verify that you have a stable internet connection.

- Storage Quota: Ensure you have not exceeded your OneDrive or SharePoint storage quota.

2. Permission Issues

If users are unable to access shared files:

- Verify Permissions: Double-check the file permissions and ensure they are set correctly.

- Update Sharing Links: If using sharing links, ensure they are not expired and have the correct access level.

- Organization Policies: Check if there are any organizational policies restricting file sharing with certain users or groups.

3. Synchronization Problems

If files are not syncing correctly between Teams and OneDrive/SharePoint:

- Check Sync Settings: Ensure that OneDrive or SharePoint sync is enabled and properly configured.

- Update Software: Make sure you are using the latest version of Teams and OneDrive.

- Restart Sync: Try restarting the sync process by pausing and resuming sync in OneDrive settings.

Conclusion

Sharing files in Microsoft Teams is a fundamental aspect of team collaboration, enabling seamless communication and productivity. By understanding the basics of file sharing, utilizing advanced features, and following best practices, you can maximize the efficiency and security of your file management processes. Whether you're working on a simple document or managing complex projects, Microsoft Teams provides the tools and integrations necessary to keep your team connected and productive.

In the next section, we will explore the features and tools available for scheduling and joining meetings in Teams, ensuring that you can effectively organize and participate in virtual meetings.

2.3.2 Co-Authoring Documents

Microsoft Teams offers robust collaboration capabilities that allow team members to co-author documents in real time. Co-authoring means multiple people can work on the same document simultaneously, seeing each other's changes as they happen, and providing feedback in real time. This feature significantly enhances productivity and ensures that everyone is on the same page.

Here's a detailed guide on how to effectively co-author documents in Microsoft Teams:

Understanding Co-Authoring in Microsoft Teams

Co-authoring in Microsoft Teams leverages the integration with Office 365 apps like Word, Excel, and PowerPoint. This integration ensures a seamless experience where team members can edit documents directly within Teams without needing to switch between different applications.

1. Creating and Sharing a Document for Co-Authoring

To start co-authoring a document in Microsoft Teams, follow these steps:

1. Create a Document:

- Open the desired team and channel in Microsoft Teams.

- Click on the "Files" tab at the top of the channel.

- Click "New" and choose the type of document you want to create (Word, Excel, PowerPoint).

- Give the document a name and click "Create."

2. Upload an Existing Document:

- If you already have a document you want to collaborate on, click "Upload" in the "Files" tab.

- Select the document from your computer and upload it to the channel.

3. Share the Document:

- Once the document is created or uploaded, click on it to open.

- Click the "Share" button to generate a shareable link.

- Copy the link and share it with your team members, or directly mention them in the channel to notify them of the document.

2. Real-Time Co-Authoring Features

When team members open the document, they can start editing it simultaneously. Microsoft Teams provides several features to enhance the co-authoring experience:

1. Presence Indicators:

- You can see who else is working on the document in real time through presence indicators.

- Each person's cursor and selection are highlighted in different colors, making it easy to track who is making changes.

2. Comments and Feedback:

- Team members can leave comments on specific parts of the document.

- To add a comment, highlight the text or object you want to comment on, right-click, and select "New Comment."

- Comments can be replied to, creating a thread for discussion.

3. Version History:

- Microsoft Teams automatically saves the document, maintaining a version history.

- You can access previous versions by clicking "File" > "Info" > "Version History" to view or restore earlier iterations of the document.

4. Chat Integration:

- While co-authoring, you can use the chat feature within Teams to discuss changes and collaborate more effectively.

- Click the "Chat" icon in the document to open a chat window without leaving the document.

3. Best Practices for Co-Authoring

To make the most out of co-authoring in Microsoft Teams, consider the following best practices:

1. Clear Communication:

- Establish guidelines for how and when team members should make changes to the document.

- Use comments and chat to communicate any major changes or suggestions.

2. Assign Roles:

- Assign specific roles or sections of the document to team members to avoid overlapping work.

- This can be managed through comments or a brief discussion before starting the co-authoring session.

3. Regular Check-Ins:

- Schedule regular check-ins to review the document's progress.

- Use Teams meetings or calls to discuss the document in detail and resolve any issues.

4. Utilize Templates:

- Use document templates to ensure consistency in formatting and structure.

- Microsoft Teams allows you to create and share templates within your team.

4. Advanced Co-Authoring Features

Microsoft Teams and Office 365 offer several advanced features that can further enhance your co-authoring experience:

1. @Mentions in Comments:

- Use @mentions in comments to draw specific team members' attention to particular sections of the document.

- This helps in getting quick feedback and ensuring that critical points are addressed promptly.

2. Integrated Task Management:

- Integrate your document with task management tools like Planner or To Do.

- Assign tasks related to the document directly from Teams to ensure accountability and track progress.

3. Accessibility Features:

- Microsoft Teams and Office 365 include accessibility features that ensure everyone, including those with disabilities, can participate in the co-authoring process.

- Utilize tools like Immersive Reader, dictation, and screen reader support to enhance accessibility.

4. Using Office 365 Apps:

- For more complex documents, you can switch to the full versions of Word, Excel, or PowerPoint.

- Changes made in the desktop apps are automatically synced with the document in Teams.

5. Troubleshooting Common Co-Authoring Issues

While co-authoring in Microsoft Teams is generally smooth, you may encounter some common issues. Here's how to troubleshoot them:

1. Document Locked for Editing:

- If a document is locked for editing, ensure no one else has it open in a conflicting application.

- Check for any unsaved changes and ensure all users are using compatible versions of Office apps.

2. Sync Issues:

- If changes aren't syncing, check your internet connection.

- Ensure that all team members are connected to the internet and working on the latest version of the document.

3. Conflicting Changes:

- If you encounter conflicting changes, review the version history to identify and resolve discrepancies.

- Communicate with team members to understand their changes and integrate them accordingly.

6. Real-World Use Cases of Co-Authoring

To illustrate the power of co-authoring in Microsoft Teams, here are a few real-world scenarios:

1. Project Proposals:

- Teams working on project proposals can collaboratively draft, review, and finalize documents.

- Using comments and real-time editing, team members can provide immediate feedback and suggestions.

2. Marketing Plans:

- Marketing teams can co-author campaign strategies, ensuring all members contribute their ideas and expertise.

- The integration with other Office 365 tools allows for seamless incorporation of data and analytics.

3. Educational Material:

- Teachers and students can work together on assignments, presentations, and reports.

- Co-authoring fosters a collaborative learning environment, allowing for peer review and group projects.

Conclusion

Co-authoring documents in Microsoft Teams transforms the way teams collaborate, making the process more efficient and interactive. By leveraging the real-time editing capabilities, presence indicators, and integration with Office 365 apps, teams can work together seamlessly, no matter where they are located. Adopting best practices and utilizing advanced features ensures that your co-authoring experience is productive and effective, ultimately enhancing your team's overall performance.

2.3.3 Integrating with OneDrive and SharePoint

Introduction to Integration

Integrating Microsoft Teams with OneDrive and SharePoint is a powerful way to enhance collaboration and streamline file management. Both OneDrive and SharePoint are integral components of the Microsoft 365 ecosystem, offering robust solutions for storing, sharing, and managing files. In this section, we will explore how to effectively integrate these tools with Microsoft Teams, enabling seamless collaboration and efficient workflows.

Understanding OneDrive and SharePoint

Before diving into the integration process, it's important to understand the distinct roles of OneDrive and SharePoint within the Microsoft 365 suite:

- OneDrive: Primarily designed for personal storage, OneDrive is an online cloud storage service where individuals can save their files and access them from any device. It supports personal file sharing and collaboration on a smaller scale.

- SharePoint: A more comprehensive platform, SharePoint is used for creating websites, managing content, and facilitating collaboration on a larger scale. SharePoint sites often serve as centralized repositories for team or project files, offering advanced document management capabilities.

Benefits of Integration

Integrating OneDrive and SharePoint with Microsoft Teams offers several benefits:

- Centralized Access: Team members can access and collaborate on files stored in OneDrive and SharePoint directly from Teams, eliminating the need to switch between multiple applications.

- Real-Time Collaboration: Integration enables real-time co-authoring of documents, ensuring that all team members are working with the most up-to-date information.

- Improved Organization: SharePoint's robust organizational features help keep files structured and easily accessible, enhancing overall productivity.

- Enhanced Security: Both OneDrive and SharePoint offer advanced security and compliance features, ensuring that sensitive information is protected.

Setting Up OneDrive Integration

To integrate OneDrive with Microsoft Teams, follow these steps:

1. Accessing OneDrive from Teams:

   - Open Microsoft Teams and navigate to the left-hand navigation pane.

   - Click on the "Files" tab to access the Files section.

   - Here, you will see an option for "OneDrive." Clicking on this will take you to your OneDrive storage, where you can view and manage your personal files.

2. Uploading Files to OneDrive:

- In the OneDrive tab within Teams, click on the "Upload" button to add new files or folders to your OneDrive storage.

- You can also drag and drop files directly into the OneDrive interface.

3. Sharing OneDrive Files in Teams:

- To share a file stored in OneDrive with your team, go to the chat or channel where you want to share the file.

- Click on the paperclip icon (Attach) in the message box, select "OneDrive," and choose the file you want to share.

- Add a message if needed, then click "Send." The file will be shared with the selected recipients, who can view and edit it based on the permissions you've set.

Setting Up SharePoint Integration

SharePoint integration with Microsoft Teams is more comprehensive and involves setting up a dedicated SharePoint site for your team. Here's how to do it:

1. Creating a SharePoint Site:

- Navigate to the Microsoft 365 admin center and select "SharePoint."

- Click on "Create site" and choose the type of site you want to create (Team site or Communication site). For team collaboration, a Team site is recommended.

- Follow the prompts to name your site, set privacy settings, and add team members.

2. Linking SharePoint to Teams:

- Open Microsoft Teams and go to the team where you want to link the SharePoint site.

- Click on the "Files" tab, then select "Add cloud storage."

- Choose "SharePoint" and follow the prompts to link your SharePoint site to the team. Once linked, team members can access and manage SharePoint files directly from the Teams interface.

3. Managing SharePoint Files in Teams:

- Within the "Files" tab of your team, you will now see a "SharePoint" section. Clicking on this will take you to the linked SharePoint site.

- You can upload, edit, and manage files just as you would directly in SharePoint, but with the added convenience of doing so from within Teams.

Collaborating with OneDrive and SharePoint Files in Teams

Once OneDrive and SharePoint are integrated with Microsoft Teams, you can take advantage of several powerful collaboration features:

1. Real-Time Co-Authoring:

- When you open a document stored in OneDrive or SharePoint from Teams, multiple team members can work on it simultaneously. Changes are saved in real time, allowing for seamless collaboration.

- Use the "Open in App" option to access the full functionality of the respective Office app (Word, Excel, PowerPoint), while still maintaining real-time collaboration.

2. Version History:

- Both OneDrive and SharePoint track changes and maintain a version history of documents. This allows you to review previous versions, restore older versions if needed, and track who made specific changes.

- To access version history, right-click on a document in Teams, select "Version history," and choose the version you want to view or restore.

3. File Sharing and Permissions:

- SharePoint allows for advanced sharing options and permission settings. You can share files with specific team members, set permission levels (view, edit, etc.), and even share files externally if allowed by your organization's policies.

- To manage permissions, go to the SharePoint site, select the file or folder, and click on the "Share" button. From here, you can add people, set permissions, and send sharing links.

4. Organizing Files and Folders:

- SharePoint's robust organizational features enable you to create libraries, folders, and metadata to keep your files structured and easy to find.

- Use metadata and columns in SharePoint to categorize files, making it easier to search and filter based on specific criteria.

Best Practices for Using OneDrive and SharePoint with Teams

To maximize the benefits of integrating OneDrive and SharePoint with Microsoft Teams, consider the following best practices:

1. Standardize Naming Conventions:

 - Implement consistent naming conventions for files and folders to ensure easy identification and retrieval.

 - Use clear, descriptive names that indicate the content and purpose of the file or folder.

2. Regularly Review and Clean Up Files:

 - Periodically review files and folders to remove duplicates, outdated documents, and unnecessary clutter.

 - Encourage team members to archive or delete files that are no longer needed to maintain an organized workspace.

3. Set Up Appropriate Permissions:

 - Ensure that file permissions are set appropriately to balance security and collaboration needs.

 - Regularly review permissions to make sure they align with current team members and roles.

4. Leverage Metadata and Tags:

 - Use metadata and tags in SharePoint to categorize and organize files. This enhances searchability and makes it easier to find specific documents.

 - Train team members on how to use and manage metadata effectively.

5. Utilize SharePoint Libraries:

 - Create dedicated document libraries in SharePoint for different projects, departments, or functions. This helps in keeping files organized and accessible.

- Set up library views to customize how files are displayed based on specific criteria or filters.

Conclusion

Integrating OneDrive and SharePoint with Microsoft Teams is a game-changer for organizations looking to enhance collaboration and streamline file management. By following the steps outlined in this section, you can set up a seamless integration that allows team members to access, share, and collaborate on files directly from Teams. Leveraging the robust features of OneDrive and SharePoint, coupled with the communication and collaboration capabilities of Teams, can significantly boost productivity and ensure that your team is always working with the most up-to-date information.

Implementing best practices for file organization, permissions, and metadata management will further enhance the efficiency and effectiveness of your integrated workspace. As you continue to explore and utilize the full potential of OneDrive and SharePoint within Teams, your organization will be well-positioned to achieve its collaboration goals and drive success in today's dynamic work environment.

CHAPTER III
Advanced Features and Customizations

3.1 Integrating Third-Party Apps and Services

3.1.1 Adding Apps to Teams

Microsoft Teams is a robust collaboration platform that not only includes the core functionalities provided by Microsoft but also allows the integration of various third-party apps to enhance productivity and streamline workflows. Adding apps to Microsoft Teams can significantly augment the platform's capabilities, enabling teams to work more efficiently by bringing their favorite tools directly into Teams. This section will guide you through the process of discovering, adding, and managing apps in Microsoft Teams.

1. Understanding the App Store in Teams

Before diving into the process of adding apps, it is essential to familiarize yourself with the Microsoft Teams App Store. The App Store is accessible from within the Teams application and contains a wide range of apps categorized based on functionality. These categories include Project Management, Analytics, Productivity, Education, and more.

1. Accessing the App Store:

- Open Microsoft Teams.

- Click on the "Apps" icon located in the left sidebar. This opens the App Store interface.

2. Browsing and Searching for Apps:

- You can browse apps by category or use the search bar at the top of the App Store to find specific apps.

- Each app has a detailed description, user ratings, and screenshots to help you understand its functionality.

2. Adding Apps to a Team

Adding an app to a specific team allows all team members to utilize the app's features. Here's how you can add an app to a team:

1. Selecting the App:

- Once you find the app you want to add, click on its icon to open its detailed page.

- Review the app's features, permissions required, and user reviews to ensure it meets your needs.

2. Adding the App:

- Click on the "Add to a team" button.

- A dialog box will appear asking you to specify the team and channel where you want to add the app. Select the appropriate team and channel.

- Click "Set up."

3. Configuring the App:

- Some apps may require additional configuration after being added. Follow the on-screen prompts to complete the setup process.

- You may need to sign in with your account credentials or provide access permissions to the app.

3. Adding Apps to a Channel

Adding apps to a specific channel within a team allows for more focused and relevant usage of the app's features in the context of that channel's activities.

1. Navigating to the Channel:

- Go to the team and select the channel where you want to add the app

2. Adding the App:

- Click on the "+" (plus) icon located at the top of the channel interface.

- This opens the "Add a tab" window where you can browse and select apps.

3. Configuring the App:

- Similar to adding an app to a team, follow the prompts to configure the app within the channel.

- Ensure that the app is set up to meet the needs of the channel's specific activities and goals.

4. Personal Apps in Teams

In addition to adding apps to teams and channels, Microsoft Teams also supports personal apps. These apps are added to your individual Teams interface and are accessible only by you.

1. Adding Personal Apps:

- Go to the App Store by clicking on the "Apps" icon in the left sidebar.

- Browse or search for the app you want to add.

- Click on the app and select "Add for me" if the option is available.

2. Accessing Personal Apps:

- Once added, personal apps appear in the left sidebar under the "..." (more) menu.

- Click on the app's icon to access its features and functionality.

5. Managing App Permissions and Settings

Managing app permissions and settings is crucial to ensure that apps function correctly and securely within your Teams environment.

1. Reviewing App Permissions:

- Before adding any app, carefully review the permissions it requires.

- Permissions can include access to your Teams data, files, and user information.

2. Setting Up Permissions:

- After adding an app, you may need to configure its permissions.

- Go to the app's settings page to grant or revoke permissions as necessary.

3. Managing App Settings:

- Each app may have its own settings page where you can customize its behavior.

- Access app settings by clicking on the app's icon and navigating to its settings or configuration menu.

6. Using Popular Third-Party Apps in Teams

To provide practical examples, let's explore how to add and use some popular third-party apps in Microsoft Teams:

1. Trello:

- Trello is a project management tool that uses boards, lists, and cards to help you organize tasks and projects.

- To add Trello to Teams, search for "Trello" in the App Store, click "Add to a team," and configure the integration by signing in with your Trello account.

- Once added, you can create, view, and manage Trello boards directly within Teams.

2. Asana:

- Asana is another project management tool that helps teams organize work and projects.

- Search for "Asana" in the App Store, add it to your team, and sign in with your Asana account to integrate it with Teams.

- Use Asana to create tasks, track progress, and collaborate with team members without leaving Teams.

3. Zoom:

- Zoom is a popular video conferencing tool that can be integrated with Teams for scheduling and joining meetings.

- Find "Zoom" in the App Store, add it to your team, and configure the integration with your Zoom account.

- Schedule, start, and join Zoom meetings directly from within Teams.

4. Polly:

- Polly is a survey and polling app that helps you gather feedback and opinions from your team.

- Add Polly to your team from the App Store and configure it to start creating polls and surveys in your channels.

- Use Polly to engage your team and make informed decisions based on their input.

7. Tips for Effective App Integration

Integrating third-party apps can significantly enhance your team's productivity. Here are some tips for effective app integration:

1. Assessing Team Needs:

- Identify the specific needs and workflows of your team before adding apps.

- Choose apps that align with your team's goals and activities.

2. Training and Adoption:

- Provide training sessions for your team to familiarize them with new apps.

- Encourage adoption by demonstrating how the apps can improve their work processes.

3. Regular Reviews:

- Periodically review the apps you have added to ensure they are still meeting your team's needs.

- Remove any apps that are no longer useful or relevant.

4. Staying Updated:

- Keep track of updates and new features for the apps you are using.

- Regularly update apps to ensure you are using the latest versions with improved functionality and security.

8. Troubleshooting App Integration Issues

While integrating apps with Teams can enhance productivity, you may encounter some issues. Here are common problems and solutions:

1. App Not Adding Correctly:

   - Ensure you have the necessary permissions to add apps to the team or channel.

   - Check your internet connection and try adding the app again.

2. App Not Functioning Properly:

   - Verify that the app is configured correctly.

   - Ensure that you have granted all required permissions for the app to function.

3. App Conflicts:

   - Some apps may conflict with each other or with existing settings in Teams.

   - Identify and resolve conflicts by reviewing app settings and configurations.

4. Getting Support:

   - If you encounter persistent issues, contact the app's support team for assistance.

   - Use Microsoft Teams support resources for additional help and troubleshooting.

9. Conclusion

Adding third-party apps to Microsoft Teams is a powerful way to enhance your team's collaboration and productivity. By following the steps outlined in this section, you can discover, add, and manage apps effectively, ensuring that your team has the tools it needs to succeed. Remember to regularly review your app integrations and stay updated on new features to continually improve your team's workflows. With the right apps in place,

Microsoft Teams can become an even more versatile and efficient platform for all your collaborative needs.

3.1.2 Using Connectors and Bots

Microsoft Teams offers a robust platform for integrating third-party apps and services, allowing users to enhance their collaboration and productivity. Two essential components of these integrations are Connectors and Bots. Understanding how to use these features effectively can significantly boost the capabilities of your Teams environment.

Connectors

Connectors are a way to get content and updates from your favorite services into your Microsoft Teams channels. They enable the seamless flow of information, helping teams stay up-to-date with critical notifications and updates without leaving the Teams environment. Here's a step-by-step guide on using Connectors in Microsoft Teams:

1. Accessing Connectors:

   - Navigate to the channel where you want to add a Connector.

   - Click on the ellipsis (...) next to the channel name.

   - Select "Connectors" from the drop-down menu.

2. Choosing a Connector:

   - Browse through the list of available Connectors or use the search bar to find a specific one.

   - Click on the "Configure" button next to the Connector you want to add.

3. Configuring the Connector:

   - Follow the on-screen instructions to configure the Connector.

   - This may involve signing into the service, selecting specific settings, and determining how and when updates should be posted to your channel.

4. Using the Connector:

- Once configured, the Connector will automatically post updates to the channel based on the settings you've specified.

- You can manage or remove the Connector at any time by revisiting the "Connectors" menu.

Popular Connectors include services like Trello, GitHub, Twitter, and RSS feeds. By integrating these tools, teams can receive updates on project management tasks, code changes, social media activity, and more directly within their Teams channels.

Bots

Bots in Microsoft Teams are powerful AI-driven tools that can automate tasks, answer questions, and provide interactive support. Bots can be used to streamline workflows, enhance productivity, and improve user engagement. Here's how to effectively use Bots in Microsoft Teams:

1. Adding Bots:

- Go to the Teams app store by clicking on "Apps" in the left sidebar.

- Use the search function or browse categories to find a Bot that suits your needs.

- Click on the Bot and select "Add to a team" or "Add to chat".

2. Interacting with Bots:

- Once added, you can start interacting with the Bot in the designated channel or chat.

- Bots typically respond to commands or queries entered as text.

- For example, the "Who" Bot can provide organizational information, while the "Calendar" Bot can assist with scheduling meetings.

3. Custom Bots:

- Organizations can develop custom Bots tailored to their specific needs using the Microsoft Bot Framework.

- Custom Bots can integrate with internal systems, databases, and APIs to provide bespoke functionalities.

4. Managing Bots:

- Bots can be managed via the Teams app store or through the Microsoft Teams admin center.

- You can adjust settings, permissions, and access controls to ensure Bots operate securely within your organization.

Best Practices for Using Connectors and Bots

1. Security Considerations:

- Ensure that Connectors and Bots comply with your organization's security policies.

- Regularly review permissions and access settings to prevent unauthorized access to sensitive information.

2. User Training:

- Provide training sessions and resources to help team members understand how to use Connectors and Bots effectively.

- Encourage users to explore and leverage these tools to enhance their workflows.

3. Monitoring and Optimization:

- Regularly monitor the activity and performance of Connectors and Bots.

- Gather feedback from users to identify areas for improvement and optimization.

4. Integration Strategy:

- Develop a strategic plan for integrating Connectors and Bots into your Teams environment.

- Prioritize integrations that will deliver the most significant benefits to your team's productivity and collaboration.

Examples of Effective Use Cases

1. Project Management:

- Use the Trello Connector to receive updates on board activities, card assignments, and due dates directly in your Teams channel.

- Deploy a project management Bot to create tasks, assign team members, and track progress without leaving Teams.

2. Development Operations:

- Integrate the GitHub Connector to get notifications about code commits, pull requests, and issues.

- Utilize a DevOps Bot to automate build and deployment processes, providing real-time updates and feedback.

3. Customer Support:

- Connect with Twitter to monitor mentions and respond to customer inquiries from within Teams.

- Implement a customer support Bot that can handle common queries, escalate issues, and provide status updates.

4. Sales and Marketing:

- Use the Salesforce Connector to receive updates on opportunities, leads, and accounts.

- Deploy a marketing Bot to schedule social media posts, track campaign performance, and provide analytics.

By effectively leveraging Connectors and Bots, teams can automate routine tasks, improve communication, and access critical information in real-time. This integration not only enhances productivity but also creates a more cohesive and efficient collaborative environment within Microsoft Teams.

3.1.3 Managing App Permissions

Managing app permissions in Microsoft Teams is crucial for maintaining security, ensuring compliance, and providing the appropriate access levels to team members. As organizations increasingly integrate third-party apps and services into Microsoft Teams, understanding how to manage these permissions effectively becomes paramount. This section will guide you through the processes and best practices for managing app permissions in Teams.

Understanding App Permissions in Microsoft Teams

App permissions in Microsoft Teams determine what an app can access and what actions it can perform within the Teams environment. Permissions can vary widely depending on the app and its intended use. Common permissions requested by apps include:

- Access to user profiles and data

- Ability to read and send messages

- Access to files and documents

- Integration with other Office 365 services (e.g., Outlook, OneDrive)

- Administrative permissions to manage settings and configurations

It is essential to understand these permissions and ensure they align with your organization's security policies and user needs.

Setting Up App Permissions

The process of setting up app permissions involves several steps, which include evaluating the app's requirements, configuring the necessary permissions, and ongoing management and monitoring. Here's a detailed guide on how to set up app permissions:

1. Evaluate the App's Requirements:

  - Review Documentation: Before integrating an app, review its documentation to understand what permissions it requires and why.

  - Security Assessment: Conduct a security assessment to ensure the app does not pose any risks to your organization's data and privacy.

  - User Needs: Consider the needs of your team and how the app will enhance productivity and collaboration.

2. Configure App Permissions:

  - Admin Center: Use the Microsoft Teams Admin Center to manage app permissions. Navigate to the "Teams apps" section and select "Permission policies."

- Create Permission Policies: Create or modify permission policies to define what apps are allowed or blocked within your Teams environment.

  - Allow All Apps: This setting allows all third-party apps to be installed, providing flexibility but potentially increasing risk.

  - Block All Apps: This setting blocks all third-party apps, offering maximum security but limiting functionality.

  - Allow Specific Apps: This setting allows only specified apps, balancing security and functionality by permitting only trusted apps.

- Assign Policies to Users: Assign these permission policies to specific users or groups based on their roles and needs.

3. Approve Apps:

- Admin Approval: Some apps require admin approval before they can be installed. Use the Teams Admin Center to review and approve these apps.

- Review Permissions: Carefully review the permissions requested by the app before granting approval.

Ongoing Management and Monitoring

Managing app permissions is not a one-time task. It requires ongoing management and monitoring to ensure continued security and compliance. Here are the steps for effective ongoing management:

1. Regular Reviews:

- Periodic Assessments: Regularly review the apps and their permissions to ensure they are still necessary and secure.

- Update Policies: Update permission policies as needed to reflect changes in organizational needs or security posture.

2. Monitoring App Usage:

- Usage Reports: Use the Teams Admin Center to generate reports on app usage. This helps in understanding which apps are actively used and if there are any unauthorized apps.

- User Feedback: Collect feedback from users about the apps they use and any issues they encounter. This can provide insights into the app's effectiveness and security concerns.

3. Responding to Security Incidents:

- Incident Response Plan: Have a plan in place for responding to security incidents related to app permissions. This includes identifying and mitigating risks, communicating with affected users, and updating policies to prevent future incidents.

- Audit Logs: Regularly review audit logs to detect any unusual or unauthorized activities involving third-party apps.

Best Practices for Managing App Permissions

To effectively manage app permissions in Microsoft Teams, consider the following best practices:

1. Least Privilege Principle:

- Minimal Permissions: Grant apps the minimal permissions necessary for their functionality. Avoid over-permissioning which can lead to security vulnerabilities.

- Role-Based Access Control: Use role-based access control to assign permissions based on user roles and responsibilities.

2. User Training and Awareness:

- Educate Users: Train users on the importance of app permissions and the potential risks associated with third-party apps.

- Clear Guidelines: Provide clear guidelines on how to request and use third-party apps within Teams.

3. Security and Compliance:

- Compliance Requirements: Ensure that the apps and their permissions comply with your organization's regulatory and compliance requirements.

- Regular Audits: Conduct regular audits to ensure ongoing compliance and identify any deviations from established policies.

4. Collaboration with IT and Security Teams:

- Cross-Functional Collaboration: Work closely with IT and security teams to manage app permissions effectively. This ensures that all aspects of security and functionality are considered.

- Shared Responsibility: Promote a culture of shared responsibility where all team members understand their role in maintaining a secure Teams environment.

Examples and Case Studies

To illustrate the importance of managing app permissions effectively, consider the following examples and case studies:

1. Case Study 1: Unauthorized Data Access:

- Scenario: A third-party app with excessive permissions was installed, leading to unauthorized access to sensitive data.

- Outcome: By reviewing and adjusting app permissions, the organization mitigated the risk and enhanced security.

2. Case Study 2: Improved Productivity with Controlled Permissions:

- Scenario: A team integrated a project management app with limited permissions, ensuring it could only access necessary data.

- Outcome: The team benefited from the app's functionality without compromising security, leading to improved productivity and collaboration.

Conclusion

Managing app permissions in Microsoft Teams is a critical aspect of maintaining a secure and efficient collaboration environment. By understanding the importance of app permissions, setting them up correctly, and implementing ongoing management and monitoring practices, organizations can harness the power of third-party apps while ensuring security and compliance. Following best practices and learning from real-world examples can help in effectively managing app permissions and enhancing overall team productivity.

3.2 Customizing Teams with Tabs

3.2.1 Adding and Removing Tabs

Customizing Microsoft Teams with tabs is a powerful way to streamline workflows, improve team collaboration, and provide easy access to essential tools and information. Tabs are an integral part of the Teams interface, allowing users to embed content from various sources directly within their team channels. This section will guide you through the process of adding and removing tabs, ensuring you can tailor the Teams experience to meet your specific needs.

Adding Tabs

Step-by-Step Guide to Adding Tabs

1. Navigate to the Desired Channel

- Open Microsoft Teams and select the team and channel where you want to add a tab. Ensure you have the necessary permissions to modify the channel settings.

2. Access the Tabs Menu

- At the top of the channel, you'll see a series of existing tabs, such as Posts and Files. Next to these tabs, click on the '+' icon to open the Add a Tab menu.

3. Choose an App or Service

- A pop-up window will display a variety of apps and services that you can add as tabs. These include built-in Microsoft apps (e.g., OneNote, Planner), third-party apps (e.g., Trello, Asana), and custom-developed apps. Browse through the available options or use the search bar to find a specific app.

4. Configure the Tab Settings

- After selecting an app, you'll need to configure its settings. This step varies depending on the app. For example, if you're adding a OneNote tab, you'll choose the specific notebook and section to display. If you're adding a website tab, you'll enter the URL of the site you want to embed.

5. Name the Tab

- Give your tab a meaningful name that clearly indicates its purpose. This name will appear at the top of the channel alongside other tabs.

6. Add the Tab

- Click the "Save" or "Add" button to complete the process. The new tab will now appear in the channel, providing quick access to the embedded app or content.

Common Use Cases for Tabs

- Project Management: Integrate tools like Planner or Trello to manage tasks and projects within your team channel. Create boards, assign tasks, and track progress without leaving Teams.

- Document Collaboration: Add a tab for SharePoint or OneDrive to facilitate collaborative editing of documents. Team members can access and edit files in real-time, ensuring everyone is working with the latest version.

- Note Taking and Knowledge Sharing: Use OneNote to create a shared notebook for meeting notes, brainstorming sessions, and knowledge sharing. This keeps all relevant information in one easily accessible location.

- Web Integration: Embed frequently used websites or web apps as tabs. For example, add a tab for your company's intranet, a project-specific dashboard, or an external tool that your team uses regularly.

Tips for Effective Tab Management

- Prioritize Tabs Based on Team Needs: Only add tabs that provide significant value to your team. Avoid cluttering the channel with unnecessary tabs, as this can make navigation more difficult.

- Organize Tabs Logically: Arrange tabs in a logical order based on their importance and usage frequency. You can reorder tabs by dragging and dropping them into the desired position.

- Provide Training and Documentation: Ensure that team members understand the purpose of each tab and how to use it effectively. Provide training sessions or create a quick reference guide to assist with onboarding.

Removing Tabs

Step-by-Step Guide to Removing Tabs

1. Navigate to the Channel

- Open the team and channel from which you want to remove a tab.

2. Access the Tab Menu

- Click on the tab you wish to remove. At the top right corner of the tab interface, you'll see a drop-down arrow or an ellipsis (three dots). Click on this to open the tab options menu.

3. Remove the Tab

- In the options menu, select "Remove" or "Delete." Confirm your decision when prompted. Note that removing a tab does not delete the underlying app or data; it merely removes the shortcut from the channel.

Considerations for Removing Tabs

- Evaluate Tab Usage: Before removing a tab, consider whether it is still being used by team members. Removing an actively used tab can disrupt workflows and cause confusion.

- Communicate Changes: Inform your team about any significant changes to the channel layout, including the removal of tabs. This helps prevent confusion and ensures everyone is aware of where to find essential tools and information.

- Backup Important Data: If the tab contains critical information or configurations, ensure you have a backup or alternative access method before removing it. For example, if you're removing a Planner tab, make sure task assignments and progress are documented elsewhere.

Common Reasons for Removing Tabs

- Redundancy: Over time, some tabs may become redundant as team needs evolve. Regularly review and clean up tabs to keep the channel streamlined and relevant.

- Reorganization: You might need to remove tabs as part of a broader effort to reorganize the team's structure or workflows. Removing outdated or less-used tabs can make room for more pertinent tools and information.

- Performance Improvement: In some cases, having too many tabs can slow down the performance of Teams, especially if they load extensive external content. Removing unnecessary tabs can improve the user experience.

Advanced Tab Customizations

- Custom Tabs Development: For teams with specific needs, consider developing custom tabs using the Microsoft Teams Developer Platform. This allows you to create tailored solutions that integrate deeply with your workflows.

- Tab Permissions Management: Control who can add, modify, or remove tabs by configuring channel permissions. This ensures that only authorized users can make changes, maintaining consistency and order within the channel.

- Automating Tab Management: Use Power Automate (formerly Microsoft Flow) to automate the addition or removal of tabs based on triggers and conditions. For example, automatically add a Planner tab when a new project is created or remove tabs associated with completed projects.

By effectively managing tabs in Microsoft Teams, you can enhance collaboration, streamline workflows, and ensure that your team has quick access to the tools and information they need. Whether adding new tabs to introduce valuable resources or removing outdated ones to keep the channel organized, understanding the best practices for tab management is crucial for maximizing the efficiency and effectiveness of your team's communication and collaboration efforts.

3.2.2 Popular Tab Integrations

One of the most powerful features of Microsoft Teams is its ability to integrate with a wide range of applications through tabs. Tabs allow users to bring important tools and resources directly into their Teams channels, creating a centralized hub for collaboration and productivity. In this section, we will explore some of the most popular tab integrations that can enhance your Teams experience.

1. Microsoft Office Suite

a. Excel

Excel is a cornerstone of data management and analysis for many organizations. By adding an Excel tab to your Teams channel, you can collaborate on spreadsheets in real-time without leaving the Teams interface. This integration supports co-authoring, allowing multiple users to edit the same document simultaneously, and includes features like cell highlighting to show who is working on specific parts of the sheet.

b. Word

Word integration in Teams enables collaborative document editing and review. Adding a Word tab allows team members to draft, revise, and finalize documents together. Features like commenting and track changes are fully supported, making it easy to manage feedback and edits.

c. PowerPoint

PowerPoint is essential for creating and presenting slideshows. With a PowerPoint tab in Teams, users can co-author presentations, share ideas, and make real-time updates. This is particularly useful for preparing collaborative presentations where input from multiple team members is required.

2. Planner

Planner is a task management tool that integrates seamlessly with Teams. By adding a Planner tab, you can create and manage task boards within your Teams channels. This integration allows you to assign tasks, set due dates, and track progress using visual boards and charts. It's a powerful way to keep your team organized and ensure that projects stay on track.

3. OneNote

OneNote is a versatile note-taking application that supports multimedia notes, including text, images, and audio. Adding a OneNote tab to your Teams channel provides a shared space for brainstorming, meeting notes, and project documentation. OneNote's integration supports real-time collaboration, allowing multiple users to edit notes simultaneously and keep track of changes.

4. SharePoint

SharePoint integration in Teams brings robust document management capabilities directly into your channels. By adding a SharePoint tab, you can access and manage documents stored in your SharePoint libraries without switching between applications. This integration supports version control, permissions management, and metadata, making it ideal for teams that rely heavily on document collaboration and storage.

5. Power BI

Power BI is a business analytics service that provides interactive visualizations and business intelligence capabilities. By adding a Power BI tab, you can embed reports and dashboards within your Teams channels. This integration allows team members to view and interact with data insights directly within Teams, facilitating data-driven decision-making and collaboration.

6. GitHub

For development teams, GitHub integration is invaluable. Adding a GitHub tab allows you to monitor repositories, view pull requests, and track issues without leaving Teams. This integration streamlines development workflows and ensures that the entire team stays informed about code changes and project progress.

7. Trello

Trello is a popular project management tool that uses boards, lists, and cards to organize tasks. By adding a Trello tab to Teams, you can bring your Trello boards into your channels.

This integration allows you to manage tasks, set due dates, and collaborate on projects within the Teams environment, providing a unified workspace for project management.

8. Asana

Asana is another project management tool that integrates well with Teams. By adding an Asana tab, you can view and manage your Asana tasks and projects directly within Teams. This integration helps streamline project tracking and ensures that team members can stay updated on their tasks without switching between applications.

9. Adobe Creative Cloud

For creative teams, integrating Adobe Creative Cloud applications like Photoshop, Illustrator, and Premiere Pro can be a game-changer. By adding an Adobe Creative Cloud tab, team members can share assets, collaborate on creative projects, and provide feedback within Teams. This integration simplifies the workflow for design and multimedia projects, ensuring that all resources and feedback are centralized.

10. Zendesk

Zendesk is a customer support and ticketing system that can be integrated into Teams via a tab. Adding a Zendesk tab allows support teams to track tickets, view customer inquiries, and manage support workflows directly within Teams. This integration helps improve response times and ensures that support staff can collaborate effectively to resolve customer issues.

11. SurveyMonkey

SurveyMonkey is a powerful survey tool that can be integrated into Teams to facilitate feedback collection and analysis. By adding a SurveyMonkey tab, you can create, distribute, and analyze surveys directly within Teams. This integration is useful for gathering team feedback, conducting market research, and running employee engagement surveys.

12. Smartsheet

Smartsheet is a work management and automation platform that integrates seamlessly with Teams. Adding a Smartsheet tab allows you to manage projects, track tasks, and automate workflows within Teams. This integration supports real-time collaboration and provides a visual way to manage complex projects and processes.

13. Jira

Jira is a popular issue and project tracking tool used by development teams. By adding a Jira tab, you can view and manage your Jira issues and projects directly within Teams. This integration helps streamline development workflows, allowing team members to stay updated on project progress and issues without leaving Teams.

14. Wiki

Teams includes a built-in Wiki tab that provides a space for team knowledge sharing and documentation. The Wiki tab is perfect for creating and organizing content such as project documentation, team guidelines, and process workflows. It supports rich text editing and can be structured into sections and pages for easy navigation.

15. Forms

Microsoft Forms integration allows you to create and share surveys, quizzes, and polls within Teams. Adding a Forms tab provides a quick way to gather input from your team, conduct assessments, and collect feedback. Responses are automatically collected and can be analyzed directly within Teams.

16. Stream

Microsoft Stream is a video service for sharing and managing corporate videos. By adding a Stream tab, you can embed videos, training sessions, and company announcements within your Teams channels. This integration supports video playback, commenting, and likes, making it a powerful tool for internal communications and training.

17. PowerApps

PowerApps allows you to build custom business applications without writing code. By adding a PowerApps tab, you can bring these custom apps directly into your Teams channels. This integration is useful for creating tailored solutions for specific business needs, such as expense reporting, inventory management, or employee onboarding.

18. Yammer

Yammer is a social networking service for enterprise communication. By adding a Yammer tab, you can integrate Yammer communities and discussions into your Teams channels. This integration helps bridge the gap between formal team collaboration and informal social networking, fostering a sense of community and engagement within the organization.

19. Poly

Poly is a tool for creating polls and surveys within Teams. Adding a Poly tab allows you to quickly gather opinions and feedback from your team. This integration supports multiple question types and provides real-time results, making it a great tool for decision-making and team engagement.

20. MindMeister

MindMeister is a mind mapping tool that helps visualize ideas and brainstorming sessions. By adding a MindMeister tab, you can create and collaborate on mind maps within Teams. This integration is useful for planning projects, developing strategies, and fostering creative thinking within your team.

3.2.3 Custom Tabs and Development

Custom tabs in Microsoft Teams provide a powerful way to extend the functionality of your workspace, integrate with other tools, and enhance collaboration. This section will guide you through the process of developing and implementing custom tabs in Teams, providing detailed steps, best practices, and examples to help you get the most out of this feature.

Understanding Custom Tabs

Custom tabs allow you to embed web content directly into Teams, making it accessible within the app. They can be added to both channels and group chats, offering a seamless way to integrate your team's most-used tools and services.

There are two types of custom tabs:

1. Static Tabs: These are added to personal apps and appear on the left-hand side navigation bar.

2. Configurable Tabs: These are added to channels and group chats, allowing users to configure the tab with specific content.

Prerequisites for Developing Custom Tabs

Before you start developing custom tabs, ensure you have the following prerequisites:

- Microsoft 365 Subscription: Access to Teams through a Microsoft 365 subscription.

- Developer Tools: Tools such as Visual Studio Code, Node.js, and the Teams Yeoman Generator.

- Basic Knowledge of Web Development: Understanding HTML, CSS, and JavaScript.

Steps to Create Custom Tabs

Step 1: Set Up Your Development Environment

1. Install Node.js and npm: Node.js is a JavaScript runtime, and npm is the Node package manager. Both are required to run and manage your project.

```
npm install -g yo generator-teams
```

2. Install the Yeoman Generator for Teams: The Yeoman generator simplifies the creation of Teams apps.

```
npm install -g generator-teams
```

3. Create a New Project: Use the generator to create a new Teams app project.

```
yo teams
```

Follow the prompts to configure your project. Select "Tab" as one of the components.

Step 2: Develop Your Custom Tab

1. Project Structure: Familiarize yourself with the project structure. The key folders include:

- `src/app/web/tab/`: Contains the code for your tab.
- `src/public/`: Hosts static files like images and stylesheets.

2. Define Your Tab Content: Edit the HTML, CSS, and JavaScript files in the `tab` folder to define what your tab will display.

For example, edit `src/app/web/tab/Tab.tsx` to include your custom content:

```
import  as React from "react";


export default class CustomTab extends React.Component {
  render() {
    return (
      <div>
        <h1>Welcome to My Custom Tab</h1>
        <p>This is a custom tab in Microsoft Teams.</p>
      </div>
    );
  }
```

```
}
```

3. Configure the Tab: Update the `manifest.json` file to define the tab's configuration.

```
{
  "staticTabs": [
    {
      "entityId": "customTab",
      "name": "Custom Tab",
      "contentUrl": "https://<your-app-url>/tab.html",
      "websiteUrl": "https://<your-app-url>/",
      "scopes": ["personal"]
    }
  ]
}
```

Step 3: Test Your Tab

1. Run Your Project: Start your project using the following command:

```
gulp serve
```

2. Use ngrok for Tunneling: Ngrok creates a secure tunnel to your localhost, making it accessible over the internet.

```
ngrok http 3007
```

Update your `manifest.json` with the ngrok URL.

3. Upload the App to Teams: Go to the Teams app, navigate to "Apps" > "Manage Apps" > "Upload a custom app" and upload the modified `manifest.json` file.

4. Test Functionality: Ensure your custom tab works as expected in the Teams interface.

Best Practices for Developing Custom Tabs

1. User Experience: Ensure your tab's UI is user-friendly and integrates seamlessly with the Teams environment. Follow Microsoft's [Fluent Design System](https://developer.microsoft.com/en-us/fluentui/) for consistency.

2. Performance Optimization: Optimize your web content for fast loading times. Use efficient coding practices and minimize external dependencies.

3. Security: Ensure your tab adheres to security best practices. Implement proper authentication and authorization mechanisms to protect sensitive data.

4. Responsive Design: Design your tab to be responsive, ensuring it works well on different devices and screen sizes.

5. Accessibility: Make your tab accessible to all users, including those with disabilities. Follow [WCAG guidelines](https://www.w3.org/WAI/standards-guidelines/wcag/) for web accessibility.

Advanced Customization and Development

1. Integrating with Microsoft Graph: Use Microsoft Graph API to integrate your tab with other Microsoft 365 services, such as retrieving user profiles, calendar events, and more.

Example: Fetching user profile data

```
import { Client } from "@microsoft/microsoft-graph-client";


const client = Client.init({
  authProvider: (done) => {
    done(null, accessToken); // Access token obtained through authentication
  }
```

```
});

client
  .api('/me')
  .get()
  .then((res) => {
    console.log(res);
  });
```

2. Implementing Authentication: Secure your tab using Microsoft identity platform for authentication. Use OAuth 2.0 and OpenID Connect protocols for user sign-in.

Example: Adding authentication with MSAL.js

```
import  as msal from "@azure/msal-browser";

const msalConfig = {
  auth: {
    clientId: "your-client-id",
    authority: "https://login.microsoftonline.com/your-tenant-id",
    redirectUri: "https://your-redirect-uri"
  }
};

const msalInstance = new msal.PublicClientApplication(msalConfig);

msalInstance.loginPopup().then((response) => {
```

```
    console.log(response);
  });
```

3. Developing Configurable Tabs: Create tabs that users can configure to meet their specific needs. Use the Teams SDK to manage configuration settings.

Example: Configurable tab setup

```
import { microsoftTeams } from "@microsoft/teams-js";


microsoftTeams.initialize();


microsoftTeams.settings.registerOnSaveHandler((saveEvent) => {
  microsoftTeams.settings.setSettings({
    contentUrl: "https://<your-app-url>/configurable-tab.html",
    entityId: "configurableTab",
    suggestedDisplayName: "Configurable Tab"
  });
  saveEvent.notifySuccess();
});


microsoftTeams.settings.setValidityState(true);
```

Real-World Examples and Use Cases

1. Project Management Dashboard: Create a custom tab that integrates with project management tools like Trello or Asana, providing a centralized dashboard for tracking project progress within Teams.

2. Sales Performance Tracker: Develop a tab that pulls data from your CRM (Customer Relationship Management) system, allowing sales teams to track their performance metrics and customer interactions directly in Teams.

3. HR Portal: Build a custom tab for the HR department to manage employee information, policies, and training resources, enhancing internal communication and resource access.

Conclusion

Developing custom tabs for Microsoft Teams can significantly enhance your team's collaboration experience by integrating external tools and providing a seamless workflow. By following the steps and best practices outlined in this guide, you can create powerful custom tabs that cater to your team's specific needs and improve overall productivity.

Remember, the key to successful custom tab development lies in understanding your users' needs, leveraging the full potential of Teams' capabilities, and continuously iterating on your solutions based on feedback and evolving requirements.

3.3 Advanced Meeting and Calling Features

3.3.1 Breakout Rooms

Breakout rooms in Microsoft Teams are a powerful feature designed to facilitate smaller group discussions within larger meetings. They enable the division of participants into separate, smaller sessions, allowing for more focused and interactive engagements. This feature is particularly useful in educational settings, workshops, brainstorming sessions, and any scenario where smaller group interactions are beneficial.

Overview of Breakout Rooms

Breakout rooms allow meeting organizers to create multiple smaller meeting spaces within the main Teams meeting. Each breakout room functions as a mini-meeting, complete with its own chat, files, and other collaborative features. Participants can be assigned to rooms either manually or automatically by the organizer.

Setting Up Breakout Rooms

1. Starting with the Main Meeting:

- Begin by scheduling your meeting as usual in Microsoft Teams.

- Once the meeting has started, ensure you are the meeting organizer or have the necessary permissions to create breakout rooms.

2. Creating Breakout Rooms:

- Click on the Breakout Rooms icon in the meeting controls. This icon looks like a small square divided into four quadrants.

- Choose the number of breakout rooms you want to create. Teams allow you to create up to 50 breakout rooms in a single meeting.

3. Assigning Participants:

- Automatically: You can choose to have Teams automatically assign participants to the rooms. This method ensures that participants are evenly distributed among the rooms.

- Manually: Alternatively, you can manually assign participants to specific rooms. This is useful if you want to group participants based on certain criteria, such as department, project team, or specific discussion topics.

Managing Breakout Rooms

Once the breakout rooms are created and participants assigned, the meeting organizer has several management options:

1. Opening and Closing Rooms:

- To start the breakout sessions, click "Start rooms." Participants will be notified and automatically moved to their assigned breakout rooms.

- You can close all rooms at any time by clicking "Close rooms." Participants will then be returned to the main meeting.

2. Joining and Leaving Rooms:

- As the organizer, you can join any breakout room at any time to monitor discussions or provide assistance. Simply click on the room you want to join and select "Join room."

- You can leave the breakout room and return to the main meeting by clicking "Leave" and selecting "Return to main meeting."

3. Broadcasting Messages:

- You can send announcements to all breakout rooms simultaneously. This is useful for providing instructions, sharing updates, or giving a countdown before closing the rooms. Click "Broadcast message," type your message, and click "Send."

4. Reassigning Participants:

- During the breakout sessions, you may need to move participants between rooms. Click on "Rooms," then select "Reassign participants." Choose the participant and the new room for reassignment.

Best Practices for Using Breakout Rooms

1. Clear Objectives:

- Ensure that each breakout room has a clear objective or task. This helps participants stay focused and productive. Provide detailed instructions before opening the rooms.

2. Facilitators:

- Consider assigning a facilitator or leader to each breakout room. This person can help guide the discussion, ensure that everyone participates, and keep the group on track.

3. Time Management:

- Set a specific duration for the breakout sessions and stick to it. Use the broadcast message feature to remind participants of the time remaining.

4. Feedback and Reporting:

- After closing the breakout rooms, reconvene in the main meeting and have a representative from each room share a summary of their discussion. This ensures that valuable insights and conclusions are shared with the entire group.

Advanced Features in Breakout Rooms

1. Room Settings:

- Customize the settings for each breakout room. You can allow participants to return to the main meeting at any time or restrict them to their assigned rooms.

2. Pre-Meeting Assignments:

- For recurring meetings or planned sessions, you can pre-assign participants to breakout rooms. This saves time and ensures that participants are already grouped when the meeting starts.

3. Persistent Rooms:

- In some cases, you might want to use the same breakout room configurations for multiple sessions. Microsoft Teams allows you to recreate previous room assignments quickly.

Use Cases for Breakout Rooms

1. Educational Sessions:

- Teachers can use breakout rooms for group projects, discussions, and peer review sessions. This enables more personalized attention and interaction among students.

2. Workshops and Training:

- Facilitators can divide participants into smaller groups for hands-on activities, role-playing, or scenario-based training. This enhances learning and engagement.

3. Brainstorming and Ideation:

- Breakout rooms are ideal for brainstorming sessions where small groups can discuss ideas in-depth before presenting them to the larger group.

4. Team Building:

- Use breakout rooms for team-building exercises, icebreakers, and social activities. This fosters stronger connections and collaboration among team members.

Conclusion

Breakout rooms in Microsoft Teams are a versatile and powerful tool for enhancing collaboration and engagement in various meeting scenarios. By understanding how to set up, manage, and effectively use breakout rooms, you can transform your meetings into more interactive and productive sessions. Whether you're conducting a classroom lesson, a corporate workshop, or a team meeting, breakout rooms provide the flexibility to meet your collaboration needs. Embrace this feature to unlock new levels of participation and efficiency in your virtual gatherings.

3.3.2 Live Events and Webinars

Microsoft Teams Live Events and Webinars provide powerful tools for hosting large-scale virtual events and delivering professional-quality presentations to a wide audience. This section will explore the features, setup process, best practices, and tips for hosting successful live events and webinars.

Understanding Live Events and Webinars

Live events in Microsoft Teams are designed for one-to-many communication where the host or a small group of presenters can broadcast video and content to a large online audience. Unlike standard Teams meetings, which are more interactive, live events are more structured, with limited interaction from attendees. Webinars, on the other hand, offer a blend of interaction and broadcast capabilities, allowing for Q&A sessions, polls, and more engaging features.

Key Features of Live Events and Webinars

1. Scalability: Live events can support thousands of attendees, making them ideal for company-wide meetings, public announcements, and large training sessions.

2. Production Options: You can produce live events using Microsoft Teams or an external app or device. Teams provides a streamlined experience, while external production tools offer more advanced features.

3. Recording and Archiving: Live events can be recorded for on-demand viewing, ensuring that those who cannot attend live can still access the content later.

4. Q&A Management: Live events feature a moderated Q&A system where attendees can submit questions, and presenters or moderators can respond in real-time.

5. Interactive Tools: Webinars offer additional interactive tools such as polls and attendee chat, enhancing engagement during the session.

6. Analytics and Reporting: After the event, detailed analytics provide insights into attendee engagement, helping to measure the event's success and gather feedback for future improvements.

Setting Up a Live Event or Webinar

1. Planning Your Event

- Define the Purpose: Clearly outline the objectives of your event. Determine whether it is an informational session, training, or a promotional webinar.

- Identify the Audience: Understand who your audience is and tailor the content and delivery to meet their needs.

- Set a Date and Time: Choose a date and time that maximizes attendance, considering different time zones if your audience is global.

2. Creating the Event

- Accessing the Live Events Feature: In Microsoft Teams, navigate to the Calendar and select the "New meeting" dropdown, then choose "Live event."

- Event Details: Fill in the event details, including the title, description, start and end times, and the event production type (Teams or external app/device).

- Invite Presenters and Producers: Add presenters and producers who will participate in the event. Presenters are responsible for delivering content, while producers manage the event logistics.

3. Configuring Event Settings

- Permissions: Determine who can attend the event—public, organization-wide, or specific people and groups.

- Event Options: Configure options such as recording, live captions, and attendee engagement tools (e.g., Q&A).

- Custom Branding: For webinars, you can customize the registration page with your company's branding, including logos, colors, and images.

4. Preparing for the Event

- Rehearsals and Dry Runs: Conduct rehearsals to ensure that all presenters are familiar with the technology and the event flow.

- Content Preparation: Prepare all the content that will be shared, such as slides, videos, and polls. Ensure that it is polished and aligns with the event's objectives.

- Technical Checks: Verify that all equipment, including cameras, microphones, and internet connections, are functioning properly.

Conducting the Live Event or Webinar

1. Starting the Event

- Producer's Role: The producer starts the live event, manages the layout, and switches between content and presenters.

- Presenters' Role: Presenters share their screens, deliver their content, and interact with attendees through the Q&A panel.

2. Managing the Event Flow

- Content Delivery: Ensure smooth transitions between different segments of the event. Use visual aids, such as slides and videos, to keep the audience engaged.

- Q&A Management: Moderators can review and publish questions, respond to queries, and manage the flow of questions to presenters.

- Interactive Elements: For webinars, use polls and other interactive tools to engage the audience and gather feedback in real-time.

3. Handling Technical Issues

- Troubleshooting On-the-Fly: Be prepared to address any technical issues that arise during the event. Have a plan for backup presenters or content if needed.

- Support Channels: Ensure that technical support is available to both presenters and attendees during the event.

Post-Event Activities

1. Follow-Up and Recording

- Recording Access: Provide attendees with access to the event recording. This allows those who missed the live session to view it later.

- Follow-Up Emails: Send follow-up emails to attendees, including a thank-you note, a link to the recording, and any additional resources or materials.

2. Analyzing Event Performance

- Event Analytics: Review the event analytics to assess engagement metrics such as the number of attendees, participation levels, and Q&A activity.

- Feedback Collection: Collect feedback from attendees through surveys to understand what worked well and what could be improved for future events.

3. Continuous Improvement

- Lessons Learned: Document the lessons learned from the event, including any technical issues encountered and the overall effectiveness of the content delivery.

- Iterative Process: Use the insights gained to refine your approach for future live events and webinars, continuously improving the experience for both presenters and attendees.

Best Practices for Successful Live Events and Webinars

1. Engage Your Audience

- Interactive Content: Use interactive content such as polls, Q&A, and chat to keep the audience engaged throughout the event.

- Dynamic Presentations: Avoid monotonous presentations by incorporating multimedia elements and varying the presentation style.

2. Professional Production Quality

- High-Quality Equipment: Use high-quality cameras, microphones, and lighting to ensure that both video and audio are clear and professional.

- Stable Internet Connection: Ensure a stable and fast internet connection to prevent interruptions and maintain the quality of the broadcast.

3. Effective Moderation

- Moderation Team: Have a dedicated moderation team to manage Q&A, handle technical issues, and support presenters.

- Clear Communication: Establish clear communication channels between the production team, presenters, and moderators.

4. Preparation and Rehearsals

- Thorough Rehearsals: Conduct multiple rehearsals to ensure that all participants are comfortable with their roles and the event flow.

- Backup Plans: Have contingency plans in place for potential technical issues or unexpected disruptions.

5. Audience Engagement Before and After the Event

- Pre-Event Promotion: Promote the event through various channels to attract a larger audience. Provide information on what attendees can expect and how to join.

- Post-Event Follow-Up: Engage with attendees after the event by providing access to recordings, additional resources, and opportunities for further interaction.

By following these guidelines and leveraging the robust features of Microsoft Teams, you can host successful live events and webinars that deliver value to your audience and enhance your organization's communication and collaboration capabilities.

3.3.3 Call Queues and Auto Attendants

Introduction to Call Queues and Auto Attendants

Call Queues and Auto Attendants are essential features for organizations that manage a high volume of incoming calls. These features streamline the call management process, ensuring that calls are directed to the right departments or individuals efficiently. In Microsoft Teams, these tools can significantly enhance your team's communication and operational efficiency.

Call Queues in Microsoft Teams

Call Queues allow incoming calls to be directed to a group of people within your organization. This feature is particularly useful for customer service teams, support centers, and sales departments where calls need to be answered promptly and distributed evenly among available agents.

Setting Up Call Queues

1. Navigate to the Microsoft Teams Admin Center: To set up a Call Queue, you need to have administrative access. Go to the Microsoft Teams Admin Center.

2. Create a New Call Queue: Under the "Voice" section, select "Call Queues" and then "Add." Here, you'll need to provide a name for your Call Queue, which should be descriptive of its purpose (e.g., "Customer Support Queue").

3. Assign a Resource Account: A resource account is required to manage the Call Queue. If you don't have one, you can create it in the Microsoft 365 Admin Center. Assign this resource account to the Call Queue.

4. Configure Greeting Message: You can upload a custom greeting message or use the default one. The greeting message is what callers will hear when they are placed in the queue.

5. Set the Call Distribution Method: Choose how you want the calls to be distributed among the agents. Options include Attendant Routing (all agents are notified simultaneously), Serial Routing (calls are routed to agents one by one), and Round Robin (calls are distributed evenly).

6. Add Agents: Select the users who will be part of this Call Queue. You can add individual users or groups.

7. Configure Overflow and Timeout Options: Set up what happens if all agents are busy or if the call is not answered within a specified time. Options include redirecting the call to another Call Queue, a voicemail, or an external number.

8. Save and Activate: Once all settings are configured, save the Call Queue. It will now be active and ready to handle incoming calls.

Managing Call Queues

1. Monitoring Performance: Regularly check the performance of your Call Queues. Use the Call Analytics and Call Quality Dashboard in the Teams Admin Center to monitor metrics such as average wait time, call volume, and agent performance.

2. Adjusting Settings: Based on the performance data, you might need to adjust the Call Queue settings. For example, you might need to add more agents during peak hours or change the call distribution method to better match your team's workflow.

3. Training Agents: Ensure that all agents are trained to handle calls efficiently. Provide them with scripts, FAQs, and guidelines to improve customer interactions.

Auto Attendants in Microsoft Teams

Auto Attendants allow you to create a menu system for incoming calls, directing callers to the appropriate department or information. This feature is useful for organizations with multiple departments or services, as it helps streamline the caller's journey.

Setting Up Auto Attendants

1. Navigate to the Microsoft Teams Admin Center: Go to the "Voice" section and select "Auto Attendants."

2. Create a New Auto Attendant: Click "Add" to create a new Auto Attendant. Provide a name and description that accurately represents its purpose.

3. Assign a Resource Account: Similar to Call Queues, an Auto Attendant requires a resource account. Create or assign a resource account to the Auto Attendant.

4. Configure General Settings: Set up the general settings, including the time zone and the language for the Auto Attendant. This will determine how the system interacts with callers.

5. Set Up Call Flow: Define the call flow for the Auto Attendant. This includes:

- Welcome Greeting: Upload a recorded welcome message or use text-to-speech to create one.

- Menu Options: Create a menu with different options (e.g., "Press 1 for Sales, Press 2 for Support"). Each option should be linked to a specific action, such as transferring to a Call Queue, playing an informational message, or connecting to a specific user.

- Business Hours and Holidays: Define the business hours during which the Auto Attendant will operate. Set up holiday schedules with special greetings and routing rules.

6. Configure Call Handling Options: Specify how calls should be handled during and outside business hours. You can set up different call flows for each scenario.

7. Save and Activate: Save the Auto Attendant settings. It will now be active and ready to handle incoming calls.

Managing Auto Attendants

1. Review Call Logs: Regularly review the call logs and analytics to understand how callers are interacting with the Auto Attendant. This data can help you identify any issues or bottlenecks in the call flow.

2. Update Menu Options: Based on the call data and feedback from callers, you may need to update the menu options. Ensure that the options are clear and lead to the correct destinations.

3. Regular Maintenance: Periodically review and update the greetings, menu options, and call handling rules to ensure they are still relevant and effective.

Best Practices for Call Queues and Auto Attendants

1. Clear and Concise Greetings: Ensure that all greetings and messages are clear and concise. Callers should easily understand their options and the actions they need to take.

2. Regular Testing: Regularly test the Call Queues and Auto Attendants to ensure they are functioning correctly. Test during both business hours and after hours to verify all scenarios.

3. Gather Feedback: Collect feedback from callers and agents to identify areas for improvement. Use surveys or direct feedback mechanisms to gather this information.

4. Continuous Training: Provide ongoing training for agents and administrators. Ensure they are familiar with the latest features and best practices for using Call Queues and Auto Attendants.

5. Optimize Call Flows: Continuously analyze call data to optimize the call flows. Look for patterns and trends that indicate where callers may be experiencing difficulties.

Conclusion

Call Queues and Auto Attendants are powerful tools within Microsoft Teams that can significantly enhance the efficiency of your organization's communication processes. By setting up and managing these features effectively, you can ensure that incoming calls are handled promptly and directed to the appropriate resources, improving overall customer satisfaction and operational efficiency. Implementing best practices and continuously monitoring and adjusting the settings will help you get the most out of these advanced features, ensuring that your team can collaborate and communicate seamlessly.

CHAPTER IV
Teams for Project Management

4.1 Setting Up Projects in Teams

4.1.1 Creating Project Teams and Channels

Creating project teams and channels in Microsoft Teams is a fundamental step in managing projects effectively. This process ensures that team members are well-organized, communication is streamlined, and collaboration tools are utilized to their fullest potential. In this section, we will delve into the step-by-step guide to creating project teams and channels, and how to optimize them for successful project management.

Understanding Project Teams

In Microsoft Teams, a "team" is a collection of people, conversations, files, and tools—all in one place. Each team is built around a specific project or organizational need. For project management, setting up a dedicated team for each project allows for focused communication and collaboration.

1. Determine the Project Scope and Requirements

- Define the Project Objectives: Clearly outline what the project aims to achieve. This includes the goals, deliverables, and deadlines.

- Identify Team Members: List all individuals who will be involved in the project. Consider their roles and responsibilities to ensure that all necessary skills are covered.

- Establish Communication Needs: Determine the types of communication (e.g., daily updates, weekly meetings) required to keep the project on track.

2. Create the Project Team

- Access Microsoft Teams: Open Microsoft Teams and navigate to the Teams section.

- Create a New Team: Click on "Join or create a team" at the bottom of the Teams list, then select "Create a team."

- Select Team Type: Choose "From scratch" to build a new team or use an existing team template if available. For most project management purposes, selecting "From scratch" is advisable for complete customization.

- Team Name and Description: Provide a meaningful name that reflects the project. Add a description to outline the project's purpose and objectives.

- Privacy Settings: Decide whether the team will be private (only accessible to invited members) or public (anyone in the organization can join). For project management, a private team is typically preferred to control access and ensure confidentiality.

- Add Members: Invite team members by entering their names or email addresses. Assign roles (Owner or Member) based on their responsibilities within the project.

3. Setting Up Channels

- Default General Channel: Every team comes with a default "General" channel. This can be used for high-level project information and announcements.

- Create Additional Channels: Based on project needs, create additional channels to organize different aspects of the project. For example:

  - Planning: For discussions and documents related to project planning and scheduling.

  - Development: For tasks, conversations, and files related to the development phase.

  - Testing: To manage activities and communications related to testing and quality assurance.

  - Documentation: For storing all project documentation and reference materials.

- Channel Naming Conventions: Use clear and consistent naming conventions for channels to make navigation intuitive. For example, prefix channels with numbers or categories (e.g., "1. Planning," "2. Development").

Optimizing Project Teams and Channels

1. Customization and Settings

- Channel Descriptions: Add descriptions to each channel to clarify its purpose and contents.

- Tabs and Apps: Utilize tabs to add important tools and files directly into channels. Common tabs include:

  - Files: A tab for easy access to relevant documents and files.

  - Planner: To integrate task management directly within the channel.

  - OneNote: For project notes and shared information.

  - Website: For linking to external resources or project management tools.

2. Permissions and Roles

- Team Owner vs. Member: Assign multiple owners to a team to ensure continuous management even if the primary owner is unavailable.

- Guest Access: If collaborating with external stakeholders, enable guest access and manage their permissions carefully to ensure data security.

- Channel Moderation: Utilize channel moderation settings to control who can post and manage content within specific channels.

3. Communication and Collaboration

- Team Meetings: Schedule regular team meetings using the "Meet Now" feature or by scheduling through the Teams calendar. Regular check-ins help keep everyone aligned and address issues promptly.

- Conversations and Mentions: Use @mentions to grab the attention of specific team members or entire channels for important updates.

- Announcements: Make use of the announcement feature in posts to highlight important messages in a visually distinct way.

Best Practices for Managing Project Teams and Channels

1. Consistent Communication

- Daily Updates: Encourage team members to provide daily updates on their progress in the relevant channels.

- Weekly Syncs: Hold weekly sync meetings to review progress, discuss challenges, and plan the upcoming week's tasks.

- Transparent Reporting: Ensure that all team members have access to project reports and updates to maintain transparency.

2. Documentation and Knowledge Sharing

- Centralized Documentation: Keep all project-related documents in the designated channels for easy access and reference.

- Version Control: Use version control features in Office 365 to track changes and maintain document integrity.

- Knowledge Base: Create a knowledge base within the team using OneNote or Wiki tabs to store important information, guidelines, and FAQs.

3. Task Management and Delegation

- Planner for Task Assignment: Use Microsoft Planner to create tasks, assign them to team members, and set deadlines. This helps in tracking task progress and accountability.

- Task Prioritization: Prioritize tasks based on their importance and deadlines. Use labels and priority tags in Planner to organize tasks efficiently.

- Regular Follow-ups: Conduct regular follow-ups on assigned tasks to ensure they are on track and address any issues that arise.

4. Feedback and Improvement

- Continuous Feedback Loop: Encourage team members to provide feedback on processes and tools used in the project. This helps in identifying areas of improvement.

- Retrospectives: Conduct regular retrospectives to review what went well, what didn't, and how processes can be improved in future projects.

- Adapt and Evolve: Be open to changing and adapting your approach based on feedback and project needs. Flexibility is key to successful project management.

Conclusion

Setting up project teams and channels in Microsoft Teams is crucial for effective project management. By following the steps outlined above, you can ensure that your team is well-organized, communication is clear, and collaboration is seamless. Customizing your team and channels to fit the specific needs of your project, along with employing best practices, will enhance your team's productivity and increase the likelihood of project success. Whether you are managing a small project or a large-scale initiative, Microsoft Teams provides the tools and features needed to keep everything on track and within reach.

4.1.2 Using Planner for Task Management

Effective task management is crucial for the success of any project. Microsoft Planner, integrated with Microsoft Teams, provides a powerful and intuitive way to organize, assign, and track tasks within your projects. This section will guide you through using Planner for task management, covering everything from creating and assigning tasks to monitoring progress and ensuring deadlines are met.

Understanding Microsoft Planner

Microsoft Planner is a task management tool that allows teams to create, assign, and track tasks in a visually organized manner. It integrates seamlessly with Microsoft Teams, providing a centralized hub for project collaboration and task tracking. Planner uses a card-based system, where tasks are represented as cards on a board, similar to other popular task management tools like Trello.

Setting Up a Planner Board

To start using Planner within Microsoft Teams, you first need to set up a Planner board for your project. Follow these steps:

1. Navigate to Your Team and Channel:

- Open Microsoft Teams and select the team and channel where you want to manage your project tasks.

2. Add Planner to the Channel:

- Click on the "+" icon at the top of the channel to add a new tab.

- Choose "Planner" from the list of available apps.

- If you already have an existing Planner board, you can link it; otherwise, create a new one.

3. Name Your Planner Board:

- Provide a name for your Planner board that clearly reflects the project or purpose it serves.

4. Create Buckets for Task Organization:

- Buckets are used to group related tasks. Create buckets based on phases of the project, task categories, or any other logical grouping that suits your project needs. For example, you might have buckets named "To Do," "In Progress," and "Completed."

Creating and Assigning Tasks

With your Planner board set up, you can now start creating and assigning tasks. Here's how:

1. Create a Task:

- Click on the "+ Add task" button within a bucket.

- Enter the task name and click "Add task." You can also specify a due date and assign the task to a team member directly from this interface.

2. Assigning Tasks:

- To assign a task, open the task card by clicking on it.

- Use the "Assign" field to select the team member(s) responsible for the task. You can assign tasks to multiple people if needed.

3. Adding Task Details:

- Within the task card, you can add more details to ensure clarity and accountability. This includes:

- Description: Provide a detailed description of the task.

- Checklist: Break down the task into smaller sub-tasks by creating a checklist.

- Attachments: Attach relevant files or documents.

- Comments: Use the comments section for ongoing communication and updates related to the task.

Tracking Task Progress

Monitoring the progress of tasks is essential for project management. Microsoft Planner offers several features to help you track and manage tasks effectively:

1. Task Status:

- Each task card has a status indicator that can be set to "Not Started," "In Progress," or "Completed." Updating the status helps team members understand the current state of each task at a glance.

2. Priority Levels:

- Assign priority levels to tasks (e.g., Urgent, Important, Medium, Low) to help team members prioritize their work.

3. Due Dates and Reminders:

- Set due dates for tasks to ensure they are completed on time. Microsoft Planner can send reminders to assignees as the due date approaches.

4. Labels:

- Use color-coded labels to categorize tasks further. Labels can represent different types of work, departments, or any other classification that aids in organizing tasks.

5. Charts and Views:

- Planner provides several views to help visualize task progress:

  - Board View: Displays tasks as cards in buckets.

  - Charts View: Offers a visual representation of task progress, including the number of tasks in each status, progress over time, and task distribution among team members.

- Schedule View: Displays tasks on a calendar, helping you see upcoming deadlines and plan accordingly.

Collaborating on Tasks

Effective collaboration is key to successful project management. Microsoft Planner facilitates collaboration through several features:

1. Comments and Updates:

- Team members can leave comments on task cards to provide updates, ask questions, or give feedback. This ensures that all communication related to a task is centralized and easily accessible.

2. Notifications:

- Team members receive notifications for task assignments, comments, and updates, keeping everyone informed and engaged.

3. Task Attachments and Links:

- Attach files directly to task cards for easy access. You can also link to documents stored in SharePoint or OneDrive, ensuring that all relevant materials are available to the team.

4. Integration with Microsoft Teams:

- Since Planner is integrated with Teams, you can discuss tasks in Teams chats and channels, ensuring seamless communication and collaboration.

Automating Task Management

Automation can significantly enhance task management efficiency. Microsoft Teams and Planner offer several automation options:

1. Power Automate:

- Use Power Automate (formerly Microsoft Flow) to create automated workflows between Planner and other applications. For example, you can set up a flow to create Planner tasks from emails or to notify a team when a task is marked as complete.

2. Task Templates:

- Create task templates for recurring tasks or projects. This saves time and ensures consistency in task creation.

3. Automated Reminders:

- Set up automated reminders for upcoming due dates or overdue tasks to keep the team on track.

Best Practices for Using Planner in Teams

To maximize the effectiveness of Microsoft Planner for task management, consider the following best practices:

1. Clear Task Naming Conventions:

- Use clear and descriptive names for tasks to ensure team members understand what each task entails at a glance.

2. Regular Updates and Reviews:

- Encourage team members to update task statuses regularly and review the Planner board frequently to stay on top of progress and potential issues.

3. Consistent Use of Labels and Buckets:

- Develop a consistent approach to using labels and buckets across the project to maintain organization and clarity.

4. Encourage Collaboration:

- Foster a culture of collaboration by encouraging team members to use comments and discussions within task cards. This ensures all communication is centralized and accessible.

5. Leverage Analytics:

- Utilize the charts and views in Planner to analyze task progress and identify bottlenecks or areas for improvement.

Example: Using Planner for a Marketing Campaign

To illustrate how Planner can be used for task management, let's consider a marketing campaign project:

1. Setting Up the Planner Board:

  - Create a Planner board named "Marketing Campaign."

  - Create buckets such as "Planning," "Content Creation," "Distribution," and "Analysis."

2. Creating Tasks:

  - Under the "Planning" bucket, create tasks like "Define Campaign Goals," "Identify Target Audience," and "Develop Campaign Strategy."

  - In the "Content Creation" bucket, add tasks such as "Write Blog Posts," "Design Graphics," and "Create Social Media Posts."

3. Assigning Tasks:

  - Assign the "Define Campaign Goals" task to the marketing manager and the "Write Blog Posts" task to the content writer.

  - Ensure each task has a clear due date and priority level.

4. Tracking Progress:

  - Regularly update task statuses as work progresses. Use checklists within tasks to break down larger tasks into smaller steps.

5. Collaborating and Communicating:

  - Use the comments section in task cards to discuss ideas, provide feedback, and share updates.

  - Attach relevant files, such as draft blog posts or graphic designs, to the appropriate tasks.

6. Automating Workflow:

  - Set up a Power Automate flow to create Planner tasks from incoming campaign ideas submitted via a Microsoft Forms survey.

By following these steps and best practices, you can effectively use Microsoft Planner within Teams to manage tasks, collaborate with your team, and ensure the success of your projects.

Conclusion

Using Microsoft Planner for task management in Microsoft Teams provides a robust and flexible solution for organizing and tracking project tasks. By setting up a Planner board, creating and assigning tasks, monitoring progress, and leveraging collaboration and automation features, you can enhance your team's productivity and ensure your projects are completed efficiently and effectively. With a structured approach and consistent use of Planner, you can streamline your task management processes and achieve your project goals with greater ease.

4.1.3 Tracking Progress and Milestones

Tracking progress and milestones in Microsoft Teams is crucial for ensuring that your project stays on schedule and meets its objectives. Microsoft Teams offers several features and integrations that make tracking progress and milestones straightforward and effective.

1. Setting Up Milestones

Milestones are significant points or events in your project timeline that indicate progress and achievement. Here's how to set up and track milestones in Microsoft Teams:

a. Define Your Milestones:

- Identify the key events or deliverables that will serve as milestones. This could include project kick-offs, deadlines for major deliverables, client approval points, or project completion.

- Clearly define what constitutes the completion of each milestone.

b. Use Planner to Track Milestones:

- Microsoft Planner, integrated within Teams, allows you to create tasks and assign them to team members. To track milestones, create a new Planner board for your project.

- Add a task for each milestone. Set due dates, assign responsible team members, and include any relevant details or attachments.

- Use labels and buckets to categorize and organize your milestones within the Planner board. For example, you could create buckets for "Upcoming Milestones," "In Progress," and "Completed Milestones."

c. Visualize Milestones on a Timeline:

- While Planner provides a list and board view, you can also use Microsoft Project or other timeline tools to visualize your milestones. Microsoft Project integrates seamlessly with Teams and allows you to create Gantt charts that visually represent your project timeline and milestones.

2. Tracking Progress

Tracking progress involves monitoring the status of tasks and milestones to ensure that the project is moving forward as planned. Here are some strategies and tools for tracking progress in Teams:

a. Regular Status Updates:

- Schedule regular status update meetings or check-ins with your team. Use these meetings to discuss the progress of tasks and milestones, address any issues or blockers, and adjust timelines as needed.

- Use the chat or meeting functionality in Teams to facilitate these updates. You can create a dedicated channel for status updates and discussions related to progress.

b. Task Management with Planner:

- In addition to tracking milestones, use Planner to manage individual tasks within your project. Create tasks for each step or deliverable required to reach your milestones.

- Assign tasks to team members, set due dates, and track their progress using the Planner board. Team members can update the status of their tasks, add comments, and attach relevant files.

c. Progress Reporting with Power BI:

- Power BI, another Microsoft tool that integrates with Teams, allows you to create detailed reports and dashboards to track project progress. You can connect Power BI to your Planner board, SharePoint lists, or other data sources to visualize task completion, team performance, and milestone achievement.

- Create custom reports that show the status of tasks and milestones, including metrics such as task completion rates, overdue tasks, and upcoming deadlines. Share these reports with your team in a Teams channel or during status update meetings.

d. Use OneNote for Progress Documentation:

- OneNote is a powerful tool for documenting progress and keeping track of project details. Create a dedicated OneNote notebook for your project and organize it into sections and pages for different aspects of your project.

- Use OneNote to document meeting notes, track decisions and action items, and store important project information. You can link OneNote pages to tasks in Planner or other project management tools for easy reference.

3. Monitoring Team Performance

Monitoring team performance is essential for ensuring that everyone is contributing effectively to the project. Here's how to use Teams to monitor and manage team performance:

a. Assign Clear Responsibilities:

- Clearly define the roles and responsibilities of each team member. Use Planner to assign tasks and ensure that everyone knows what they are accountable for.

- Use the Teams chat or meeting functions to communicate expectations and provide feedback on performance.

b. Track Task Completion:

- Use Planner and Power BI to monitor task completion rates and identify any tasks that are falling behind schedule. Review task progress regularly and address any issues or delays promptly.

- Celebrate task completions and milestone achievements to keep the team motivated and engaged.

c. Conduct Performance Reviews:

- Schedule regular performance reviews with team members to discuss their progress and address any challenges they are facing. Use the meeting functionality in Teams to conduct these reviews virtually.

- Provide constructive feedback and support to help team members improve their performance and stay on track.

4. Managing Risks and Issues

Effective project management involves identifying and managing risks and issues that could impact your project. Here's how to use Teams to manage risks and issues:

a. Risk Identification and Assessment:

- Use a dedicated Teams channel or OneNote notebook to document potential risks and issues. Encourage team members to report any risks or concerns they identify.

- Assess the impact and likelihood of each risk and prioritize them based on their potential impact on the project.

b. Develop Risk Mitigation Plans:

- Create mitigation plans for each identified risk. Use Planner to create tasks for implementing mitigation strategies and assign them to team members.

- Monitor the status of mitigation tasks and update your risk assessment as needed.

c. Issue Tracking and Resolution:

- Use Planner or a dedicated SharePoint list to track issues that arise during the project. Assign responsibility for resolving each issue and set deadlines for resolution.

- Regularly review the status of issues during team meetings and provide support to team members as needed to resolve them promptly.

5. Continuous Improvement

Continuous improvement is key to successful project management. Here's how to use Teams to drive continuous improvement in your projects:

a. Conduct Post-Project Reviews:

- Schedule a post-project review meeting with your team to discuss what went well, what didn't, and what could be improved in future projects. Use Teams to facilitate this meeting and document the discussion in OneNote.

- Identify lessons learned and best practices that can be applied to future projects.

b. Implement Feedback Loops:

- Create feedback loops within your team to continuously gather input and suggestions for improvement. Use the Teams chat or dedicated channels for team members to share their feedback.

- Review feedback regularly and make adjustments to your project management processes as needed.

c. Leverage Analytics and Reporting:

- Use Power BI and other reporting tools to analyze project performance data. Identify trends and patterns that indicate areas for improvement.

- Share insights and recommendations with your team and stakeholders to drive continuous improvement.

6. Utilizing Templates and Standard Operating Procedures (SOPs)

Templates and SOPs can streamline project management processes and ensure consistency. Here's how to create and use them in Teams:

a. Create Project Templates:

- Develop templates for common project documents, such as project plans, status reports, and meeting agendas. Store these templates in a SharePoint library or a dedicated Teams channel for easy access.

- Use these templates to ensure consistency and save time when setting up new projects.

b. Develop Standard Operating Procedures:

- Document your project management processes in a OneNote notebook or SharePoint library. Include detailed instructions and guidelines for each process, such as task management, risk assessment, and progress tracking.

- Share these SOPs with your team and provide training to ensure that everyone follows the same procedures.

By effectively tracking progress and milestones in Microsoft Teams, you can ensure that your projects stay on schedule, meet their objectives, and deliver successful outcomes. Leveraging the various tools and features available in Teams, such as Planner, OneNote, Power BI, and integration with other Microsoft products, will enhance your project management capabilities and drive better collaboration and productivity within your team.

4.2 Collaboration Tools for Project Management

4.2.1 Using OneNote for Project Notes

Microsoft OneNote is a powerful tool that can be seamlessly integrated with Microsoft Teams to enhance project management and collaboration. OneNote allows project teams to create, share, and organize notes in a central location, ensuring that all team members have access to the most up-to-date information. This section will provide a detailed guide on how to use OneNote for project notes, covering setup, features, best practices, and tips for effective use.

1. Introduction to OneNote

OneNote is a digital notebook that provides a flexible platform for creating and organizing notes. It can be used for various purposes, including project management, meeting notes, brainstorming sessions, and more. OneNote notebooks can be shared with team members, allowing for real-time collaboration and easy access to information.

2. Setting Up OneNote in Microsoft Teams

To start using OneNote in Microsoft Teams, follow these steps:

2.1 Adding OneNote to a Team

1. Navigate to the desired team: Open Microsoft Teams and go to the team where you want to add OneNote.

2. Add a new tab: Click on the plus (+) icon at the top of the channel to add a new tab.

3. Select OneNote: From the list of available apps, select OneNote.

4. Choose or create a notebook: You can either select an existing OneNote notebook or create a new one for your team.

5. Name the tab: Give the tab a relevant name, such as "Project Notes" or "Meeting Notes."

6. Save: Click "Save" to add OneNote to your team.

2.2 Structuring Your OneNote Notebook

A well-organized OneNote notebook is crucial for effective project management. Here are some tips for structuring your notebook:

1. Create sections: Divide your notebook into sections based on different aspects of your project, such as "Project Overview," "Meeting Notes," "Task Lists," "Research," and "Brainstorming."

2. Add pages: Within each section, create pages for specific topics or meetings. For example, under "Meeting Notes," you could have pages for each team meeting with the date and agenda.

3. Use section groups: For larger projects, use section groups to further organize your notebook. For example, you might have a section group for each project phase, such as "Planning," "Execution," and "Closure."

3. Features of OneNote for Project Management

OneNote offers a variety of features that make it an excellent tool for managing project notes:

3.1 Note-Taking

1. Text notes: Easily create text notes by clicking anywhere on a page and typing. OneNote's free-form canvas allows you to position text boxes wherever you need them.

2. Rich text formatting: Use rich text formatting options, such as bold, italics, underlining, highlighting, and bullet points, to make your notes clear and organized.

3. Tags: Use tags to categorize and prioritize your notes. OneNote offers various built-in tags, such as "To Do," "Important," "Question," and "Idea." You can also create custom tags to suit your needs.

3.2 Multimedia Integration

1. Images: Insert images into your notes by clicking "Insert" and selecting "Pictures." This is useful for including diagrams, screenshots, or photos of whiteboard sessions.

2. Audio recordings: Record audio directly within OneNote by clicking "Insert" and selecting "Audio." This feature is great for capturing meeting discussions or brainstorming sessions.

3. Files and attachments: Attach files to your notes by clicking "Insert" and selecting "File Attachment." This allows you to keep relevant documents and resources easily accessible.

3.3 Collaboration

1. Real-time collaboration: Multiple team members can edit the same OneNote notebook simultaneously. Changes are synced in real-time, making it easy to collaborate on notes and documents.

2. Comments and annotations: Use comments and annotations to provide feedback on notes or to ask questions. This is particularly useful for reviewing meeting notes or project plans.

3. Sharing: Share your OneNote notebook with team members by clicking "File" and selecting "Share." You can choose to share the entire notebook or specific sections or pages.

3.4 Search and Organization

1. Search: Use the search bar to quickly find notes by keywords or tags. OneNote's powerful search capabilities make it easy to locate specific information within large notebooks.

2. Page templates: Use page templates to create consistent and professional-looking notes. OneNote offers a variety of built-in templates, such as meeting agendas, project plans, and to-do lists.

3. Linked notes: Link notes to other pages or sections within your notebook, or to external resources, such as websites or documents. This helps you create a connected and organized information network.

4. Best Practices for Using OneNote in Project Management

To get the most out of OneNote for project management, consider the following best practices:

4.1 Standardize Note-Taking

1. Create a note-taking template: Develop a standard template for taking project notes. This might include sections for meeting agendas, action items, decisions, and follow-ups.

2. Consistent formatting: Use consistent formatting across all notes to make them easy to read and understand. This includes using the same font size, color, and heading styles.

3. Tagging system: Establish a tagging system to categorize and prioritize notes. This helps team members quickly identify important information and action items.

4.2 Regular Updates

1. Weekly reviews: Schedule regular reviews of your OneNote notebook to ensure that notes are up-to-date and that action items are being tracked and completed.

2. Meeting summaries: After each meeting, create a summary page that includes key decisions, action items, and next steps. Share this summary with the team to ensure everyone is on the same page.

3. Archiving: Periodically archive old notes and sections to keep your notebook organized and focused on current project activities.

4.3 Integration with Other Tools

1. Planner integration: Link OneNote pages to Planner tasks to ensure that action items are tracked and completed. This helps you create a seamless workflow between note-taking and task management.

2. Microsoft Project integration: Use OneNote to capture meeting notes and project updates, and then link these notes to your Microsoft Project plan. This ensures that project documentation is consistent and easily accessible.

3. Power BI integration: Create OneNote pages that link to Power BI dashboards and reports. This allows you to include real-time project data and analytics in your notes.

5. Tips for Effective Use of OneNote

Here are some additional tips to help you make the most of OneNote for project management:

5.1 Keyboard Shortcuts

1. Quick note creation: Use the keyboard shortcut Ctrl + N to quickly create a new page.

2. Tagging: Use Ctrl + 1 through Ctrl + 5 to quickly apply tags to your notes.

3. Search: Press Ctrl + E to open the search bar and quickly find notes.

5.2 Customizing OneNote

1. Custom tags: Create custom tags to suit your project needs. This can help you categorize and prioritize notes more effectively.

2. Page templates: Develop custom page templates for different types of notes, such as meeting agendas, project plans, and brainstorming sessions.

3. Notebook organization: Regularly review and reorganize your notebook to ensure that it remains structured and easy to navigate.

5.3 Leveraging OneNote for Remote Teams

1. Shared notebooks: Use shared notebooks to ensure that all team members have access to the latest project information. This is especially important for remote teams.

2. Real-time collaboration: Encourage team members to use OneNote's real-time collaboration features to work together on notes and documents.

3. Regular updates: Schedule regular updates and reviews of your OneNote notebook to keep everyone informed and aligned.

Conclusion

Using OneNote for project notes in Microsoft Teams can significantly enhance your team's ability to collaborate and manage projects effectively. By setting up OneNote correctly, taking advantage of its features, following best practices, and integrating it with other tools, you can ensure that your project documentation is organized, accessible, and useful for all team members. Whether you are managing a small project or a large, complex initiative, OneNote can be a valuable addition to your project management toolkit.

4.2.2 Integrating with Microsoft Project

Integrating Microsoft Project with Microsoft Teams can significantly enhance project management capabilities by combining the robust project planning features of Microsoft Project with the collaborative and communication functionalities of Microsoft Teams. This integration facilitates seamless communication, real-time updates, and better tracking of project progress. Below, we will explore in detail how to integrate Microsoft Project with Microsoft Teams and leverage its features for effective project management.

Overview of Microsoft Project Integration

Microsoft Project is a powerful tool designed for project management, offering comprehensive functionalities for planning, scheduling, resource allocation, and tracking project progress. Integrating it with Microsoft Teams allows project managers and team members to:

- Centralize project communication and collaboration.

- Access project plans and schedules directly within Teams.

- Receive real-time updates and notifications on project milestones and tasks.

- Utilize advanced reporting and analytics tools for better decision-making.

Steps to Integrate Microsoft Project with Microsoft Teams

1. Add Microsoft Project to Your Team

  - Open Microsoft Teams and navigate to the desired team.

  - Click on the "+" icon (Add a tab) at the top of the channel.

  - Search for "Project" and select "Project" from the list of available apps.

  - Follow the prompts to sign in and grant necessary permissions.

  - Select the existing project you want to integrate or create a new project.

  - Once added, the project will appear as a tab within the selected team channel.

2. Configure Project Settings

  - Click on the newly added Project tab to open Microsoft Project within Teams.

  - Configure project settings such as timelines, milestones, tasks, and resource assignments.

  - Customize the project view to display Gantt charts, task lists, or board views according to your preference.

- Ensure all team members have the appropriate permissions to view and edit project details.

3. Assign Tasks and Responsibilities

- Use Microsoft Project's task assignment features to allocate tasks to team members.

- Set deadlines, priorities, and dependencies for each task.

- Enable notifications to ensure team members receive updates on task assignments and changes.

4. Monitor Project Progress

- Utilize the various views in Microsoft Project to monitor project progress.

- Track task completion, resource utilization, and project timelines.

- Use the reporting tools within Microsoft Project to generate status reports and performance metrics.

5. Collaborate and Communicate

- Use Microsoft Teams' chat and channel features to discuss project updates and collaborate on tasks.

- Share files, documents, and project plans directly within Teams.

- Schedule and conduct project meetings using Microsoft Teams' meeting features.

Leveraging Advanced Features

1. Using Power Automate for Automation

- Integrate Power Automate with Microsoft Project and Teams to automate repetitive tasks and workflows.

- Create flows to automatically update project status, send reminders, and trigger notifications based on project events.

2. Integrating with Microsoft Planner

- Combine Microsoft Project and Planner to create a hybrid project management environment.

- Use Planner for task management and Microsoft Project for detailed project planning and scheduling.

- Sync tasks and updates between Planner and Project for consistent and up-to-date information.

3. Utilizing Power BI for Reporting

- Integrate Power BI with Microsoft Project to create dynamic and interactive project dashboards.

- Use Power BI to visualize project data, track KPIs, and generate custom reports.

- Embed Power BI dashboards within Microsoft Teams for easy access and sharing.

Best Practices for Integrating Microsoft Project with Microsoft Teams

1. Maintain Clear Communication

- Ensure all team members are aware of the integration and how to use it effectively.

- Conduct training sessions to familiarize the team with the features and functionalities of both Microsoft Project and Teams.

2. Regularly Update Project Information

- Keep project plans, tasks, and schedules up-to-date to reflect the current status of the project.

- Regularly review and adjust project timelines and resource allocations as needed.

3. Utilize Templates for Consistency

- Create and use project templates to standardize project management practices.

- Templates can help ensure consistency across different projects and teams.

4. Monitor and Analyze Project Performance

- Use the reporting and analytics tools available in Microsoft Project and Power BI to monitor project performance.

- Analyze project data to identify trends, risks, and opportunities for improvement.

5. Encourage Collaboration and Feedback

- Foster a collaborative environment by encouraging team members to share ideas, feedback, and updates.

- Use Teams' chat and channel features to facilitate open communication and discussion.

Conclusion

Integrating Microsoft Project with Microsoft Teams creates a powerful project management ecosystem that combines detailed project planning with robust communication and collaboration tools. By following the steps outlined above and leveraging the advanced features of both platforms, project managers and teams can achieve greater efficiency, improve project outcomes, and enhance overall productivity. This integration not only streamlines project management processes but also fosters a collaborative and transparent work environment, essential for the success of any project.

4.2.3 Using Power BI for Reporting

Power BI is a powerful business analytics tool that allows users to visualize data and share insights across an organization. When integrated with Microsoft Teams, it enhances the project management experience by providing real-time data visualizations and interactive reports. This section will guide you through the process of integrating Power BI with Teams, creating effective reports, and utilizing these reports to improve project outcomes.

Integrating Power BI with Microsoft Teams

1. Adding Power BI to Teams:

- To integrate Power BI with Teams, you first need to add the Power BI app to your Teams environment. Go to the Microsoft Teams app store, search for "Power BI," and add it to your team. Once added, you can pin it to your sidebar for easy access.

- You can also add Power BI reports to specific channels by clicking on the "+" icon at the top of the channel, selecting Power BI, and choosing the report you want to display.

2. Connecting Power BI to Your Data Sources:

- Power BI can connect to a variety of data sources, including Excel files, SharePoint lists, SQL databases, and more. Ensure your data sources are up-to-date and accurately reflect your project data.

- In Power BI Desktop, go to "Home" -> "Get Data" to connect to your desired data source. Follow the prompts to authenticate and import your data into Power BI.

3. Publishing Reports to Power BI Service:

- Once your reports are created in Power BI Desktop, publish them to the Power BI service. Click on "File" -> "Publish" -> "Publish to Power BI," and select your workspace.

- After publishing, your reports are available in the Power BI service and can be shared with your team in Microsoft Teams.

Creating Effective Power BI Reports for Project Management

1. Designing Your Reports:

- Start by identifying the key metrics and KPIs that are important for your project. Common metrics include project progress, budget tracking, resource allocation, and task completion rates.

- Use visualizations such as bar charts, line graphs, pie charts, and Gantt charts to represent your data. Power BI offers a variety of visualizations that can be customized to fit your needs.

2. Using Filters and Slicers:

- Filters and slicers allow you to interact with your data and drill down into specific details. Add slicers to your report to filter by project phase, team member, or task status.

- Use the filter pane to set up page-level or report-level filters, providing a more dynamic and interactive reporting experience.

3. Creating Dashboards:

- Dashboards in Power BI provide a high-level overview of your project data. Pin visualizations from different reports to a single dashboard to create a comprehensive view of your project's health.

- Customize your dashboard by arranging tiles, setting alerts, and adding notes or comments to provide context for your team.

Utilizing Power BI Reports in Teams

1. Embedding Reports in Channels:

- Embed your Power BI reports directly into Teams channels for easy access. This ensures that all team members have real-time visibility into project data without leaving the Teams environment.

- To embed a report, click on the "+" icon in the channel, select Power BI, and choose the report you want to add. You can adjust the report's settings to control access and permissions.

2. Collaborating on Reports:

- Use Teams' chat and conversation features to discuss the insights from your Power BI reports. Tag team members, start conversations around specific data points, and share feedback directly within the Teams interface.

- Schedule regular meetings to review the reports, discuss progress, and make data-driven decisions. Use the integrated Power BI visuals during your meetings to provide a clear and concise overview of the project's status.

3. Setting Up Alerts and Notifications:

- Power BI allows you to set up data alerts that notify you when specific conditions are met. For example, you can set an alert to notify you when a project's budget exceeds a certain threshold or when a milestone is approaching.

- Configure these alerts to be delivered directly to your Teams channel, ensuring that your team is always informed about critical changes or updates in real time.

Best Practices for Using Power BI in Project Management

1. Regularly Update Your Data:

- Ensure that your data sources are regularly updated to provide accurate and current information in your reports. Set up scheduled refreshes in Power BI to automate this process and minimize manual updates.

- Regular updates help maintain the integrity of your reports and ensure that your team is working with the most recent data.

2. Maintain Consistency in Reporting:

- Use standardized templates and visualizations across your reports to maintain consistency and make it easier for team members to interpret the data.

- Consistent reporting helps build familiarity and trust in the data, enabling more effective decision-making.

3. Train Your Team:

- Provide training and resources to help your team members understand how to use Power BI and interpret the reports. This could include formal training sessions, tutorials, or documentation.

- A well-informed team is better equipped to leverage the insights provided by Power BI and contribute to the project's success.

4. Leverage Advanced Analytics:

- Utilize Power BI's advanced analytics features, such as AI and machine learning capabilities, to gain deeper insights into your project data. Predictive analytics can help you identify potential risks and opportunities, allowing for proactive project management.

- Explore features like the "Analyze in Excel" option or integrating with Azure Machine Learning for more sophisticated analysis.

Case Studies: Successful Use of Power BI in Project Management

1. Case Study 1: Construction Project Management

- A construction company used Power BI to track project progress, manage budgets, and monitor resource allocation. By embedding Power BI reports in Teams, they achieved real-time collaboration and improved decision-making.

- Key metrics included project completion rates, budget variance, and resource utilization. The interactive dashboards allowed project managers to quickly identify issues and take corrective actions.

2. Case Study 2: IT Project Implementation

- An IT services firm integrated Power BI with Microsoft Teams to manage the implementation of a large-scale software project. Power BI provided visibility into task completion, issue tracking, and team performance.

- The firm used Power BI to generate reports on project milestones, risk assessments, and client satisfaction. This approach led to improved project delivery times and client satisfaction.

3. Case Study 3: Marketing Campaign Management

- A marketing agency used Power BI to manage and analyze data from multiple campaigns. By integrating Power BI with Teams, the agency could share real-time insights with clients and adjust strategies on the fly.

- Reports included metrics on campaign performance, ROI, and audience engagement. The interactive visualizations helped the agency make data-driven decisions and optimize campaign outcomes.

Conclusion

Integrating Power BI with Microsoft Teams provides a powerful combination of data visualization and collaboration tools that can significantly enhance project management. By following the steps outlined in this section, you can create effective reports, foster team collaboration, and make informed decisions based on real-time data insights. Whether you are managing a small project or a large-scale initiative, leveraging Power BI in your Teams environment will help you achieve better outcomes and drive project success.

4.3 Managing Project Meetings

Effective project management requires structured and well-managed meetings. Microsoft Teams offers a suite of tools and features to schedule, manage, and document meetings, ensuring all stakeholders are on the same page. This section will provide detailed guidance on scheduling regular meetings using Microsoft Teams, focusing on best practices to enhance productivity and collaboration.

4.3.1 Scheduling Regular Meetings

Regular meetings are the backbone of successful project management, providing a platform for team members to discuss progress, address challenges, and plan next steps. Microsoft Teams simplifies the process of scheduling these meetings, making it easy to coordinate with team members and ensure that everyone is informed and prepared.

Step-by-Step Guide to Scheduling Regular Meetings in Microsoft Teams

1. Open Microsoft Teams: Launch the Microsoft Teams application and navigate to the appropriate team and channel where you want to schedule the meeting.

2. Go to the Calendar: Click on the "Calendar" icon on the left-hand menu. This opens the calendar view, where you can see your upcoming meetings and schedule new ones.

3. Schedule a New Meeting: Click on the "New meeting" button at the top right corner of the calendar. This will open a form to fill in the details of the meeting.

4. Enter Meeting Details:

- Title: Provide a clear and concise title for the meeting. For example, "Weekly Project Update" or "Sprint Planning Meeting."

- Attendees: Add the email addresses of the team members who need to attend the meeting. You can also add entire distribution lists or teams to ensure no one is left out.

- Date and Time: Select the date and time for the meeting. Use the scheduling assistant to check the availability of all attendees.

- Repeat Option: For regular meetings, select the "Repeat" option and choose the frequency (daily, weekly, bi-weekly, etc.). This will automate the scheduling of future meetings.

5. Location: If the meeting is virtual, select "Microsoft Teams Meeting" to generate a meeting link. If it's in-person or hybrid, specify the physical location.

6. Add Description and Agenda: Use the description box to provide an agenda or any preparatory information. This helps attendees know what to expect and come prepared.

7. Save and Send Invites: Once all details are filled in, click "Save." This will send invitations to all attendees and add the meeting to their calendars.

Best Practices for Scheduling Regular Meetings

1. Set a Clear Objective: Every meeting should have a clear purpose. Whether it's a project update, brainstorming session, or problem-solving meeting, defining the objective helps keep the meeting focused and productive.

2. Prepare an Agenda: An agenda sets the tone for the meeting and ensures all critical topics are covered. Share the agenda in advance so attendees can prepare their input and questions.

3. Choose the Right Time: Select a time that works for all attendees, especially if the team is spread across different time zones. The scheduling assistant in Teams can help find the optimal time.

4. Limit Meeting Length: Keep meetings as short as possible to maintain engagement and productivity. An hour is generally sufficient for most meetings; consider 30 minutes for shorter updates.

5. Ensure Required Attendees are Available: Use the scheduling assistant to check the availability of key stakeholders. If critical members are unavailable, reschedule to ensure their participation.

6. Send Reminders: Teams will automatically send notifications, but it's also helpful to send a reminder a day before the meeting, especially for important discussions.

Enhancing Meeting Effectiveness

1. Pre-Meeting Preparation: Encourage attendees to review the agenda and any preparatory materials beforehand. This allows for more informed discussions and decision-making.

2. Use Collaborative Tools: Leverage Teams' integration with OneNote for note-taking, Planner for task management, and SharePoint for document storage. These tools enhance collaboration during and after meetings.

3. Assign Roles: Designate roles such as facilitator, timekeeper, and note-taker. This ensures the meeting runs smoothly and key points are documented.

4. Encourage Participation: Foster an inclusive environment where all team members feel comfortable sharing their ideas and feedback. Use the raise hand feature or round-robin format to ensure everyone has a chance to speak.

5. Stay on Topic: Follow the agenda closely and avoid deviating into unrelated topics. If new issues arise, note them for discussion in a separate meeting.

6. Summarize Key Points and Action Items: At the end of the meeting, summarize the key points discussed and list the action items. Assign responsibilities and set deadlines for each task.

Using Teams Features to Enhance Meeting Management

1. Meeting Notes: Utilize the Meeting Notes feature in Teams to document discussions, decisions, and action items in real-time. These notes are accessible to all attendees and can be referenced in future meetings.

2. Recording Meetings: Record meetings to capture the discussion for those who couldn't attend or for future reference. Teams automatically saves the recording to the meeting chat, where it can be accessed by all participants.

3. Screen Sharing and Whiteboard: Use screen sharing to present documents, slides, or other materials during the meeting. The Whiteboard feature allows for real-time brainstorming and visualization of ideas.

4. Polling and Q&A: Use the Polls app to gather input or make decisions during the meeting. The Q&A feature can manage questions from attendees, ensuring a structured and interactive session.

5. Breakout Rooms: For larger meetings or workshops, use breakout rooms to divide participants into smaller groups for focused discussions. This is particularly useful for brainstorming or problem-solving sessions.

6. Follow-Up Meetings: Schedule follow-up meetings directly from the current meeting to discuss ongoing issues or to check on the progress of action items. This ensures continuity and accountability.

Managing Meeting Logistics

1. Technical Setup: Ensure that all attendees have the necessary technical setup, including a stable internet connection, functioning microphone, and camera. Conduct a test meeting if needed.

2. Accessibility: Consider the accessibility needs of all participants. Teams offers features such as live captions and transcription to support attendees with hearing impairments.

3. Time Management: Start and end meetings on time. Respecting the schedule helps build a culture of punctuality and efficiency.

4. Post-Meeting Follow-Up: Send a summary email or message in Teams with the meeting notes, action items, and any relevant documents. This reinforces accountability and keeps everyone informed.

Case Study: Effective Use of Teams for Project Meetings

Scenario: A software development team uses Microsoft Teams to manage their bi-weekly sprint planning meetings.

Approach:

- Preparation: The Scrum Master creates an agenda in OneNote, detailing the sprint goals, backlog items, and discussion points.

- Scheduling: The Scrum Master schedules the meeting in Teams, using the repeat feature for bi-weekly occurrences.

- During the Meeting: Team members use the Planner integration to review and assign tasks. The Scrum Master shares the screen to display the backlog and progress charts. Notes are taken in real-time using the Meeting Notes feature.

- Post-Meeting: The Scrum Master sends a follow-up message in the Teams channel with the meeting notes, assigned tasks, and deadlines. The meeting recording is also shared for reference.

Outcome: The team maintains clear communication and accountability, resulting in improved efficiency and successful sprint completions.

In conclusion, scheduling regular meetings in Microsoft Teams is a straightforward process that, when executed with best practices, significantly enhances team collaboration and project management. By leveraging the powerful features of Teams, project managers can ensure that meetings are productive, engaging, and effective in driving project success.

4.3.2 Using Meeting Templates

Managing project meetings effectively is crucial to the success of any project. Meeting templates in Microsoft Teams can significantly streamline this process, ensuring consistency, efficiency, and clarity. In this section, we will delve into the importance of using meeting templates, how to create and use them in Microsoft Teams, and best practices for maximizing their benefits.

1. The Importance of Meeting Templates

Meeting templates serve as predefined frameworks that outline the structure and content of a meeting. They help ensure that all necessary topics are covered, reduce the time spent on meeting preparation, and maintain consistency across meetings. Using templates can lead to more productive meetings by keeping participants focused and organized.

2. Creating Meeting Templates in Microsoft Teams

Creating a meeting template in Microsoft Teams involves several steps. Here's a detailed guide:

Step 1: Define the Purpose and Agenda

Before creating a template, determine the purpose of the meeting and outline the key agenda items. Common project meeting types include:

- Project Kick-off Meetings
- Weekly Status Meetings
- Milestone Reviews
- Risk Management Meetings
- Retrospectives

Each type of meeting will have a different focus and agenda. For example, a weekly status meeting might include agenda items such as progress updates, upcoming tasks, potential issues, and resource needs.

Step 2: Create a Standard Meeting Outline

Develop a standard outline that includes the essential components of your meetings. This might involve:

- Meeting Title
- Date and Time
- Participants
- Agenda Items
  - Topic 1
  - Topic 2
  - Topic 3
- Discussion Points
- Action Items
- Follow-up Tasks

Step 3: Utilize Microsoft Teams and OneNote

Microsoft Teams integrates seamlessly with OneNote, making it an excellent tool for creating and managing meeting templates. Here's how to set up a meeting template using OneNote:

- Open Microsoft Teams and navigate to the team or channel where you want to create the meeting template.

- Click on the "Files" tab, then select "Open in SharePoint."

- In SharePoint, create a new OneNote notebook or open an existing one.

- In OneNote, create a new section for meeting templates.

- Add pages for each meeting type, with the standard meeting outline you defined earlier.

Step 4: Create a Teams Meeting Link

To facilitate easy access to the meeting template, include a link to a Microsoft Teams meeting within the OneNote template. This allows participants to join the meeting directly from the template.

Step 5: Save and Share the Template

Once your template is complete, save it in a location accessible to all team members. Share the template with your team and provide guidance on how to use it for upcoming meetings.

3. Using Meeting Templates in Microsoft Teams

Using meeting templates in Microsoft Teams involves several practical steps to ensure they are effectively integrated into your project management workflow:

Step 1: Schedule the Meeting

- Open Microsoft Teams and navigate to the "Calendar" tab.

- Click "New Meeting" and fill in the meeting details such as title, date, time, and participants.

- In the meeting description, provide a brief overview of the meeting's purpose and a link to the meeting template in OneNote.

Step 2: Share the Agenda

- Prior to the meeting, share the agenda with participants. This can be done by copying the relevant sections from the OneNote template and pasting them into the meeting invitation or a Teams channel.

- Encourage participants to review the agenda and add any additional topics or questions they may have.

Step 3: Conduct the Meeting

- During the meeting, refer to the template to ensure all agenda items are covered. Use the template to take notes, record discussion points, and document action items.

- If you're using OneNote, you can update the template in real-time and share the notes with participants immediately after the meeting.

Step 4: Follow Up

- After the meeting, review the notes and ensure all action items are assigned to the appropriate team members.

- Update the meeting template with any adjustments or improvements based on feedback from participants.

4. Best Practices for Using Meeting Templates

To maximize the effectiveness of meeting templates, consider the following best practices:

Consistency and Standardization

- Use the same template for similar types of meetings to maintain consistency and make it easier for participants to follow along.

- Standardize the format and structure of your templates to ensure they are easy to read and understand.

Customization and Flexibility

- While consistency is important, be flexible and customize templates as needed to fit the specific needs of each meeting.

- Allow team members to suggest changes or additions to the template to ensure it remains relevant and useful.

Regular Review and Improvement

- Periodically review and update your meeting templates to reflect any changes in your project management processes or team dynamics.

- Gather feedback from participants to identify areas for improvement and make necessary adjustments to the templates.

Integration with Other Tools

- Integrate meeting templates with other project management tools and software to streamline your workflow. For example, link action items in the template to tasks in Microsoft Planner or Azure DevOps.

- Use Microsoft Teams' built-in features, such as @mentions and file sharing, to enhance collaboration and communication during meetings.

Training and Adoption

- Provide training and guidance to team members on how to use meeting templates effectively. This can include creating a short training video or hosting a workshop.

- Encourage the adoption of meeting templates by demonstrating their benefits and showing how they can save time and improve meeting outcomes.

5. Example Meeting Templates

Here are a few example meeting templates to illustrate how you can structure different types of project meetings:

Weekly Status Meeting Template

- Meeting Title: Weekly Project Status Meeting
- Date and Time: [Date], [Time]
- Participants: [List of Participants]
- Agenda Items:
  - Project Updates
  - Completed Tasks
  - Upcoming Tasks
  - Issues and Risks
  - Resource Needs
- Discussion Points: [Detailed Notes]
- Action Items: [List of Action Items]
- Follow-up Tasks: [List of Follow-up Tasks]

Project Kick-off Meeting Template

- Meeting Title: Project Kick-off Meeting
- Date and Time: [Date], [Time]
- Participants: [List of Participants]
- Agenda Items:
  - Project Overview
  - Objectives and Goals
  - Key Milestones
  - Roles and Responsibilities
  - Communication Plan
- Discussion Points: [Detailed Notes]

- Action Items: [List of Action Items]

- Follow-up Tasks: [List of Follow-up Tasks]

Risk Management Meeting Template

- Meeting Title: Risk Management Meeting

- Date and Time: [Date], [Time]

- Participants: [List of Participants]

- Agenda Items:

  - Risk Identification

  - Risk Assessment

  - Mitigation Strategies

  - Monitoring and Reporting

- Discussion Points: [Detailed Notes]

- Action Items: [List of Action Items]

- Follow-up Tasks: [List of Follow-up Tasks]

By using these templates and following the guidelines provided, you can ensure that your project meetings are well-organized, productive, and focused on achieving project goals. Meeting templates not only save time but also help maintain consistency and clarity across your project management efforts, ultimately contributing to the success of your projects.

4.3.3 Capturing Meeting Minutes and Action Items

Efficient project management relies heavily on effective communication and meticulous documentation. One of the most critical aspects of this process is capturing meeting minutes and action items during project meetings. Microsoft Teams offers a suite of tools that can help ensure all meeting details are accurately recorded and action items are tracked to completion. This section will provide a comprehensive guide on capturing meeting minutes and action items using Microsoft Teams, highlighting best practices, tools, and techniques to streamline this process.

1. The Importance of Meeting Minutes and Action Items

Meeting minutes serve as an official record of what was discussed and decided during a meeting. They provide a reference for participants and stakeholders who may not have been present and serve as a reminder for tasks and decisions made. Action items are specific tasks assigned to individuals or teams during the meeting, which need to be tracked and followed up on to ensure project progress. Properly capturing and managing these elements is crucial for accountability, transparency, and project success.

2. Preparing for the Meeting

Preparation is key to capturing accurate and comprehensive meeting minutes. Here are some steps to prepare effectively:

- Create a Meeting Agenda: Develop a clear agenda outlining the topics to be discussed. This helps guide the meeting and ensures all important topics are covered.

- Assign Roles: Designate someone to take minutes and track action items. This person should be familiar with the project and the meeting agenda.

- Set Up the Meeting in Teams: Schedule the meeting in Microsoft Teams, ensuring all relevant participants are invited and have access to the meeting materials.

3. Capturing Meeting Minutes in Microsoft Teams

Microsoft Teams provides several tools and features that facilitate the capturing of meeting minutes:

- Use OneNote: OneNote is an excellent tool for capturing meeting minutes. It allows for organized note-taking and integrates seamlessly with Microsoft Teams.

- Creating a Meeting Notes Section: Before the meeting, create a section in OneNote specifically for the meeting. You can do this by selecting the meeting in Teams, clicking on the "Meeting Notes" tab, and creating a new notes section.

- Organizing Notes: During the meeting, take notes in a structured format. Use headings for different agenda items and bullet points for discussion points and decisions.

- Adding Tags: Use OneNote tags to highlight important points, such as decisions, action items, and follow-up tasks.

- Recording the Meeting: Microsoft Teams allows you to record meetings. This is particularly useful for capturing detailed discussions and ensuring nothing is missed.

- Starting the Recording: To start recording, click on the "More actions" (three dots) button in the meeting toolbar and select "Start recording."

- Accessing the Recording: After the meeting, the recording will be available in the meeting chat and can be reviewed to fill in any gaps in the minutes.

4. Tracking Action Items

Capturing action items is crucial for ensuring tasks are completed and progress is made. Here's how to effectively track action items using Microsoft Teams:

- Using Planner: Microsoft Planner is a powerful tool for managing tasks and action items.

- Creating a Planner Board: Create a Planner board for your project team. Within this board, create buckets for different categories of tasks (e.g., "To Do," "In Progress," "Completed").

- Adding Tasks: During the meeting, add action items as tasks in Planner. Assign these tasks to specific team members, set due dates, and add any relevant details.

- Tracking Progress: Use Planner to monitor the progress of tasks. Team members can update the status of their tasks, and you can easily see which tasks are on track and which need attention.

- Using To-Do Lists: For smaller projects or simpler task management, Microsoft To-Do can be used.

- Creating Lists: Create a list for your project and add tasks as action items.

- Assigning Tasks: Assign tasks to team members and set due dates.

- Tracking Completion: Team members can mark tasks as complete, and you can track overall progress.

5. Best Practices for Capturing Meeting Minutes and Action Items

To ensure the effectiveness of your meeting documentation, follow these best practices:

- Be Concise: Capture key points and decisions without going into excessive detail. Focus on what's important and actionable.

- Be Clear: Use clear and straightforward language. Ensure that action items are specific, with clearly defined tasks, responsible parties, and deadlines.

- Review and Distribute: After the meeting, review the minutes and action items for accuracy. Distribute the minutes to all participants and relevant stakeholders as soon as possible.

- Follow Up: Regularly review action items and follow up with responsible parties to ensure tasks are completed. Use the task management tools in Teams to track and monitor progress.

6. Integrating with Other Tools

Microsoft Teams integrates with various other tools that can enhance your ability to capture and track meeting minutes and action items:

- Integrating with SharePoint: Store meeting minutes and related documents in SharePoint for easy access and collaboration.

- Creating a SharePoint Library: Create a document library in SharePoint for your project. Store all meeting minutes and related documents here.

- Linking in Teams: Link the SharePoint library to your Teams channel for easy access.

- Using Power Automate: Automate the process of capturing and distributing meeting minutes.

- Creating Workflows: Use Power Automate to create workflows that automatically save meeting notes, distribute them to participants, and create follow-up tasks in Planner.

- Streamlining Processes: Automating these processes reduces manual effort and ensures consistency.

7. Case Study: Effective Meeting Management in Practice

To illustrate the importance and effectiveness of capturing meeting minutes and action items, let's look at a case study:

Case Study: ABC Construction Project

Background: ABC Construction is managing a large construction project involving multiple teams and stakeholders. Effective communication and task management are critical to the project's success.

Challenge: The project team struggled with keeping track of decisions made during meetings and ensuring action items were followed up on.

Solution: The project manager implemented Microsoft Teams for all project communication and documentation. They used OneNote for capturing meeting minutes and Planner for tracking action items.

Implementation:

- Meeting Preparation: Before each meeting, the project manager created a detailed agenda and shared it with all participants via Teams.

- During the Meeting: The designated note-taker used OneNote to capture key discussion points, decisions, and action items. The meeting was recorded for reference.

- After the Meeting: The meeting minutes were reviewed and distributed to all participants. Action items were added to Planner, assigned to team members, and tracked to completion.

Results: The team saw significant improvements in communication and task management. Meeting minutes were clear and concise, and action items were consistently followed up on. This led to increased accountability and progress on project tasks.

Conclusion

Capturing meeting minutes and action items is a vital component of effective project management. Microsoft Teams provides a robust set of tools to facilitate this process, ensuring that all discussions, decisions, and tasks are accurately documented and tracked. By following the best practices and utilizing the tools outlined in this chapter, you can enhance your project meetings' effectiveness, improve communication, and ensure that all team members are aligned and accountable.

CHAPTER V
Teams for Education

5.1 Setting Up Teams for Classrooms

5.1.1 Creating Class Teams

Microsoft Teams has revolutionized the educational landscape, providing educators and students with a powerful platform for collaboration, communication, and management. Creating class teams in Microsoft Teams is the foundational step towards building a dynamic and interactive learning environment. In this section, we will walk you through the detailed process of creating class teams, ensuring that your virtual classroom is set up for success.

Step-by-Step Guide to Creating Class Teams

1. Accessing Microsoft Teams:

- Start by logging into Microsoft Teams. Ensure that you have the necessary permissions to create teams. Typically, educators will have these permissions, but it's always a good practice to confirm with your IT administrator.

- From the Microsoft Teams interface, navigate to the 'Teams' section on the left-hand side of the screen. This is your central hub for all team-related activities.

2. Initiating Team Creation:

- Click on the 'Join or create a team' button located at the bottom of the Teams panel. This will bring up options for creating a new team or joining an existing one.

- Select the 'Create team' button to start the process of setting up your new class team.

3. Choosing the Team Type:

- Microsoft Teams offers several team types, including Class, PLC (Professional Learning Community), Staff, and Other. For educational purposes, select 'Class.'

- The 'Class' team type is specifically designed for educators and students, offering features such as assignments, grades, and class notebooks that are tailored to the educational context.

4. Naming Your Team and Adding a Description:

- Enter a meaningful name for your class team. This should be specific and clear, such as 'Math 101 - Spring 2024' or 'History Class - Grade 8.'

- Optionally, add a description that provides more details about the class. This can help students and parents understand the purpose and scope of the team.

5. Adding Students and Co-Teachers:

- After naming your team, you will be prompted to add students and co-teachers. You can add members by typing their names or email addresses. Microsoft Teams is integrated with your institution's directory, making it easy to find and add users.

- Adding co-teachers can be beneficial for collaborative teaching and ensuring that there is always a backup for class management.

6. Setting Up Channels for Organization:

- Once your team is created, it's time to set up channels. Channels help organize the content and activities within your class team. By default, a 'General' channel is created.

- Create additional channels based on subjects, units, projects, or any other organizational method that suits your teaching style. For example, you could have channels like 'Homework,' 'Group Projects,' 'Exams,' and 'Resources.'

- Channels can be public (accessible to all team members) or private (accessible to specific members). Use private channels for group work or sensitive discussions.

7. Customizing Team Settings:

- Access the team settings by clicking on the ellipsis (...) next to your team name and selecting 'Manage team.' Here, you can adjust settings related to member permissions, guest access, and team code.

- Set clear guidelines and permissions to ensure that the class team runs smoothly. Decide who can post messages, create channels, or add apps.

8. Integrating Class Notebooks:

- Microsoft Teams integrates seamlessly with OneNote Class Notebooks, providing a versatile tool for note-taking, collaboration, and organization.

- Set up your Class Notebook by navigating to the 'General' channel, clicking on the 'Class Notebook' tab, and following the setup instructions. This will create sections for collaboration space, content library, and individual student notebooks.

9. Configuring Assignments and Grades:

- Utilize the 'Assignments' tab to create, distribute, and grade assignments. This feature simplifies the process of managing student work and provides a centralized location for all assignment-related activities.

- The 'Grades' tab allows you to track student progress and maintain a grade book within Teams. This ensures transparency and helps students stay informed about their performance.

10. Enhancing Communication:

- Encourage students to use the 'Posts' tab in each channel for discussions, questions, and announcements. This fosters an interactive and engaging learning environment.

- Utilize the chat feature for direct communication with individual students or small groups. This can be particularly useful for providing personalized feedback or addressing specific concerns.

Best Practices for Creating and Managing Class Teams

1. Clear Communication:

- Establish clear communication guidelines and expectations from the start. Let students know how and when they can contact you, the appropriate channels for different types of communication, and the expected response times.

2. Consistent Organization:

- Maintain a consistent organizational structure across all your class teams. This helps students navigate the platform more easily and reduces confusion. Use a similar naming convention for channels, assignments, and resources.

3. Engaging Content:

- Keep your content engaging and varied. Use a mix of text, videos, interactive elements, and external resources to keep students interested and motivated.

4. Regular Updates:

- Regularly update your class team with new materials, announcements, and assignments. This keeps the team dynamic and ensures that students have access to the latest information.

5. Encourage Collaboration:

- Foster a collaborative learning environment by encouraging students to work together on projects, participate in discussions, and share their insights. Use the collaboration space in Class Notebooks and create group assignments to promote teamwork.

6. Monitor and Support:

- Actively monitor the class team to ensure that students are participating and adhering to guidelines. Provide timely support and feedback to keep them on track.

7. Leverage Analytics:

- Use the analytics tools available in Microsoft Teams to track student engagement and participation. This data can help you identify students who may need additional support and adjust your teaching strategies accordingly.

By following these detailed steps and best practices, you can effectively create and manage class teams in Microsoft Teams, providing a structured, interactive, and supportive online learning environment for your students. This foundational setup will pave the way for a successful and enriching educational experience, harnessing the full potential of Microsoft Teams in the classroom.

5.1.2 Organizing Channels for Subjects and Units

Organizing channels in Microsoft Teams for educational purposes involves creating a structured and logical setup that facilitates efficient communication and collaboration. This section will guide you through the process of organizing channels for subjects and units within your class teams, ensuring that both teachers and students can easily access and interact with the relevant materials.

Step-by-Step Guide to Organizing Channels

1. Understand the Structure and Requirements

- Identify the Subjects and Units: Before creating channels, identify the subjects you will be teaching and the units or topics under each subject. This clarity helps in structuring the channels logically.

- Plan the Channel Layout: Decide on the primary structure of your channels. Typically, channels can be organized by subjects (e.g., Mathematics, Science, History) and further divided into units or topics within each subject.

2. Create Channels for Each Subject

- Navigate to Your Class Team: Open Microsoft Teams and go to the specific class team you want to organize.

- Add a New Channel: Click on the ellipsis (three dots) next to the team name and select "Add channel."

- Name the Channel: Give the channel a clear and concise name that represents the subject (e.g., "Mathematics").

- Set the Channel Type: Choose whether the channel should be "Standard" (visible to everyone) or "Private" (only accessible to specific members). For most educational purposes, standard channels are preferred.

- Describe the Channel: Provide a brief description of the channel to indicate its purpose, such as "Mathematics subject discussions and resources."

3. Organize Channels by Units or Topics

- Subdivide Channels for Units: Within each subject channel, consider creating sub-channels for different units or topics. Since Microsoft Teams doesn't support nested channels directly, you can use a naming convention or tab structure.

- Using Tabs for Organization: Instead of creating multiple channels, use tabs within a channel to organize content by units. For example, in the "Mathematics" channel, add tabs named "Unit 1: Algebra," "Unit 2: Geometry," etc.

- Naming Convention: If you prefer separate channels, use a naming convention like "Mathematics - Algebra" and "Mathematics - Geometry" to keep related topics together.

4. Set Up Initial Content and Guidelines

- Upload Initial Resources: Populate each channel or tab with initial resources such as syllabus outlines, reading materials, and introductory notes.

- Post Guidelines: Create a pinned post or a tab with guidelines on how students should use the channel. This might include rules for posting, how to label assignments, and any specific formats to follow.

5. Utilize Class Notebooks for Organization

- Set Up Class Notebooks: Within each channel, you can use OneNote Class Notebooks for more detailed and organized note-taking. Set up sections within the Class Notebook for each unit or topic.

- Share Notebooks with Students: Ensure that all students have access to the Class Notebooks and understand how to use them. This can be a central repository for lecture notes, additional reading materials, and collaborative student work.

6. Encourage Consistent Use

- Regular Updates: Regularly update each channel with new materials, assignments, and announcements to keep the students engaged.

- Student Participation: Encourage students to actively participate in each channel by posting questions, sharing insights, and collaborating on projects.

Detailed Example: Setting Up a Mathematics Class Team

To illustrate the process, let's consider a detailed example of setting up a Mathematics class team.

1. Creating the Mathematics Team

- Team Name: "Grade 10 Mathematics"

- Channels:

  - General

- Algebra
- Geometry
- Calculus
- Statistics

2. Setting Up the Algebra Channel

- Name: "Mathematics - Algebra"
- Description: "Discussions and resources for Algebra topics."
- Initial Resources:
  - Syllabus outline for Algebra
  - Introductory notes on basic algebraic concepts
  - Links to online resources and textbooks

3. Organizing Content within the Algebra Channel

- Tabs:
  - Unit 1: Linear Equations: Upload lecture notes, problem sets, and related resources.
  - Unit 2: Quadratic Equations: Provide resources, assignments, and additional reading materials.
  - Assignments: Use the Assignments tab to post homework and project instructions.
- Class Notebook:
  - Sections: Linear Equations, Quadratic Equations, Polynomials
  - Pages: Detailed lecture notes, example problems, student collaboration spaces

4. Establishing Guidelines and Best Practices

- Posting Etiquette: Encourage students to use specific titles for their posts, such as "Question on Quadratic Equations Homework."
- Resource Sharing: Allow students to share useful links and resources, fostering a collaborative learning environment.

- Q&A Sessions: Schedule regular Q&A sessions where students can ask questions and clarify doubts.

5. Monitoring and Managing the Channel

- Regular Check-Ins: Teachers should regularly check the channels to ensure that discussions stay on topic and that any questions are promptly addressed.

- Feedback: Provide regular feedback on student posts and contributions to encourage active participation.

Advanced Tips for Effective Channel Management

1. Use Announcements Wisely

- Important Updates: Use the "Announcement" feature in the General channel for major updates, deadlines, and important information. Announcements can be highlighted with colorful banners to grab attention.

2. Pinning Posts

- Key Resources: Pin essential posts, such as the syllabus, important dates, and rules, so they remain easily accessible at the top of the channel.

3. Leverage the Power of Apps and Bots

- Third-Party Integrations: Integrate apps like Kahoot for quizzes, Flipgrid for video discussions, and Quizlet for flashcards to make the learning experience more interactive.

- Bots for Automation: Use bots like Polly for polls and surveys to gather student feedback and make classes more engaging.

4. Create Private Channels for Group Projects

- Group Work: For group projects, create private channels where small groups can collaborate independently. This ensures focused discussions and better management of group activities.

5. Conducting Virtual Office Hours

- Office Hours Channel: Create a dedicated channel for virtual office hours where students can drop in to ask questions. Schedule regular times and use the meeting feature to facilitate these sessions.

By following these guidelines and utilizing the advanced features of Microsoft Teams, educators can create an organized, interactive, and engaging learning environment. Properly organized channels not only streamline communication but also enhance the overall educational experience for both teachers and students.

5.1.3 Adding Students and Teachers

Adding students and teachers to your class team in Microsoft Teams is a crucial step to ensure that everyone involved in the learning process can access the resources they need, participate in discussions, and stay updated on assignments and grades. This process can be broken down into a few key steps to ensure that it's done efficiently and correctly.

1. Preparing the Class Roster

Before adding students and teachers, it's important to have a well-prepared class roster. This roster should include:

- Full names of all students and teachers.

- Email addresses (preferably those associated with your school or institution).

- Any specific groups or sections within the class, if applicable.

Having this information organized in a spreadsheet or a document can simplify the process of adding users to Teams.

2. Adding Students to the Class Team

2.1 Manually Adding Students

To manually add students to your class team, follow these steps:

1. Open Microsoft Teams and navigate to the specific class team where you want to add students.

2. Click on the "More options" button (three dots) next to the team name.

3. Select "Add member" from the dropdown menu.

4. In the "Add members" window, enter the email addresses of the students you want to add. As you type, Teams will suggest matching addresses. You can select these or continue typing the full email address.

5. Once you have entered all the email addresses, click "Add."

2.2 Adding Students via Bulk Upload

If you have a large number of students, manually adding each one can be time-consuming. Instead, you can use a bulk upload method:

1. Prepare a CSV file with the list of student email addresses. Each email address should be on a separate line.

2. Navigate to the class team and click on "Manage team."

3. Select "Members" and then choose "Bulk add."

4. Upload your CSV file. Teams will process the file and add all listed students to the team.

2.3 Inviting Students via a Join Code

For a more self-service approach, you can create a join code for your class team:

1. Go to the class team and select "Manage team."

2. Navigate to the "Settings" tab.

3. Under "Team code," click "Generate."

4. Share the generated code with your students. They can use this code to join the team by selecting "Join or create a team" and entering the code.

3. Adding Teachers to the Class Team

Teachers, like students, can be added to the team in a few different ways. Depending on their role, teachers can be added as owners or members.

3.1 Manually Adding Teachers

To manually add teachers:

1. Open the class team and click on the "More options" button next to the team name.

2. Select "Add member."

3. Enter the email addresses of the teachers. Ensure that they are added as owners if they need to manage the team and its settings.

4. Click "Add."

3.2 Using Bulk Upload or Join Code for Teachers

The same bulk upload and join code methods used for students can also be applied to add teachers. Ensure that you assign appropriate roles (owner or member) to teachers during this process.

4. Assigning Roles and Permissions

Once students and teachers are added, it's important to review and assign roles and permissions:

- Owners: Typically, the class teacher or lead educator should be an owner. Owners can manage team settings, add/remove members, and create/delete channels.

- Members: Students and additional teachers can be members. Members can participate in discussions, access resources, and submit assignments.

To assign roles:

1. Go to the class team and select "Manage team."

2. Under the "Members" tab, you'll see a list of all team members.

3. Use the dropdown menu next to each name to change their role (e.g., from member to owner).

5. Setting Up Groups within the Class Team

If your class has different sections or groups, you can set up private channels within the team for these groups:

1. Go to the class team and select "More options" next to the team name.

2. Choose "Add channel."

3. Enter the channel name (e.g., Group A, Group B).

4. Under "Privacy," select "Private – Accessible only to a specific group of people within the team."

5. Add the relevant students and teachers to each private channel.

6. Communicating the Process to Students and Teachers

Ensure that all students and teachers are aware of how to access Microsoft Teams and understand the basic functionalities:

- Send out an introductory email with login instructions, links to tutorials, and contact information for technical support.

- Schedule a kickoff meeting or orientation session to walk through the Teams interface and answer any questions.

- Provide ongoing support and resources, such as a FAQ document or a dedicated support channel within the team.

7. Troubleshooting Common Issues

Be prepared to address common issues that students and teachers might encounter:

- Login Problems: Ensure that all users are using the correct email addresses and passwords. Verify that they have access to the necessary Microsoft 365 subscriptions.

- Access Issues: Check that students and teachers are added to the correct teams and have the appropriate roles.

- Technical Difficulties: Provide resources for troubleshooting technical issues, such as internet connectivity problems, device compatibility, and software updates.

8. Maintaining the Roster

Regularly update the class roster to reflect changes, such as new students joining or others leaving:

- Periodically review the team membership to ensure accuracy.

- Use the bulk upload feature to add multiple new students or teachers at once if needed.

- Communicate any changes to the team promptly to avoid confusion.

Conclusion

Adding students and teachers to your class team in Microsoft Teams is a foundational step for effective classroom management and collaboration. By following these detailed steps and best practices, you can ensure a smooth setup process, enabling a seamless learning experience for all participants. As you continue to use Teams, keep refining your approach to meet the evolving needs of your classroom.

5.2 Assignments and Grades

5.2.1 Creating and Managing Assignments

In the digital age, education is increasingly incorporating technology to enhance the learning experience. Microsoft Teams offers a robust platform for creating and managing assignments, which simplifies the process for both teachers and students. This section provides a comprehensive guide to setting up, distributing, and tracking assignments in Microsoft Teams.

1. Introduction to Assignments in Microsoft Teams

Assignments in Microsoft Teams are designed to streamline the process of assigning, collecting, and grading student work. This feature allows educators to create assignments with due dates, provide necessary resources, and give feedback all within a single platform. By leveraging Teams, educators can save time, improve organization, and foster better communication with students.

2. Setting Up Your Class Team

Before diving into creating assignments, ensure your Class Team is set up correctly. Each class team should have designated channels for various subjects or units, where assignments can be posted.

Creating Class Teams:

- Navigate to Teams on the left sidebar of the Microsoft Teams app.
- Click on "Join or create a team" at the bottom of the Teams list.
- Select "Create team" and choose the "Class" option.
- Follow the prompts to enter your class name, description, and add students and teachers.

Organizing Channels:

- Use channels to organize your class content. For example, you can create channels for "Math," "Science," "Homework," etc.

- Click on the three dots next to the class team name, then select "Add channel."

- Name the channel, add a description if necessary, and set privacy settings.

3. Creating Assignments

Creating assignments in Microsoft Teams involves several steps, from drafting the assignment to specifying details like due dates and points. Here's a step-by-step guide:

1. Accessing the Assignments Tab:

- Go to the desired class team.

- Click on the "Assignments" tab at the top of the channel.

2. Creating a New Assignment:

- Click on the "Create" button and select "Assignment" from the dropdown menu.

- Enter the title and instructions for the assignment. Be clear and concise to ensure students understand the requirements.

3. Adding Resources:

- You can attach files, links, or other resources that students will need to complete the assignment.

- Click on "Add resources," then select the type of resource you want to add. You can upload files from your computer, OneDrive, or link to online resources.

4. Setting Due Dates and Times:

- Specify the due date and time for the assignment. Click on the calendar icon to select the date, and use the time field to set the submission deadline.

- You can also set a "Close date" after which students can no longer submit the assignment. This is optional but useful for maintaining deadlines.

5. Assigning Points:

- If you are grading the assignment, enter the total points possible in the "Points" field.

- You can also use rubrics for more detailed grading criteria. Click on "Add rubric" to create or attach a rubric.

4. Distributing Assignments

Once the assignment is created, it needs to be distributed to students. Microsoft Teams allows for flexible distribution options, enabling you to assign work to the entire class, individual students, or specific groups.

1. Assigning to the Whole Class:

- By default, the assignment is set to be distributed to all students in the class. Simply click "Assign" to distribute it.

2. Assigning to Individual Students or Groups:

- To assign to specific students, click on the "All students" dropdown and select the students or groups you want to assign the work to.

- You can create groups within Teams if needed. Go to the "Teams" tab, click on the class team, then "Manage team" and "Add group."

5. Managing Assignments

Managing assignments in Microsoft Teams involves monitoring submission status, providing feedback, and making adjustments as needed. The Assignments tab provides a comprehensive view of all assignments and their statuses.

1. Viewing Assignment Status:

- Go to the "Assignments" tab and select the assignment you want to review.

- You will see a list of students and the status of their submissions (Not turned in, Turned in, Returned).

2. Providing Feedback:

- Click on a student's submission to view their work.

- You can add comments directly on the document or use the feedback field to provide overall comments.

- Use the rubric (if applicable) to grade the assignment. Click on the rubric criteria to assign points.

3. Returning Assignments:

- After reviewing and grading, click "Return" to send the graded assignment back to the student.

- You can return assignments individually or to multiple students at once by selecting their names and clicking "Return" at the top.

6. Tracking Student Progress

Tracking progress is crucial for understanding how students are performing and identifying areas where they might need additional support. Microsoft Teams offers several tools for monitoring student progress.

1. Using the Grades Tab:

- The "Grades" tab provides an overview of all assignments and their statuses.

- Click on the tab to see a grid view of student names, assignments, and grades.

2. Exporting Grades:

- You can export grades to an Excel file for further analysis. Click on "Export to Excel" in the "Grades" tab.

- Use this file to track progress over time, identify trends, and share with parents or administrators.

3. Analytics and Insights:

- Microsoft Teams provides insights into student engagement and performance. Go to the "Insights" tab to view detailed analytics.

- Use these insights to inform your teaching strategies and provide targeted support to students.

7. Best Practices for Creating and Managing Assignments

To make the most of the assignment features in Microsoft Teams, consider the following best practices:

1. Clear Instructions:

- Provide detailed instructions and expectations for each assignment. This helps students understand what is required and reduces confusion.

2. Consistent Deadlines:

- Set consistent due dates and times for assignments. This helps students manage their time effectively and develop good study habits.

3. Timely Feedback:

- Provide feedback promptly to keep students engaged and motivated. Timely feedback helps students understand their mistakes and improve.

4. Use of Rubrics:

- Utilize rubrics for grading to ensure fairness and transparency. Rubrics provide clear criteria for evaluation and help students understand how they are being assessed.

5. Regular Monitoring:

- Regularly check the status of assignments and follow up with students who are falling behind. This proactive approach helps address issues before they become major problems.

8. Leveraging Technology for Enhanced Learning

Microsoft Teams integrates with various educational tools and technologies to enhance the learning experience. Consider incorporating these tools into your assignments:

1. Class Notebook:

- Use Class Notebook for collaborative note-taking and sharing. This tool is integrated with Teams and provides a digital space for students to organize their notes.

2. Immersive Reader:

- Immersive Reader helps students with reading difficulties by providing tools like text-to-speech and customizable reading settings. Enable this feature in assignments to support diverse learning needs.

3. Third-Party Apps:

- Explore third-party apps that integrate with Microsoft Teams to enhance assignments. Apps like Kahoot!, Flipgrid, and Quizlet offer interactive learning experiences.

Conclusion

Creating and managing assignments in Microsoft Teams is a powerful way to streamline the educational process and enhance student learning. By following the steps outlined in this guide, educators can effectively set up, distribute, and track assignments, providing a seamless and efficient experience for both teachers and students. Embracing these tools and best practices will not only improve organization and communication but also foster a more engaging and productive learning environment.

5.2.2 Grading and Providing Feedback

Grading and providing feedback are critical components of the educational process, as they guide students' learning, reinforce concepts, and identify areas that need improvement. Microsoft Teams offers robust tools to facilitate these tasks efficiently, allowing educators to streamline their workflow and focus more on student engagement.

Overview of the Grading Process

1. Accessing Assignments:

- To start grading, navigate to the Assignments tab in the General channel of your class team.

- Select the assignment you wish to grade. You will see a list of students and the status of their submissions (e.g., Not Turned In, Turned In, Graded).

2. Reviewing Submissions:

- Click on a student's name to view their submission. This opens the assignment in the Teams interface.

- Depending on the type of assignment (e.g., document, video, quiz), you can view and interact with the student's work directly within Teams or download it for offline review.

Providing Grades

1. Grading Criteria:

- Before assigning grades, ensure you have a clear grading rubric or criteria. Microsoft Teams allows you to attach rubrics to assignments, providing transparency and consistency in grading.

- Rubrics can be created and customized in Teams, specifying different criteria and levels of achievement. This helps students understand how their work will be evaluated.

2. Assigning Grades:

- In the student's assignment view, you will find a grading panel where you can enter the grade. This can be a numerical score, letter grade, or other grading scale as defined in your assignment setup.

- If using a rubric, select the appropriate level for each criterion. Teams will automatically calculate the total grade based on the rubric.

3. Feedback Comments:

- In addition to grades, providing written feedback is crucial for student development. Teams allows you to add comments directly on the student's submission.

- Highlight specific parts of their work and provide constructive feedback, suggesting areas for improvement and praising well-done sections.

- Use the feedback box to give overall comments on the assignment, summarizing your detailed feedback and encouraging further effort.

Enhancing Feedback with Digital Tools

1. Annotation Tools:

- Microsoft Teams integrates with OneNote, allowing you to use digital ink to annotate directly on submissions.

- Highlight text, draw diagrams, and make notes on students' work. These visual cues can help students better understand your feedback.

2. Audio and Video Feedback:

- For more personalized feedback, consider using audio or video comments. Teams enables you to record short messages directly within the assignment grading interface.

- This method can be especially effective for complex feedback or for students who may benefit from auditory learning.

3. Rubric Feedback:

- If you've attached a rubric to the assignment, use it to provide detailed, criterion-based feedback. This helps students see precisely where they excelled and where they need improvement.

- Microsoft Teams makes it easy to click and score each criterion, providing a clear and structured way to deliver feedback.

Tracking Student Progress

1. Gradebook Integration:

- All grades and feedback provided in Teams are automatically saved and organized in the class gradebook.

- Access the Grades tab in the General channel to view an overview of all student grades for the course. This tab allows you to see individual student progress and overall class performance.

2. Progress Reports:

- Generate progress reports to share with students and parents. Teams can export grade data, which can be used to create detailed progress reports.

- These reports can highlight strengths, identify areas for improvement, and track changes over time.

3. Student Access to Feedback:

- Once graded, students can access their grades and feedback through the Assignments tab.

- Encourage students to review their feedback carefully. Provide opportunities for them to discuss their grades and feedback with you if they have questions or need further clarification.

Continuous Improvement

1. Student Reflections:

- Encourage students to reflect on the feedback they receive. You can create assignments specifically for reflection, where students can write about what they learned from the feedback and how they plan to improve.

- Reflection assignments can be a valuable tool for metacognition, helping students become more self-aware and proactive in their learning.

2. Re-submissions and Revisions:

- Allow students to revise and resubmit their work based on your feedback. This iterative process can lead to deeper learning and better mastery of the subject matter.

- Microsoft Teams supports multiple submissions for the same assignment, making it easy to track changes and improvements over time.

3. Feedback on Feedback:

- Gather feedback from students on the feedback you provide. Ask them what types of feedback they find most helpful and adjust your approach accordingly.

- Continuous improvement in your feedback methods can lead to better student engagement and success.

Best Practices for Effective Feedback

1. Timeliness:

- Provide feedback as promptly as possible. Timely feedback helps students make connections between their work and your comments while the material is still fresh in their minds.

- Microsoft Teams notifications ensure that students are alerted when their work has been graded and feedback is available.

2. Specificity:

- Be specific in your feedback. Rather than saying "Good job," explain what specifically was done well (e.g., "Your thesis statement is clear and well-supported by evidence").

- Specific feedback helps students understand exactly what they did right and what needs improvement.

3. Balanced Approach:

- Use a balanced approach in your feedback, providing both positive comments and constructive criticism.

- Highlight strengths to boost confidence and motivation, and address weaknesses with actionable suggestions for improvement.

4. Consistency:

- Be consistent in your grading and feedback. Use rubrics and grading criteria to ensure fairness and transparency.

- Consistency helps build trust and ensures that all students are evaluated by the same standards.

Conclusion

Grading and providing feedback are essential tasks for educators using Microsoft Teams. By leveraging the platform's robust tools and following best practices, you can deliver meaningful, constructive, and timely feedback that supports student growth and learning. Whether through written comments, digital annotations, or personalized audio and video messages, your feedback can significantly impact your students' academic journey. Through continuous improvement and engagement, you can create a supportive and effective learning environment in Microsoft Teams.

5.2.3 Tracking Student Progress

Tracking student progress in Microsoft Teams is an essential part of the educational process, providing educators with the tools they need to monitor, assess, and support student learning effectively. This section will guide you through the steps and best practices for utilizing Microsoft Teams to track student progress comprehensively.

Overview of Tracking Student Progress

Tracking student progress involves collecting data on student performance, engagement, and participation over time. This data helps educators identify areas where students excel and where they may need additional support. Microsoft Teams offers several features to facilitate this process, including the Grades tab, assignment analytics, and integration with other Microsoft tools such as OneNote and Excel.

Setting Up the Grades Tab

The Grades tab in Microsoft Teams is a centralized location where educators can view and manage student grades for all assignments within a team. Here's how to set it up and use it effectively:

1. Accessing the Grades Tab:

- Navigate to the team where you have created assignments.
- Click on the "Grades" tab located at the top of the channel.
- The Grades tab will display a list of all assignments and students, along with their respective grades.

2. Viewing Assignment Status:

- The Grades tab provides a clear overview of which assignments have been completed, are pending, or are missing.
- This visual representation helps educators quickly identify students who may be falling behind or need additional support.

3. Updating Grades:

- To update grades, click on the cell corresponding to the student and assignment.
- Enter the grade and any feedback if necessary.
- Changes are automatically saved and reflected in the student's view.

Using Assignment Analytics

Assignment analytics in Microsoft Teams provide insights into student performance and engagement. Here's how to make the most of these analytics:

1. Accessing Analytics:

- Navigate to the "Assignments" tab in your team.

- Click on "Insights" to view analytics for your assignments.

2. Analyzing Data:

- Insights provide information on assignment submission rates, average grades, and individual student performance.

- Use this data to identify trends, such as assignments that many students found challenging or those that were completed quickly.

3. Taking Action:

- Based on the analytics, you can adjust your teaching strategies, provide additional resources, or offer extra support to students who may be struggling.

- Share insights with students to help them understand their progress and areas for improvement.

Integrating OneNote for Progress Tracking

OneNote is a powerful tool for tracking student progress, offering features such as individual notebooks, collaboration spaces, and digital portfolios. Here's how to use OneNote in conjunction with Microsoft Teams:

1. Setting Up Class Notebooks:

- In your team, navigate to the "Class Notebook" tab.

- Set up a class notebook with sections for each student, collaboration spaces, and content libraries.

2. Using Individual Notebooks:

- Encourage students to use their individual notebooks to take notes, complete assignments, and reflect on their learning.

- Regularly review student notebooks to monitor progress and provide feedback.

3. Creating Digital Portfolios:

- Use OneNote to create digital portfolios where students can showcase their work and track their progress over time.

- Portfolios can include a variety of content, such as written assignments, multimedia projects, and reflective journals.

Utilizing Excel for Advanced Tracking

Excel is an excellent tool for advanced tracking and data analysis. Here's how to use Excel in conjunction with Microsoft Teams to track student progress:

1. Exporting Data:

- In the Grades tab, click on "Export to Excel" to download a spreadsheet of student grades and assignment data.

- Open the exported file in Excel for further analysis.

2. Analyzing Data in Excel:

- Use Excel's powerful data analysis tools, such as pivot tables and charts, to gain deeper insights into student performance.

- Create custom reports to share with students, parents, and administrators.

3. Automating Data Updates:

- Set up formulas and macros in Excel to automate data updates and streamline the tracking process.

- Integrate Excel with other tools, such as Power BI, for advanced data visualization and reporting.

Best Practices for Tracking Student Progress

To effectively track student progress in Microsoft Teams, consider the following best practices:

1. Consistency and Regularity:

- Consistently update grades and feedback to ensure students have a clear understanding of their progress.

- Regularly review assignment analytics and take action based on the insights.

2. Transparency and Communication:

- Maintain transparency with students about how their progress is being tracked and assessed.

- Communicate regularly with students about their performance, providing constructive feedback and encouragement.

3. Using Multiple Tools:

- Leverage the various tools available in Microsoft Teams, such as the Grades tab, OneNote, and Excel, to create a comprehensive tracking system.

- Integrate additional tools, such as Forms for quizzes and surveys, to gather more data on student learning.

4. Engaging Students in the Process:

- Encourage students to take an active role in tracking their own progress.

- Use features such as self-assessments and peer reviews to help students develop a sense of ownership over their learning.

5. Continuous Improvement:

- Continuously refine your tracking methods based on feedback and data analysis.

- Stay updated on new features and best practices in Microsoft Teams to enhance your tracking system.

Case Study: Effective Progress Tracking

To illustrate the practical application of tracking student progress in Microsoft Teams, let's explore a case study of an educator who successfully implemented these strategies.

Case Study: Mrs. Smith's High School Biology Class

Mrs. Smith, a high school biology teacher, wanted to improve how she tracked her students' progress. She decided to leverage Microsoft Teams and its various tools to create a comprehensive tracking system.

1. Setting Up the Grades Tab:

- Mrs. Smith set up the Grades tab for her biology class, entering all assignments and their respective due dates.

- She regularly updated the Grades tab with student grades and feedback, ensuring students were aware of their performance.

2. Using Assignment Analytics:

- Mrs. Smith accessed the Insights tab to analyze assignment data.

- She noticed that many students struggled with a particular assignment, indicating a need for additional instruction on the topic.

3. Integrating OneNote:

- Mrs. Smith set up a class notebook in OneNote, with sections for each student to take notes and complete assignments.

- She reviewed student notebooks weekly, providing feedback and identifying areas where students needed more support.

4. Utilizing Excel for Advanced Tracking:

- Mrs. Smith exported grade data to Excel and created custom reports to share with parents during parent-teacher conferences.

- She used Excel to track trends in student performance over time, helping her identify long-term progress and areas for improvement.

5. Engaging Students in the Process:

- Mrs. Smith encouraged her students to use OneNote to track their own progress and reflect on their learning.

- She implemented self-assessments and peer reviews, fostering a collaborative and reflective learning environment.

By following these strategies, Mrs. Smith was able to create a robust system for tracking student progress, ultimately leading to improved student outcomes and a more transparent and supportive learning environment.

5.3 Enhancing Classroom Interaction

5.3.1 Using Class Notebook

Using Class Notebook within Microsoft Teams offers an innovative and interactive way to enhance classroom interaction. Class Notebook, a feature integrated from OneNote, is designed specifically for educational purposes, providing a versatile and dynamic tool for both teachers and students. This section will provide a comprehensive guide on how to set up and utilize Class Notebook effectively in your virtual classroom.

Setting Up Class Notebook

Creating a Class Notebook:

1. Accessing Class Notebook:

- Open Microsoft Teams and navigate to the specific class team where you want to create a notebook.

- Click on the "Class Notebook" tab at the top of the channel. If it's not visible, you may need to add it by clicking on the "+" sign and selecting Class Notebook from the list of apps.

2. Initial Setup:

- When you first click on Class Notebook, you'll be prompted to set up a new notebook. Click on "Set up a OneNote Class Notebook."

- Follow the on-screen instructions to create sections for students, which include:

  - Collaboration Space: Where everyone in the class can share, organize, and collaborate.

  - Content Library: A read-only space for handouts, readings, and other materials.

  - Student Notebooks: Private notebooks shared between the teacher and each individual student. Only the teacher can see all students' notebooks.

3. Customizing Sections:

- You can customize the sections in each student's notebook to include areas like Homework, Class Notes, Handouts, and Quizzes. These sections can be tailored to meet the specific needs of your curriculum and teaching style.

Setting Permissions:

- Permissions in Class Notebook are critical for maintaining privacy and managing collaboration.

- Teachers have full access to all parts of the notebook, while students can only access their own sections and the shared spaces (Collaboration Space and Content Library).

- Adjust permissions as necessary to suit different activities, such as allowing students to contribute to the Collaboration Space during group projects.

Utilizing Class Notebook for Classroom Interaction

Creating and Distributing Content:

1. Adding Content to the Content Library:

- The Content Library is an ideal place to distribute course materials. You can add text, images, audio, video, and links to web resources.

- To add content, simply click on the Content Library section, then click on the desired page, and start typing or insert various media.

2. Distributing Pages to Students:

- One of the most powerful features of Class Notebook is the ability to distribute pages to all students or specific groups.

- To distribute a page, create or select the page you want to share, click "Class Notebook" on the toolbar, and select "Distribute Page." You can then choose to distribute it to all students or a particular group.

Encouraging Collaboration:

1. Using the Collaboration Space:

- The Collaboration Space is where students can work together on projects, group assignments, or any collaborative activity.

- Teachers can create sections for different groups or projects and monitor progress in real-time.

- Encourage students to use the Collaboration Space for brainstorming, sharing ideas, and peer feedback.

2. Facilitating Discussions:

- Use the Collaboration Space to facilitate class discussions. Pose a question or a topic, and let students contribute their thoughts and responses.

- You can organize discussions by creating a new section for each topic or week.

Monitoring and Providing Feedback:

1. Reviewing Student Work:

- Teachers can access each student's notebook to review their work and provide feedback.

- Use tags and highlights to mark important sections, add comments, and give constructive feedback directly on their pages.

2. Real-Time Feedback:

- Providing real-time feedback is crucial for student engagement and improvement. Use the commenting feature to leave notes and suggestions as students work on their assignments.

- You can also schedule one-on-one meetings using Teams to discuss their progress and address any issues.

Advanced Features of Class Notebook

Incorporating Multimedia:

1. Adding Audio and Video:

- Class Notebook supports the addition of audio and video, making it easier to provide diverse content.

- Teachers can record lectures or explanations and embed them directly into the notebook pages. This is particularly useful for language learning, music education, or providing detailed instructions.

2. Interactive Content:

- Use interactive elements like quizzes, polls, and forms to engage students. These can be embedded into notebook pages to make learning more interactive and fun.

- Utilize Microsoft Forms to create surveys and quizzes, and link them within the notebook for seamless access.

Using Templates and Pre-Made Content:

1. Pre-Made Templates:

- Class Notebook offers a variety of pre-made templates that can save time and ensure consistency across your class materials.

- Templates for lesson plans, homework assignments, project outlines, and more can be customized to fit your specific needs.

2. Creating Your Own Templates:

- Teachers can create their own templates for recurring assignments or activities. Once a template is created, it can be saved and reused, ensuring uniformity and efficiency.

Integration with Other Microsoft Tools:

1. Using OneDrive:

- Class Notebook seamlessly integrates with OneDrive, allowing for easy sharing and storage of files.

- Teachers and students can attach files from OneDrive directly into the notebook, ensuring that all resources are easily accessible and organized.

2. Connecting with Teams Meetings:

- Schedule and link Teams meetings within Class Notebook pages. This is particularly useful for setting up virtual office hours, study groups, or additional support sessions.

- Meeting notes and recordings can be stored in the notebook, providing a comprehensive resource for students.

Accessibility and Inclusivity:

1. Immersive Reader:

- The Immersive Reader tool in Class Notebook aids students with different learning needs by enhancing text readability. It offers features like text-to-speech, translation, and highlighting.

- Encourage students to use this tool to improve comprehension and engagement with the material.

2. Supporting Diverse Learning Styles:

- Class Notebook's flexibility supports various learning styles, whether visual, auditory, or kinesthetic.

- Provide content in multiple formats – text, audio, video, and interactive elements – to cater to the diverse needs of your students.

Best Practices for Using Class Notebook

Organizing Your Notebook:

1. Consistency in Naming Conventions:

- Use consistent naming conventions for sections and pages to keep the notebook organized and easy to navigate.

- Clearly label each section and page with the topic, date, and any other relevant information.

2. Regular Maintenance:

- Regularly review and update the notebook to ensure that all information is current and relevant.

- Archive old sections and pages to keep the notebook uncluttered.

Engaging Students:

1. Interactive Assignments:

- Design assignments that require students to use different features of Class Notebook, such as inserting multimedia, collaborating with peers, and using the drawing tools.

- Encourage creativity and critical thinking through interactive and dynamic assignments.

2. Student Feedback:

- Regularly seek feedback from students on how Class Notebook is working for them and what could be improved.

- Use this feedback to make adjustments and enhance the learning experience.

Professional Development:

1. Training and Workshops:

- Attend training sessions and workshops on Microsoft Teams and Class Notebook to stay updated on new features and best practices.

- Share your knowledge with colleagues to foster a collaborative teaching environment.

2. Continuous Learning:

- Explore online resources, tutorials, and communities dedicated to Microsoft Teams and Class Notebook.

- Engage in continuous learning to enhance your skills and stay current with technological advancements.

In conclusion, using Class Notebook in Microsoft Teams can significantly enhance classroom interaction, foster collaboration, and improve the overall learning experience. By effectively setting up, utilizing, and continuously improving your use of Class Notebook, you can create a dynamic and engaging virtual classroom environment that supports diverse learning styles and needs.

5.3.2 Conducting Virtual Lectures and Discussions

Conducting virtual lectures and discussions using Microsoft Teams is a powerful way to create an engaging and interactive learning environment. This section will guide you through the process of setting up, conducting, and optimizing virtual lectures and discussions to ensure that your students receive the best possible educational experience.

Setting Up Virtual Lectures

1. Scheduling Your Lecture:

- Using the Calendar:

Start by opening the Microsoft Teams application and navigating to the Calendar tab. Click on "New meeting" to schedule your lecture. Enter the details, including the title of the lecture, the date and time, and any necessary recurrence settings. Add the students or class team as participants to ensure everyone receives an invitation.

- Inviting Guests:

If you have guest lecturers or external participants, ensure they are added to the meeting. You can do this by entering their email addresses in the "Invite people" field. Guests will receive an email invitation with a link to join the lecture.

2. Preparing Your Content:

- Slide Decks and Visual Aids:

Create a slide deck or other visual aids to enhance your lecture. PowerPoint is seamlessly integrated with Microsoft Teams, allowing you to share your slides directly within the meeting.

- Multimedia Elements:

Incorporate multimedia elements such as videos, audio clips, and interactive content to make your lecture more engaging. These can be shared via screen sharing or uploaded as files in the meeting chat.

3. Setting Up Your Environment:

- Technical Check:

Ensure your computer, webcam, and microphone are working correctly. Perform a test call to check audio and video quality. Ensure you have a stable internet connection to avoid disruptions.

- Minimizing Distractions:

Choose a quiet, well-lit location for your lecture. Inform family members or roommates of your lecture schedule to minimize interruptions. Use a virtual background if your surroundings are not conducive to a professional appearance.

Conducting the Lecture

1. Starting the Lecture:

- Join Early:

Join the meeting a few minutes before the scheduled start time to greet students as they join and address any technical issues that may arise.

- Record the Lecture:

Start the recording by clicking on the "More actions" (three dots) button and selecting "Start recording." This allows students who cannot attend the live session to review the lecture later.

2. Engaging with Students:

- Interactive Polls and Quizzes:

Use the "Forms" app to create polls and quizzes during your lecture. This can help assess students' understanding of the material and keep them engaged.

- Q&A Sessions:

Encourage students to ask questions by using the chat feature or raising their hand. Allocate specific times during the lecture for Q&A sessions to address these questions.

3. Sharing Content:

- Screen Sharing:

Share your screen to display your slide deck or other materials. Click on the "Share content" button and choose the screen or window you want to share. Ensure you have all necessary materials open and ready before starting the share.

- Using Whiteboard:

Utilize the Whiteboard feature to illustrate concepts dynamically. This tool allows you to draw, write, and collaborate with students in real-time.

4. Managing the Classroom:

- Muting Participants:

To minimize background noise, mute all participants at the beginning of the lecture. You can allow students to unmute themselves when they need to speak.

- Breakout Rooms:

For group discussions or activities, use the Breakout Rooms feature. This allows you to divide students into smaller groups for more focused interaction. Set a timer for breakout sessions and provide clear instructions for the tasks they need to complete.

Conducting Virtual Discussions

1. Creating a Safe and Inclusive Environment:

- Establishing Ground Rules:

Set clear ground rules for discussions at the beginning of the semester. Encourage respectful communication and active listening. Address any inappropriate behavior immediately to maintain a positive environment.

- Encouraging Participation:

Use various techniques to encourage participation, such as calling on students by name, using the chat feature for responses, and encouraging the use of emojis or reactions to express agreement or understanding.

2. Facilitating Discussions:

- Prompting Questions:

Prepare a list of open-ended questions to stimulate discussion. Encourage students to think critically and express their opinions. For example, "What are your thoughts on...?" or "Can someone explain why...?"

- Group Activities:

Incorporate group activities that require collaboration and discussion. This can include case studies, role-playing, or problem-solving tasks.

3. Utilizing Discussion Tools:

- Channels and Threads:

Use specific channels for different topics or units. Within each channel, create threads to organize discussions. This helps keep conversations focused and easy to follow.

- OneNote Class Notebook:

Leverage the OneNote Class Notebook for collaborative note-taking and discussion documentation. This allows students to contribute their thoughts and review notes at any time.

4. Providing Feedback:

- Timely Responses:

Provide timely and constructive feedback on students' contributions. Acknowledge their input and provide additional insights or resources to further their understanding.

- Peer Feedback:

Encourage students to provide feedback to each other. This not only fosters a sense of community but also helps students develop critical thinking and evaluation skills.

Enhancing Interaction with Additional Tools

1. Integrating Third-Party Apps:

- Kahoot!:

Use Kahoot! for interactive quizzes and games. This can make learning fun and reinforce key concepts.

- Padlet:

Padlet allows for collaborative brainstorming and idea sharing. Create boards where students can post their thoughts, questions, and reflections.

2. Utilizing Microsoft Forms:

- Surveys and Feedback:

Create surveys to gather feedback on your lectures and discussions. Use this feedback to improve future sessions.

- Assessment Tools:

Use Microsoft Forms for formative assessments. Create quizzes and polls to gauge student understanding and adapt your teaching accordingly.

3. Leveraging Insights for Education:

- Monitoring Student Engagement:

Use the Insights app to track student engagement and participation. This provides valuable data on attendance, participation, and assignment completion.

- Identifying At-Risk Students:

Identify students who may be struggling based on their engagement levels and provide additional support as needed.

Best Practices for Virtual Lectures and Discussions

1. Continuous Improvement:

- Reflecting on Sessions:

After each lecture or discussion, take time to reflect on what went well and what could be improved. Seek feedback from students to identify areas for enhancement.

- Professional Development:

Engage in professional development opportunities to stay updated on best practices for virtual teaching. Participate in webinars, online courses, and communities of practice.

2. Building Community:

- Virtual Office Hours:

Offer virtual office hours to provide additional support and build rapport with students. Use these sessions to address individual concerns and foster a sense of community.

- Social Interaction:

Create opportunities for social interaction, such as virtual coffee breaks or informal discussion sessions. This helps build a supportive and connected classroom environment.

By following these detailed guidelines, educators can effectively conduct virtual lectures and discussions using Microsoft Teams. This not only enhances the learning experience for students but also ensures that they remain engaged and motivated throughout their educational journey.

5.3.3 Sharing Educational Resources

In the modern educational environment, sharing educational resources efficiently and effectively is crucial for enhancing classroom interaction and ensuring that students have access to the materials they need to succeed. Microsoft Teams provides a robust platform for educators to share resources, foster collaboration, and create an interactive learning experience. This section will guide you through the various ways to share educational resources within Microsoft Teams, including best practices for organizing and distributing materials, integrating third-party resources, and utilizing Teams' built-in features to enhance student engagement.

Organizing Educational Resources

1. Creating a Central Repository

One of the key features of Microsoft Teams is the ability to create a central repository for all class materials. This repository can be organized within the 'Files' tab of each channel. To set up an efficient repository:

- Folders and Subfolders: Organize your materials into folders and subfolders based on subjects, units, or weeks. For example, you might have a main folder for 'Science' with subfolders for 'Biology,' 'Chemistry,' and 'Physics.'

- Naming Conventions: Use clear and consistent naming conventions for files and folders. This helps students easily find what they need. For example, files could be named by topic and date (e.g., "Photosynthesis_2023-09-01").

- Access Permissions: Ensure that the appropriate permissions are set so that students can view and download the materials they need without compromising the security of your content.

2. Utilizing Class Notebook

The Class Notebook in Microsoft Teams is a powerful tool for organizing and sharing resources. It provides a digital binder where you can distribute notes, assignments, and other educational content.

- Teacher-Only Section: This section is visible only to the teacher and can be used to store lesson plans, notes, and other preparatory materials.

- Content Library: A read-only section for students where you can share important documents, reference materials, and instructional content.

- Student Notebooks: Individual sections for each student that allow for personalized distribution of resources and assignments.

Distributing Educational Resources

1. Using the 'Posts' Tab

The 'Posts' tab in each channel is an excellent place to share resources directly with your students. Here, you can post announcements, share links to files, and embed multimedia resources.

- Announcements and Updates: Use @mentions to draw attention to important resources and updates. For example, "@Class, I've uploaded the new assignment on photosynthesis. Check the Files tab!"

- Pinned Posts: Pin important posts to the top of the channel for easy access. This is particularly useful for key resources that students need to refer to frequently.

2. Assignments and Grades

The 'Assignments' tab is a dedicated space for distributing and managing assignments. This feature allows you to attach resources directly to assignments, ensuring students have all the necessary materials.

- Attaching Resources: When creating an assignment, you can attach files from your computer, OneDrive, or the Class Notebook. This ensures that all resources related to the assignment are centralized.

- Rubrics and Guidelines: Include rubrics and guidelines within the assignment to help students understand the expectations and grading criteria.

3. Collaborative Spaces

Microsoft Teams offers several collaborative tools that can enhance the sharing of resources:

- Wiki: Each channel includes a Wiki tab by default, which can be used to create and share collaborative documents. The Wiki is ideal for group projects and class notes.

- Whiteboard: During meetings and virtual lectures, use the Whiteboard feature to share diagrams, illustrations, and notes in real-time. The Whiteboard can be saved and shared for later reference.

Integrating Third-Party Resources

1. Educational Apps and Tools

Microsoft Teams integrates with a wide range of third-party educational apps and tools, allowing you to enhance your resource sharing capabilities.

- Kahoot!: Use Kahoot! to create interactive quizzes and games. Share the links to these resources within Teams to engage students in a fun and interactive way.

- Quizlet: Share Quizlet flashcards and study sets directly within Teams to provide students with additional study aids.

- Flipgrid: Use Flipgrid to create video discussions and share these resources within your class channels.

2. External Resource Links

In addition to internal resources, you can share links to external educational resources. This includes online articles, videos, and interactive content from trusted educational websites.

- Embedding Videos: Use the 'Posts' tab to share links to educational videos from platforms like YouTube or Vimeo. These can be used to supplement lessons and provide visual explanations of complex topics.

- Online Articles and Journals: Share links to online articles and academic journals that are relevant to your lessons. This encourages students to engage in further reading and research.

Best Practices for Resource Sharing

1. Consistency and Clarity

Consistency is key when it comes to sharing educational resources. Ensure that all resources are shared in a consistent manner, whether through the 'Files' tab, Class Notebook, or 'Posts' tab.

- Clear Instructions: Provide clear instructions on where to find resources and how to use them. For example, "Please refer to the 'Files' tab under the 'Biology' folder for today's lecture notes."

- Regular Updates: Keep the resource repository updated with the latest materials. Regularly check for outdated resources and remove or archive them as necessary.

2. Engaging Students

Engaging students in the resource-sharing process can enhance their learning experience. Encourage students to share their own resources and collaborate on creating a comprehensive repository.

- Student Contributions: Allow students to contribute to the Class Notebook or Wiki. This could include sharing their own notes, research, or additional resources they find helpful.

- Peer Reviews: Use the 'Assignments' tab to facilitate peer reviews. Students can share their work with classmates for feedback, fostering a collaborative learning environment.

3. Feedback and Adaptation

Collect feedback from students on the effectiveness of the shared resources. This feedback can help you adapt and improve your resource-sharing strategy.

- Surveys and Polls: Use Microsoft Forms to create surveys and polls to gather feedback on the resources. Questions could include "How helpful did you find the lecture notes?" or "What additional resources would you like to see?"

- Adjusting Strategies: Based on feedback, adjust your resource-sharing methods to better meet the needs of your students. This might involve reorganizing the repository, adding new types of resources, or changing the way you distribute materials.

Conclusion

Sharing educational resources effectively in Microsoft Teams enhances classroom interaction, supports student learning, and creates a collaborative educational environment. By organizing resources efficiently, utilizing the built-in tools of Teams, and integrating third-party apps, educators can ensure that students have access to a wealth of materials that enrich their learning experience. Consistency, engagement, and adaptability are key to creating a dynamic and supportive educational space in Microsoft Teams.

CHAPTER VI
Teams for Remote Work

6.1 Setting Up for Remote Work

6.1.1 Configuring Teams for Remote Access

As remote work becomes increasingly common, it's essential to configure Microsoft Teams to support seamless remote access. This involves a combination of technical setup, user training, and ensuring that all necessary tools and features are accessible and functioning correctly. Below are the detailed steps and best practices for configuring Teams for remote access.

1. Setting Up Microsoft Teams for Remote Access

To begin, ensure that all users have access to Microsoft Teams. This involves provisioning licenses for all employees who need to use the platform. Typically, organizations opt for Office 365 subscriptions that include Teams. Make sure that each user has an account and that they can log in from their remote location.

2. Ensuring Proper Device Configuration

Remote access requires that all users have devices that are properly configured. This includes:

- Up-to-date Operating Systems: Ensure that all devices have the latest operating system updates. This helps avoid compatibility issues and ensures security.

- Installed Microsoft Teams App: While Teams can be accessed via a web browser, the desktop or mobile app provides a more robust experience. Users should install the Teams app on their devices.

- Functional Hardware: Ensure that users have working microphones, speakers, or headsets, and webcams if video conferencing is required.

3. Network Configuration and Security

Reliable and secure internet access is critical for remote work. Organizations should:

- VPN Access: Provide VPN access if necessary to ensure secure connections to company resources.

- Bandwidth Considerations: Ensure users have sufficient bandwidth. Video calls and file sharing require more bandwidth than basic text communication.

- Firewall and Security Settings: Adjust firewall settings to allow Teams traffic. Implement security protocols to protect data.

4. User Access and Permissions

Proper user access and permissions are crucial for maintaining security and functionality:

- Assigning Roles and Permissions: Define roles within Teams, such as owners, members, and guests, and assign appropriate permissions.

- Access to Necessary Channels and Files: Ensure that users have access to the channels, files, and tools they need to perform their duties. This can be managed through Teams' admin center.

5. Integration with Other Tools

Teams' strength lies in its integration capabilities with other Microsoft and third-party tools:

- Office 365 Integration: Ensure that Teams is integrated with Office 365 apps like Outlook, OneDrive, and SharePoint for seamless file sharing and collaboration.

- Third-Party Apps: Configure third-party apps that are essential for your organization. This might include project management tools, CRM systems, or other business-critical applications.

6. User Training and Support

Configuring Teams for remote access also involves training users on how to use the platform effectively:

- Training Sessions: Conduct training sessions to familiarize users with Teams features and best practices for remote work.

- Support Resources: Provide access to support resources, such as help desks, FAQs, and user manuals.

7. Ongoing Maintenance and Updates

Regular maintenance and updates ensure that Teams remains functional and secure:

- Software Updates: Regularly update Teams to the latest version to benefit from new features and security improvements.

- Monitoring and Troubleshooting: Continuously monitor performance and address any technical issues promptly.

Best Practices for Remote Collaboration

Effective remote collaboration involves more than just technical setup. It also requires establishing best practices to ensure productive and efficient teamwork.

1. Clear Communication Guidelines

Establish clear guidelines for communication to avoid misunderstandings and ensure everyone is on the same page:

- Response Times: Define expected response times for messages and emails.

- Preferred Communication Channels: Specify which communication channels to use for different types of communication (e.g., chat for quick questions, email for detailed discussions).

2. Regular Check-Ins and Meetings

Regular check-ins help maintain team cohesion and ensure everyone is aligned:

- Daily Stand-Ups: Hold daily stand-up meetings to discuss progress, challenges, and plans.

- Weekly Team Meetings: Schedule weekly meetings to review goals, track progress, and address any issues.

3. Collaborative Tools and Features

Leverage Teams' collaborative tools to enhance productivity:

- Shared Files and Documents: Use SharePoint and OneDrive for file sharing and collaboration. Encourage co-authoring documents in real-time.

- Planner and Tasks: Use Planner to assign tasks, set deadlines, and track progress. This helps keep projects organized and ensures accountability.

4. Building a Remote Work Culture

Building a positive remote work culture is essential for long-term success:

- Virtual Social Interactions: Encourage virtual social interactions, such as coffee breaks or team-building activities, to foster team spirit.

- Recognition and Rewards: Recognize and reward achievements to keep morale high.

Managing Remote Teams

Managing remote teams effectively requires a combination of leadership skills and strategic use of technology.

1. Setting Clear Goals and Expectations

Clearly define goals and expectations to ensure that everyone knows what is expected of them:

- SMART Goals: Set SMART (Specific, Measurable, Achievable, Relevant, Time-bound) goals for the team and individual members.

- Performance Metrics: Establish performance metrics to track progress and evaluate performance.

2. Providing Regular Feedback

Regular feedback is crucial for continuous improvement and development:

- One-on-One Meetings: Schedule regular one-on-one meetings to provide feedback, discuss progress, and address any concerns.

- Constructive Feedback: Provide constructive feedback that is specific, actionable, and supportive.

3. Encouraging Collaboration and Innovation

Encourage collaboration and innovation to drive creativity and problem-solving:

- Brainstorming Sessions: Hold brainstorming sessions to generate new ideas and solutions.

- Cross-Functional Teams: Create cross-functional teams to leverage diverse skills and perspectives.

4. Leveraging Analytics and Insights

Use analytics and insights to make data-driven decisions and optimize team performance:

- Teams Analytics: Utilize Teams analytics to monitor usage, identify trends, and measure engagement.

- Productivity Insights: Analyze productivity insights to identify areas for improvement and implement necessary changes.

Maintaining Work-Life Balance

Maintaining a healthy work-life balance is essential for employee well-being and productivity.

1. Setting Boundaries

Encourage employees to set boundaries between work and personal life:

- Work Hours: Define clear work hours and encourage employees to adhere to them.

- Breaks and Downtime: Encourage regular breaks and downtime to avoid burnout.

2. Promoting Wellness

Promote wellness initiatives to support employee health and well-being:

- Physical Activity: Encourage physical activity and provide resources for virtual fitness classes.

- Mental Health: Provide mental health resources and support, such as access to counseling services.

3. Flexibility and Autonomy

Offer flexibility and autonomy to help employees manage their work and personal commitments:

- Flexible Schedules: Allow flexible work schedules to accommodate personal needs.

- Autonomous Work: Encourage autonomous work and trust employees to manage their tasks effectively.

By following these detailed steps and best practices, organizations can configure Microsoft Teams for remote access, facilitate effective remote collaboration, and support the well-being and productivity of remote teams.

6.1.2 Best Practices for Remote Collaboration

Remote collaboration has become a cornerstone of modern work environments, especially in light of recent global events. Microsoft Teams provides a robust platform for facilitating seamless remote work, but to maximize its effectiveness, it is essential to follow best practices. This section explores key strategies to enhance collaboration when working remotely using Microsoft Teams.

1. Establish Clear Communication Channels

Effective communication is crucial in remote settings. Establishing clear channels within Microsoft Teams helps avoid confusion and ensures everyone is on the same page.

- Team Channels: Create dedicated channels for different projects, departments, or topics. This organization helps team members easily find relevant conversations and files.

- Announcements: Use the "Announcement" post type in Teams to highlight important updates. This feature makes key information stand out and ensures it's seen by all team members.

- Status Updates: Encourage team members to regularly update their status and use the "Out of Office" feature when necessary. This transparency helps manage expectations and ensures colleagues know when someone is unavailable.

2. Set Expectations for Responsiveness

Clear guidelines on communication expectations can prevent misunderstandings and ensure timely responses.

- Response Time: Define expected response times for different types of communication. For example, urgent messages might require a response within an hour, while less critical ones could have a 24-hour window.

- Availability Hours: Establish core working hours when team members are expected to be available. This practice can help coordinate efforts and schedule meetings at convenient times for all.

3. Utilize Video Conferencing Effectively

Video meetings are a vital component of remote collaboration, providing a more personal connection compared to text-based communication.

- Regular Check-Ins: Schedule regular video check-ins to maintain team cohesion and address any issues promptly. These meetings can be daily, weekly, or bi-weekly, depending on the team's needs.

- Agenda and Minutes: Always have a clear agenda for video meetings to ensure they are productive. Assign someone to take minutes and share them in the relevant Teams channel afterward.

- Virtual Backgrounds: Encourage the use of virtual backgrounds to maintain professionalism and privacy during video calls.

4. Encourage Collaboration Tools

Microsoft Teams integrates with various collaboration tools that can significantly enhance remote work efficiency.

- Co-Authoring Documents: Use the Office 365 integration to co-author documents in real-time. This feature allows multiple team members to work on the same document simultaneously, improving collaboration and productivity.

- Planner and To-Do: Utilize Microsoft Planner for task management within Teams. Assign tasks, set deadlines, and track progress in a visually intuitive way. Similarly, Microsoft To-Do can help individuals keep track of their personal tasks.

- Whiteboard: The Microsoft Whiteboard app is excellent for brainstorming sessions. It allows team members to sketch ideas and collaborate visually in real time.

5. Promote a Culture of Inclusivity

Inclusivity is key to fostering a collaborative remote work environment. Ensuring all team members feel valued and heard can enhance engagement and productivity.

- Equal Participation: Encourage equal participation in meetings and discussions. Actively seek input from quieter team members and ensure everyone has the opportunity to contribute.

- Cultural Sensitivity: Be mindful of cultural differences and time zones. Schedule meetings at times that are reasonable for all participants, and be respectful of diverse working styles.

- Feedback Mechanisms: Create avenues for anonymous feedback to allow team members to voice concerns or suggestions without fear of reprisal. This practice can help identify issues and improve the remote work experience.

6. Foster Team Building and Social Interaction

Maintaining a sense of team spirit and camaraderie is challenging but essential in remote settings.

- Virtual Social Events: Organize virtual team-building activities such as online games, quizzes, or informal coffee chats. These events can help maintain a sense of connection and morale.

- Recognition and Rewards: Recognize and reward team members' efforts and achievements. Public acknowledgment in team channels can boost morale and motivation.

- Wellness Programs: Promote wellness by encouraging regular breaks and sharing resources on mental and physical health. Consider organizing virtual wellness sessions such as yoga or meditation.

7. Leverage Analytics and Reporting

Using analytics to track collaboration patterns and productivity can provide insights into how the team is functioning and where improvements are needed.

- Teams Analytics: Microsoft Teams offers analytics that provide insights into usage patterns. Use these reports to understand how often team members are engaging with Teams, the frequency of meetings, and the overall activity.

- Feedback Surveys: Conduct regular surveys to gather feedback on the remote work experience. Use this data to make informed decisions about process improvements and address any issues.

8. Ensure Data Security and Privacy

Data security and privacy are paramount, especially in remote work settings where sensitive information is often shared digitally.

- Secure Access: Implement multi-factor authentication (MFA) to enhance security. Ensure that only authorized personnel have access to sensitive information.

- Data Encryption: Use end-to-end encryption for meetings and file sharing to protect data from unauthorized access.

- Compliance: Ensure compliance with relevant regulations and standards, such as GDPR or HIPAA, depending on the nature of your business.

9. Provide Continuous Training and Support

Ongoing training and support are essential to help team members make the most of Microsoft Teams and stay updated with new features.

- Training Sessions: Regularly conduct training sessions to educate team members on new features, best practices, and efficient use of Microsoft Teams.

- Support Resources: Create a repository of support resources, including FAQs, how-to guides, and video tutorials. Make these resources easily accessible within Teams.

- Peer Support: Foster a culture of peer support where team members can share tips and assist each other with any challenges they encounter.

10. Adapt and Evolve

Remote collaboration practices should evolve based on feedback and changing needs.

- Regular Reviews: Periodically review and update collaboration practices to ensure they remain effective. Gather input from team members to identify areas for improvement.

- Flexibility: Be flexible and open to experimenting with new tools and methods. What works for one team may not work for another, so adaptability is key.

- Future Trends: Stay informed about future trends in remote collaboration and technology advancements. Being proactive in adopting new solutions can keep your team ahead of the curve.

6.1.3 Managing Remote Teams

Managing remote teams effectively requires a combination of technology, communication skills, and leadership strategies. In this section, we will explore how to use Microsoft Teams to its fullest potential to manage remote teams, ensuring productivity, engagement, and collaboration.

1. Establish Clear Communication Channels

Clear communication is paramount in remote team management. With Microsoft Teams, you can set up various communication channels to ensure everyone is on the same page.

- Team and Channel Structure: Create specific teams and channels for different projects, departments, or topics. This helps in organizing conversations and keeping relevant information accessible.

- Channel Naming Conventions: Use consistent naming conventions for channels to make it easy for team members to find and follow discussions. For example, use prefixes like "Project_", "Team_", or "Dept_" followed by the specific project or department name.

- Pinned Channels and Tabs: Pin important channels and tabs for quick access. This is especially useful for frequently used documents, apps, or websites.

2. Regular Check-ins and Meetings

Frequent check-ins and meetings help in maintaining alignment and addressing issues promptly.

- Daily Stand-ups: Use the chat or meeting feature in Teams to hold daily stand-up meetings. This is a quick way for team members to share updates, discuss roadblocks, and plan their day.

- Weekly Team Meetings: Schedule regular team meetings to review progress, discuss upcoming tasks, and foster team spirit. Use the calendar feature in Teams to set recurring meetings.

- One-on-One Meetings: Conduct one-on-one meetings with team members to discuss their individual progress, provide feedback, and address any concerns. This helps in building rapport and understanding personal challenges.

3. Task Management and Tracking

Effective task management and tracking are crucial for remote teams to stay productive and meet deadlines.

- Microsoft Planner: Integrate Microsoft Planner with Teams to assign tasks, set deadlines, and track progress. Each task can have detailed descriptions, attachments, and checklists, making it easy for team members to understand their responsibilities.

- To-Do Lists: Encourage team members to use Microsoft To-Do to manage their personal tasks. To-Do integrates with Teams, allowing users to see all their tasks in one place.

- Project Management Tools: For complex projects, consider integrating project management tools like Trello, Asana, or Jira with Teams. These tools offer advanced features for task management, project tracking, and collaboration.

4. File Sharing and Collaboration

Efficient file sharing and collaboration are essential for remote teams to work together seamlessly.

- OneDrive and SharePoint Integration: Store and share files using OneDrive and SharePoint. This ensures that all team members have access to the latest versions of documents, and changes are synchronized automatically.

- Co-Authoring: Leverage the co-authoring feature in Microsoft Teams to allow multiple team members to work on the same document simultaneously. This is particularly useful for collaborative tasks like report writing, presentation creation, and data analysis.

- Version Control: Use version control to keep track of changes made to documents. This helps in maintaining a history of edits and reverting to previous versions if needed.

5. Encouraging Team Engagement

Keeping remote teams engaged and motivated is challenging but essential for maintaining productivity and job satisfaction.

- Virtual Team Building Activities: Organize virtual team building activities such as online games, quizzes, or informal chats. Use the meeting or chat features in Teams to host these activities.

- Recognition and Rewards: Recognize and reward team members for their contributions. Use Teams to announce achievements, share positive feedback, and celebrate milestones.

- Social Channels: Create channels dedicated to non-work-related topics where team members can share hobbies, interests, or personal updates. This helps in building a sense of community and fostering relationships.

6. Providing Support and Resources

Providing the necessary support and resources is crucial for remote teams to perform effectively.

- IT Support: Ensure that team members have access to IT support for resolving technical issues. Use the help desk integration in Teams or create a dedicated support channel.

- Training and Development: Offer training and development opportunities to enhance skills and knowledge. Use Teams to share training materials, organize webinars, and facilitate online courses.

- Health and Well-being: Promote health and well-being by encouraging breaks, sharing tips on maintaining a healthy work-life balance, and providing access to mental health resources.

7. Monitoring and Evaluating Performance

Regularly monitoring and evaluating performance helps in identifying areas for improvement and recognizing achievements.

- Performance Metrics: Define clear performance metrics and track them using Teams analytics and reporting tools. Metrics can include task completion rates, meeting attendance, and collaboration levels.

- Feedback Mechanisms: Implement feedback mechanisms to gather input from team members. Use Teams to conduct surveys, polls, or feedback forms.

- Continuous Improvement: Use the insights gained from performance evaluations to implement continuous improvement initiatives. Share best practices, address challenges, and adapt strategies as needed.

8. Ensuring Security and Compliance

Maintaining security and compliance is critical for protecting sensitive information and adhering to regulations.

- Data Security: Implement data security measures such as encryption, access controls, and multi-factor authentication. Use the security features in Teams and related Microsoft 365 services to protect data.

- Compliance Policies: Ensure that remote work practices comply with relevant regulations and company policies. Use Teams to communicate policies, provide training, and monitor compliance.

- Incident Response: Develop and communicate an incident response plan for addressing security breaches or compliance issues. Use Teams to coordinate response efforts and communicate with relevant stakeholders.

9. Adapting to Change

Remote work environments are dynamic and may require frequent adjustments.

- Flexibility and Adaptability: Encourage flexibility and adaptability in team members. Use Teams to communicate changes, provide updates, and offer support.

- Continuous Learning: Promote a culture of continuous learning and improvement. Use Teams to share resources, organize learning sessions, and encourage knowledge sharing.

- Feedback and Iteration: Regularly gather feedback from team members and use it to iterate and improve remote work practices. Use Teams to facilitate discussions, conduct surveys, and implement changes.

By leveraging the features and tools provided by Microsoft Teams, managers can effectively lead remote teams, ensuring that they remain productive, engaged, and connected. Implementing these strategies will help in overcoming the challenges of remote work and creating a successful, collaborative remote work environment.

6.2 Communication and Engagement

6.2.1 Keeping Teams Connected

Effective communication is the cornerstone of successful remote work. With the proliferation of remote working environments, tools like Microsoft Teams have become indispensable in ensuring seamless interaction among team members. This section will explore strategies and features within Microsoft Teams that help keep remote teams connected and engaged.

Understanding the Importance of Connectivity

In a remote work setting, maintaining connectivity goes beyond having a stable internet connection. It involves fostering an environment where team members feel engaged and informed, despite the physical distance. Connectivity in this context includes regular communication, access to shared resources, and a sense of belonging to the team.

Leveraging Microsoft Teams for Communication

1. Chat Features:

Microsoft Teams offers a robust chat feature that facilitates instant messaging among team members. Here's how to make the most out of it:

- Direct Messages: Use direct messages for quick, informal communications. This feature is ideal for clarifications, quick questions, and casual conversations.

- Group Chats: Create group chats for discussions that involve multiple team members. This is useful for departmental discussions, project-specific conversations, or brainstorming sessions.

- Persistent Chat History: Teams keeps a history of your chats, which means you can always go back to previous conversations to retrieve information or context.

2. Channels:

Channels are a fundamental feature in Microsoft Teams that organize team conversations by topic, project, or department. Each team can have multiple channels, and each channel can be tailored to specific needs.

- General Channel: Typically, every team has a General channel by default, which can be used for broad announcements and general discussions.

- Topic-Specific Channels: Create channels based on specific projects, tasks, or topics to keep conversations organized and focused.

- Private Channels: For sensitive discussions that should only be accessible to a subset of team members, use private channels.

3. Meetings and Video Calls:

Meetings and video calls are critical for maintaining face-to-face communication, which helps build stronger relationships and reduces the feeling of isolation among remote workers.

- Scheduling Meetings: Use the calendar feature to schedule regular check-ins, team meetings, and one-on-ones. Consistent meetings help maintain a rhythm and ensure that everyone stays aligned.

- Video Calls: Encourage the use of video during calls to enhance engagement. Seeing facial expressions and body language helps in better understanding and fosters a sense of connection.

- Meeting Chats: Utilize the chat feature during meetings for side conversations, sharing links, and posting relevant documents without interrupting the flow of the meeting.

Enhancing Engagement

Keeping remote teams engaged requires a blend of good communication practices and the effective use of Microsoft Teams features.

1. Interactive Meetings:

Engage your team during meetings with interactive tools:

- Polls and Surveys: Use the Forms app to create quick polls and surveys to gather opinions or feedback during meetings.

- Whiteboard: The Whiteboard feature allows team members to collaborate visually in real-time. It's especially useful for brainstorming sessions and planning.

- Breakout Rooms: For larger meetings, use breakout rooms to split participants into smaller groups for more focused discussions.

2. Regular Updates and Announcements:

Keep your team informed with regular updates and announcements:

- Announcements in Channels: Use the announcement feature in channels to share important news, updates, and milestones. Announcements stand out from regular messages and are more likely to be noticed.

- Email Integration: For critical updates that require immediate attention, consider using the email integration feature to send channel messages as emails.

3. Recognition and Rewards:

Recognizing and rewarding team members is crucial for maintaining morale and motivation:

- Praise Feature: Use the Praise app within Teams to send recognition to team members. It's a simple way to acknowledge someone's efforts publicly.

- Celebrations: Celebrate birthdays, work anniversaries, and significant achievements through dedicated channels or during meetings to build a positive and inclusive team culture.

Tools and Techniques for Effective Remote Engagement

1. Asynchronous Communication:

Not all communication needs to happen in real-time, especially when working across different time zones. Encourage the use of asynchronous communication where appropriate:

- Recorded Meetings: Record meetings for team members who can't attend in real-time. They can watch the recording at their convenience and stay informed.

- Threaded Conversations: Use threaded conversations in channels to keep discussions organized and make it easier for team members to follow along and contribute when they're available.

2. Status and Availability:

Respecting team members' availability is crucial in a remote setting:

- Status Indicators: Encourage team members to update their status indicators (e.g., available, busy, away) to reflect their current availability.

- Do Not Disturb Mode: During focused work periods or outside working hours, use the Do Not Disturb mode to minimize interruptions.

3. Social Interaction:

Fostering social interactions helps build stronger relationships and a sense of community:

- Virtual Coffee Breaks: Schedule informal virtual coffee breaks where team members can chat about non-work topics.

- Team Building Activities: Organize virtual team building activities such as online games, quizzes, or virtual escape rooms.

- Casual Channels: Create channels dedicated to casual conversations, hobbies, or interests where team members can share and connect on a personal level.

Challenges and Solutions

1. Overcoming Communication Barriers:

Remote work can sometimes lead to communication barriers due to different time zones, cultural differences, or technological issues. Address these challenges by:

- Setting Clear Expectations: Establish clear communication guidelines, including response times, preferred communication channels, and meeting etiquette.

- Cultural Sensitivity: Be mindful of cultural differences and encourage open communication to address any misunderstandings.

- Technical Support: Ensure team members have access to technical support to resolve any issues with connectivity or software.

2. Maintaining Team Cohesion:

Maintaining a cohesive team spirit in a remote environment requires deliberate effort:

- Regular Check-Ins: Schedule regular check-ins with team members to discuss their progress, address any concerns, and offer support.

- Inclusive Practices: Make sure all team members feel included and valued by encouraging participation and recognizing contributions from everyone.

- Building Trust: Foster trust by being transparent, reliable, and supportive. Trust is the foundation of a strong remote team.

3. Balancing Work and Personal Life:

Remote work can blur the boundaries between work and personal life, leading to burnout. Encourage a healthy work-life balance by:

- Setting Boundaries: Encourage team members to set clear boundaries between work and personal time. Respect these boundaries by avoiding out-of-hours communication.

- Flexible Schedules: Offer flexible working hours to accommodate different personal commitments and time zones.

- Mental Health Support: Provide resources and support for mental health, such as access to counseling services or wellness programs.

By leveraging Microsoft Teams' features and adopting effective communication and engagement strategies, remote teams can overcome the challenges of distance and maintain a connected, motivated, and productive workforce.

6.2.2 Virtual Team Building Activities

Virtual team building activities are essential for fostering a sense of community and camaraderie among remote team members. These activities can help break down barriers, encourage collaboration, and boost morale. Here are several effective virtual team building activities that can be implemented using Microsoft Teams:

1. Virtual Coffee Breaks

Virtual coffee breaks are informal meetings where team members can catch up and socialize, similar to a physical office coffee break. Schedule a regular time each week for a virtual coffee break, allowing team members to join a Teams meeting for casual conversation. This helps recreate the spontaneous interactions that often happen in an office setting.

How to Implement:

- Schedule a recurring meeting in Teams, labeled "Virtual Coffee Break."

- Encourage team members to join with their favorite beverage.

- Keep the agenda open-ended to foster organic conversations.

2. Online Game Sessions

Playing games together can be a fun and effective way to build team spirit. There are numerous online games that can be played via Microsoft Teams, ranging from trivia quizzes to collaborative puzzle-solving games.

How to Implement:

- Use the "Microsoft Teams Quiz" or "Kahoot!" apps for trivia games.

- Organize a "Pictionary" game using the Whiteboard feature in Teams.

- Schedule game sessions as part of a regular team-building calendar.

3. Virtual Happy Hours

Virtual happy hours are social gatherings held after work hours, where team members can relax and unwind together. These events can include activities like sharing a drink, playing games, or simply chatting about non-work topics.

How to Implement:

- Schedule a Teams meeting for a time that suits the majority of the team.

- Encourage team members to join with a drink of their choice.

- Include activities like virtual tours, music sessions, or themed parties.

4. Show and Tell

Show and Tell sessions allow team members to share something personal or interesting from their lives. This activity can help team members learn more about each other and build stronger personal connections.

How to Implement:

- Schedule regular "Show and Tell" sessions during team meetings.

- Ask team members to prepare a short presentation on a hobby, recent experience, or interesting fact.

- Encourage questions and discussions to foster engagement.

5. Virtual Team Challenges

Virtual team challenges can include a variety of activities, such as fitness challenges, cooking contests, or book clubs. These challenges promote team bonding and healthy competition.

How to Implement:

- Create a dedicated channel in Teams for the challenge.

- Set clear rules and guidelines for the challenge.

- Encourage participation and provide regular updates on progress.

6. Icebreaker Questions

Icebreaker questions are a simple yet effective way to start meetings and help team members get to know each other better. These questions can range from light-hearted and fun to more thoughtful and reflective.

How to Implement:

- Start each team meeting with an icebreaker question.

- Rotate the responsibility of choosing and asking the question among team members.

- Allow time for everyone to respond and discuss their answers.

7. Virtual Lunch and Learn

Virtual Lunch and Learn sessions combine team building with professional development. Team members can share their expertise on various topics while enjoying a meal together.

How to Implement:

- Schedule a regular Lunch and Learn session.

- Invite team members to volunteer to present on topics of interest.

- Encourage interactive discussions and Q&A sessions.

8. Photo Contests

Photo contests are a fun way to engage team members and encourage creativity. Themes can vary from nature photography to pet photos, and team members can vote for their favorites.

How to Implement:

- Announce a photo contest with a specific theme.

- Create a channel or thread in Teams for submissions.

- Allow team members to vote using the "Like" feature or conduct a formal poll.

9. Virtual Escape Rooms

Virtual escape rooms are interactive puzzle-solving activities that require teamwork and collaboration. These can be a thrilling way to enhance problem-solving skills and team cohesion.

How to Implement:

- Choose a virtual escape room provider that integrates with Teams.

- Schedule a session and divide team members into groups if necessary.

- Encourage collaboration and communication to solve the puzzles.

10. Peer Recognition Programs

Recognizing and appreciating team members' efforts is vital for maintaining motivation and morale. Peer recognition programs can be formalized through Microsoft Teams channels where team members can publicly acknowledge each other's contributions.

How to Implement:

- Create a dedicated "Recognition" channel in Teams.

- Encourage team members to post shout-outs and kudos.

- Consider implementing a points system or awarding virtual badges.

Benefits of Virtual Team Building Activities

Virtual team building activities offer several benefits that contribute to a positive remote work environment:

1. Improved Morale and Motivation: Regular social interactions and fun activities can boost team morale and keep motivation high.

2. Enhanced Team Cohesion: These activities help build trust and strengthen relationships among team members.

3. Increased Engagement: Engaging activities keep team members interested and involved in the team's dynamics.

4. Reduced Feelings of Isolation: Social interactions and team bonding help mitigate the isolation that can come with remote work.

5. Better Communication: Regular team building activities improve overall communication and collaboration skills.

Best Practices for Implementing Virtual Team Building Activities

To maximize the effectiveness of virtual team building activities, consider the following best practices:

1. Consistency is Key: Schedule activities regularly to ensure they become a routine part of the team culture.

2. Inclusivity Matters: Choose activities that everyone can participate in, regardless of their location or time zone.

3. Solicit Feedback: Regularly ask team members for feedback on the activities to ensure they are enjoyable and beneficial.

4. Keep it Light: While some activities can be work-related, ensure there are plenty of opportunities for light-hearted fun.

5. Celebrate Successes: Acknowledge and celebrate team achievements and milestones during these activities to boost morale further.

Conclusion

Virtual team building activities are essential for maintaining a strong, connected, and motivated remote team. Microsoft Teams provides a versatile platform to host a variety of engaging and interactive activities that can bring your team closer together, even when working apart. By implementing these activities thoughtfully and consistently, you can create a positive remote work environment that fosters collaboration, trust, and productivity.

This detailed guide on virtual team building activities should help you effectively engage and connect your remote team using Microsoft Teams, ensuring that they remain cohesive, motivated, and productive.

6.2.3 Maintaining Work-Life Balance

Maintaining a healthy work-life balance is essential, especially in a remote work environment where the lines between personal and professional life can easily blur. Microsoft Teams provides several features and tools that can help users manage their time effectively and ensure that work does not encroach on their personal life. This section will guide you through various strategies and best practices to maintain work-life balance using Microsoft Teams.

Setting Boundaries and Managing Availability

One of the first steps to maintaining a work-life balance is setting clear boundaries between work hours and personal time. Microsoft Teams offers several features to help you manage your availability:

1. Status Settings: Use the status settings in Teams to indicate your availability. You can set your status to Available, Busy, Do Not Disturb, or Away. Make it a habit to set your status to Do Not Disturb during non-working hours. This will silence notifications and help you avoid work interruptions.

2. Custom Status Messages: You can set custom status messages to inform your colleagues of your working hours. For example, you can set a status message that says, "I am available from 9 AM to 5 PM. Please leave a message if it's urgent."

3. Scheduling Quiet Hours: Teams allows you to schedule quiet hours and days, during which you won't receive notifications. This is particularly useful for ensuring that your evenings and weekends are free from work-related distractions. To set quiet hours, go to the Notifications settings in Teams and configure your preferred quiet hours and days.

Managing Notifications

Managing notifications effectively is crucial for maintaining a healthy work-life balance. Teams provides several options to customize your notification preferences:

1. Notification Settings: Go to the Settings menu and select Notifications. Here, you can customize how and when you receive notifications. For instance, you can choose to receive notifications only for direct messages and mentions, and mute notifications for less critical channels.

2. Channel Notifications: For each channel, you can customize notification settings. This allows you to prioritize important channels and mute those that are less relevant to your work.

3. Email Notifications: If you prefer to keep notifications out of your Teams app during non-working hours, you can opt to receive email summaries instead. This way, you can catch up on important updates without being constantly interrupted.

Time Management Strategies

Effective time management is key to maintaining work-life balance. Microsoft Teams offers several tools to help you organize your tasks and manage your time:

1. Tasks by Planner and To Do: Integrate Tasks by Planner and To Do into Teams to keep track of your tasks and deadlines. This integration allows you to create and manage tasks, set due dates, and categorize tasks by priority. By keeping a clear task list, you can better plan your day and avoid working late.

2. Calendar Integration: Use the calendar feature in Teams to schedule your workday. Block out time for focused work, meetings, and breaks. By planning your day in advance, you can ensure that you have dedicated time for both work and personal activities.

3. Time Blocking: Practice time blocking by setting aside specific time slots for different types of work. For example, you can block out the first two hours of your day for focused work, followed by a meeting block, and then another block for emails and administrative tasks. This helps you stay organized and prevents work from spilling over into your personal time.

Encouraging Healthy Habits

Promoting healthy habits is essential for maintaining work-life balance. Microsoft Teams can support you in building and maintaining these habits:

1. Break Reminders: Set reminders to take regular breaks throughout the day. Use the task management tools in Teams to schedule short breaks and lunch breaks. Taking regular breaks can help you stay focused and reduce stress.

2. Wellness Activities: Encourage wellness activities among your team members. Create a channel dedicated to wellness where you can share tips on exercise, meditation, and healthy eating. You can also schedule virtual wellness activities, such as group stretches or mindfulness sessions.

3. End-of-Day Rituals: Develop end-of-day rituals to signal the end of your workday. This could include tidying up your workspace, creating a to-do list for the next day, or logging out of Teams. Establishing a routine can help you mentally transition from work to personal time.

Leveraging Teams Analytics

Microsoft Teams Analytics can provide insights into your work patterns and help you make adjustments to improve work-life balance:

1. Activity Reports: Use the activity reports in Teams to monitor your activity levels. These reports can show you how much time you spend in meetings, on calls, and in chats.

Analyzing this data can help you identify areas where you can reduce unnecessary meetings or communications.

2. Focus Time Insights: Teams can provide insights into your focus time. This feature analyzes your calendar and suggests times for focused work. By blocking out these suggested times, you can ensure that you have uninterrupted periods for deep work, reducing the need to work late.

3. Wellbeing Insights: Utilize wellbeing insights provided by Teams and MyAnalytics (if available in your organization). These insights can offer recommendations on how to improve your work habits, such as taking more breaks, reducing after-hours work, and improving your meeting practices.

Promoting a Culture of Balance

Maintaining work-life balance is not just an individual responsibility but also an organizational one. Here are some ways to promote a culture of balance using Microsoft Teams:

1. Lead by Example: Leaders and managers should model healthy work-life balance by adhering to set work hours, taking breaks, and respecting employees' personal time. By setting a positive example, leaders can encourage their team members to do the same.

2. Encourage Flexibility: Promote flexible work arrangements that allow employees to manage their work schedules around their personal commitments. Use Teams to facilitate asynchronous communication and collaboration, enabling team members to work at times that suit them best.

3. Recognize and Reward Balance: Acknowledge and reward employees who demonstrate good work-life balance practices. Use Teams to share success stories and recognize individuals who are effectively managing their work and personal lives.

4. Provide Support Resources: Create a Teams channel dedicated to work-life balance resources. Share articles, videos, and tips on managing stress, maintaining a healthy lifestyle, and balancing work and personal responsibilities. Encourage employees to participate in discussions and share their own tips.

Conclusion

Maintaining work-life balance in a remote work environment requires intentional effort and the right tools. Microsoft Teams offers a range of features and best practices that can help you manage your time, set boundaries, and promote healthy habits. By leveraging these tools and strategies, you can ensure that you remain productive while also enjoying a fulfilling personal life. Remember, a balanced approach to work and life not only benefits individual well-being but also contributes to overall team productivity and satisfaction.

6.3 Productivity Tools and Tips

6.3.1 Using To-Do Lists and Tasks

Introduction

In a remote work environment, staying organized and managing tasks efficiently is crucial for maintaining productivity and ensuring that projects are completed on time. Microsoft Teams offers several features to help you keep track of your tasks and to-do lists. This section will provide a comprehensive guide on how to use these tools effectively within Microsoft Teams.

Understanding the Importance of To-Do Lists

To-do lists are a fundamental part of productivity management. They help you prioritize tasks, keep track of deadlines, and ensure that nothing falls through the cracks. In a remote work setting, where communication can sometimes be fragmented, having a clear list of tasks is even more critical. To-do lists provide the following benefits:

- Clarity and Focus: They help you identify what needs to be done and in what order.

- Time Management: By listing tasks, you can allocate time more effectively.

- Accountability: To-do lists make it easier to track progress and hold yourself accountable.

- Reduction of Stress: Knowing exactly what needs to be done can reduce the mental load and stress associated with managing multiple tasks.

Using Microsoft To Do within Teams

Microsoft To Do is an app that integrates seamlessly with Microsoft Teams, providing a simple yet powerful way to manage your tasks and to-do lists. Here's how to get started:

Setting Up Microsoft To Do

1. Adding the To Do App:

  - Open Microsoft Teams.

  - Click on the "Apps" icon in the left sidebar.

  - Search for "To Do" and click on it.

  - Click "Add" to integrate it with Teams.

2. Creating Tasks:

  - Once the To Do app is added, you can start creating tasks.

  - Click on the To Do app icon in the sidebar.

  - Click "Add a task" and enter the task name.

  - Press Enter to add the task to your list.

3. Organizing Tasks:

  - You can create different lists to organize tasks by project or category.

  - Click "New list" and give your list a name.

  - Add tasks to the appropriate list.

Managing Tasks in To Do

Setting Due Dates and Reminders:

- Each task can have a due date to help you stay on track.

- Click on a task to open its details.

- Set a due date and, if needed, a reminder.

- You can also set recurring tasks for regularly scheduled activities.

Prioritizing Tasks:

- To Do allows you to prioritize tasks by marking them as "Important."

- Click the star icon next to a task to mark it as important.

- Important tasks will appear in the "Important" section for easy access.

Adding Steps to Tasks:

- For complex tasks, you can add steps to break them down into smaller, manageable parts.

- Click on a task to open its details.

- Click "Add step" and enter the step name.

- You can check off each step as you complete it.

Integrating To Do with Planner

For teams working on collaborative projects, Microsoft Planner is a powerful tool that can be integrated with To Do for enhanced task management. Planner allows you to create plans, assign tasks to team members, and track progress. Here's how to use Planner within Teams:

Adding Planner to Teams:

- Open Microsoft Teams.

- Go to the team where you want to add Planner.

- Click on the "+" icon at the top of the channel.

- Search for "Planner" and click on it.

- Choose to create a new plan or use an existing one.

Creating and Assigning Tasks in Planner:

- Within Planner, you can create tasks and assign them to team members.

- Click "Add task," enter the task name, set a due date, and assign it to a team member.

- Tasks in Planner can have labels, priority levels, and attachments.

Tracking Progress:

- Planner provides visual charts to track progress.

- You can view tasks by status, assignee, or due date.

- Use the "Board" view to see tasks organized in buckets, similar to a Kanban board.

Syncing Planner with To Do:

- Tasks assigned to you in Planner will automatically appear in your To Do list under "Assigned to Me."

- This integration allows you to manage both personal and team tasks from one place.

Best Practices for Using To-Do Lists and Tasks in Teams

1. Consistent Review and Update:

- Regularly review your to-do lists to ensure they are up-to-date.

- Add new tasks as they come up and mark tasks as complete when done.

- Weekly reviews can help you stay on top of your workload.

2. Prioritize Effectively:

- Use the priority feature to focus on high-impact tasks.

- Consider the Eisenhower Matrix (urgent vs. important) to help prioritize tasks.

3. Delegate When Possible:

- In a team setting, delegate tasks that can be handled by others.

- Use Planner to assign tasks to team members and track their progress.

4. Set Realistic Deadlines:

- Ensure that the due dates you set are realistic and achievable.

- Avoid overloading your to-do list with too many tasks at once.

5. Utilize Reminders and Notifications:

- Take advantage of reminders and notifications to stay on track.

- Set reminders for tasks with specific deadlines.

6. Break Down Large Tasks:

- Large tasks can be overwhelming; break them down into smaller, manageable steps.

- Use the steps feature in To Do to outline the smaller components of a task.

7. Sync Across Devices:

- Microsoft To Do syncs across all your devices, ensuring you have access to your tasks wherever you are.

- Install the To Do app on your smartphone and other devices.

8. Collaborate with Your Team:

- Use shared lists in To Do for collaborative tasks.

- Communicate with your team about task progress and any potential roadblocks.

Case Study: Improving Productivity with To-Do Lists and Tasks

Let's consider a case study to illustrate how using To Do and Planner in Microsoft Teams can improve productivity:

Scenario:

A marketing team is working remotely on a campaign for a new product launch. The team includes a project manager, content creators, graphic designers, and social media specialists. The project involves multiple tasks, including content creation, graphic design, social media planning, and client meetings.

Implementation:

1. Setting Up To Do and Planner:

- The project manager sets up a new team in Microsoft Teams for the campaign.

- Within the team, they add the Planner app and create a plan named "Product Launch Campaign."

- The project manager also adds the To Do app for personal task management.

2. Creating Tasks in Planner:

- The project manager creates tasks in Planner for each phase of the campaign, such as "Content Creation," "Graphic Design," "Social Media Planning," and "Client Meetings."

- Each task is assigned to the relevant team member, with due dates and priority levels set.

3. Managing Individual Tasks with To Do:

- Team members use To Do to manage their personal tasks.

- They create tasks in To Do for their assigned responsibilities, breaking down larger tasks into smaller steps.

- Tasks assigned to them in Planner automatically appear in their To Do list under "Assigned to Me."

4. Tracking Progress and Collaboration:

- The team uses Planner's visual charts to track progress and ensure tasks are on schedule.

- Regular check-ins and virtual meetings are scheduled in Teams to discuss progress and address any challenges.

- Shared to-do lists are created in To Do for collaborative tasks, allowing team members to update and mark off completed items.

Outcome:

By using To Do and Planner in Microsoft Teams, the marketing team successfully manages their tasks and maintains productivity throughout the campaign. The integration of these tools allows for clear task delegation, efficient tracking of progress, and effective collaboration among team members. The project is completed on time, and the product launch is a success.

Conclusion

Using to-do lists and tasks effectively in Microsoft Teams can significantly enhance productivity and ensure that remote work runs smoothly. Microsoft To Do and Planner provide robust tools for managing individual and team tasks, keeping everyone organized and focused. By implementing best practices and leveraging the integration of these tools, remote teams can achieve their goals efficiently and maintain high levels of productivity. Whether you are managing personal tasks or leading a team project, Microsoft Teams offers the features you need to stay on track and succeed in a remote work environment.

6.3.2 Time Management Strategies

Managing time effectively is crucial for remote work, where the boundaries between professional and personal life often blur. Microsoft Teams offers various features and integrations to help users manage their time efficiently. In this section, we will explore several strategies and tools that can help improve time management within Microsoft Teams.

1. Setting Clear Objectives and Priorities

Effective time management begins with setting clear objectives and priorities. Knowing what needs to be accomplished and in what order can help you stay focused and avoid wasting time on less important tasks.

- Defining Goals: Use the Planner app within Microsoft Teams to define your goals and break them down into manageable tasks. Assign due dates and priorities to each task to keep track of your progress.

- Daily and Weekly Planning: At the start of each day or week, use the Tasks app to outline what you need to accomplish. Review your task list regularly to stay on track.

2. Creating a Structured Work Schedule

Remote work can sometimes lead to irregular work hours, which can affect productivity and work-life balance. Creating a structured work schedule helps establish a routine and ensures that you allocate enough time for both work and personal activities.

- Calendar Integration: Utilize the Calendar feature in Microsoft Teams to schedule your work hours, meetings, and breaks. Sync your Teams calendar with Outlook to have a unified view of your schedule.

- Time Blocking: Allocate specific blocks of time for focused work, meetings, and breaks. This method, known as time blocking, helps you concentrate on one task at a time and reduces distractions.

3. Leveraging Meetings and Communication Tools

Efficient communication is essential for remote teams. Using Microsoft Teams' communication tools effectively can save time and reduce misunderstandings.

- Effective Meeting Management: Schedule meetings with clear agendas and objectives. Use the Meeting Notes feature to record important points and action items during meetings. Limit the number of meetings to avoid meeting fatigue.

- Asynchronous Communication: Not all communication needs to happen in real-time. Use Teams' chat and channels to share updates and collaborate asynchronously. This approach can help accommodate different time zones and work schedules.

4. Utilizing To-Do Lists and Task Management

To-do lists and task management tools help you keep track of what needs to be done and ensure that nothing falls through the cracks.

- Tasks by Planner and To-Do: Integrate Microsoft To-Do with Teams to create and manage your to-do lists. Use the Tasks by Planner and To-Do app to organize tasks by project, set due dates, and track progress.

- Prioritizing Tasks: Prioritize tasks based on their urgency and importance. Use the Eisenhower Matrix (urgent-important matrix) to categorize tasks and focus on what truly matters.

5. Minimizing Distractions

Distractions can significantly impact productivity, especially when working remotely. Microsoft Teams offers several features to help minimize distractions and stay focused.

- Do Not Disturb Mode: Use the Do Not Disturb mode to block notifications during focus periods or important meetings. This feature helps you concentrate without interruptions.

- Quiet Hours: Configure quiet hours in Teams to disable notifications during non-working hours. This setting helps maintain a healthy work-life balance and prevents burnout.

6. Time Tracking and Analysis

Tracking how you spend your time can provide valuable insights into your work habits and help identify areas for improvement.

- Teams Analytics: Use the built-in analytics in Teams to monitor your activity and understand how you spend your time on various tasks and meetings. Review these insights regularly to make informed adjustments to your schedule.

- Third-Party Integrations: Consider integrating third-party time tracking tools like Toggl or Clockify with Teams to gain a detailed understanding of your time usage. These tools can help you analyze productivity patterns and optimize your workflow.

7. Taking Breaks and Managing Workload

Regular breaks are essential for maintaining productivity and preventing burnout. Managing your workload effectively ensures that you stay productive without feeling overwhelmed.

- Pomodoro Technique: Implement the Pomodoro Technique, where you work for a set period (e.g., 25 minutes) followed by a short break (e.g., 5 minutes). Use a timer or Pomodoro app to keep track of work and break intervals.

- Managing Workload: Avoid overloading yourself with too many tasks. Use the Tasks app to allocate tasks evenly and set realistic deadlines. Communicate with your team to manage expectations and delegate tasks when necessary.

8. Continuous Improvement and Adaptation

Effective time management is an ongoing process that requires continuous improvement and adaptation. Regularly evaluate your time management strategies and make adjustments as needed.

- Reflection and Feedback: Take time to reflect on your productivity and time management practices. Seek feedback from colleagues and supervisors to identify areas for improvement.

- Adapting to Changes: Be flexible and adaptable to changes in your work environment or schedule. Adjust your time management strategies to accommodate new challenges and opportunities.

6.3.3 Leveraging Teams Analytics

In today's remote work environment, understanding how your team interacts and collaborates through Microsoft Teams is crucial for enhancing productivity and engagement. Microsoft Teams Analytics provides valuable insights into user activities, app usage, and overall team engagement, helping leaders make informed decisions that can drive performance and collaboration. This section will explore how to effectively leverage Teams Analytics, covering key metrics, tools, and strategies for maximizing your team's potential.

Understanding Microsoft Teams Analytics

Microsoft Teams Analytics refers to the tools and reports available within the Teams platform that allow users to track and analyze various metrics related to team collaboration and communication. These analytics can help organizations:

- Measure User Engagement: Understanding how frequently users engage with Teams can help identify areas for improvement.

- Assess Collaboration: Monitoring how often team members collaborate through chats, meetings, and file sharing can reveal the effectiveness of teamwork.

- Evaluate App Usage: Analyzing which apps are used most frequently can provide insights into what tools your team finds valuable.

Key Metrics to Monitor

1. Active Users:

- Definition: The number of users who actively engage with Teams within a specified timeframe (daily, weekly, or monthly).

- Importance: Monitoring active users can help gauge overall team engagement and identify trends over time. If the number of active users is declining, it may signal disengagement or issues with remote collaboration.

2. Messages Sent:

- Definition: The total number of messages sent in chat, channels, and private conversations.

- Importance: This metric provides insight into how communication flows within the team. A sudden drop in messaging could indicate a lack of collaboration or a communication breakdown.

3. Meetings Held:

- Definition: The number of meetings scheduled and conducted through Teams.

- Importance: Tracking meetings can help assess whether teams are utilizing virtual face-to-face interactions effectively. High meeting counts may indicate strong collaboration, while low counts may suggest a need for more regular check-ins.

4. File Sharing Activity:

- Definition: The amount of files shared and collaborated on within Teams.

- Importance: Analyzing file sharing helps understand how often teams are collaborating on documents, presentations, and other shared resources. A decrease in file sharing may indicate a lack of collaboration or reliance on email instead.

5. Usage of Apps and Integrations:

- Definition: The frequency of app usage integrated with Teams, such as Planner, OneNote, or third-party tools.

- Importance: Understanding which apps are most utilized can help optimize workflows and encourage the use of tools that enhance productivity.

Accessing Teams Analytics

Microsoft Teams provides a variety of analytics and reporting tools that can be accessed by administrators and users with the appropriate permissions. Here's how to access them:

1. Using the Admin Center:

- Step 1: Navigate to the Microsoft Teams Admin Center.

- Step 2: Go to the "Analytics & Reports" section.

- Step 3: Choose from various report options, including user activity, app usage, and meeting reports.

2. Microsoft Teams App Insights:

- Step 1: Open Microsoft Teams.

- Step 2: Click on your profile picture and select "Settings."

- Step 3: Navigate to the "Analytics" tab to view personal insights on your activity and collaboration patterns.

3. Power BI for Custom Reports:

- Step 1: Use Microsoft Power BI to create custom reports using Teams data.

- Step 2: Connect Power BI to your Microsoft Teams environment to visualize data in customizable dashboards.

- Step 3: Share insights with team members to encourage data-driven decision-making.

Strategies for Leveraging Teams Analytics

To effectively leverage Teams Analytics for enhancing productivity and engagement, consider the following strategies:

1. Set Clear Goals:

- Before diving into analytics, establish clear objectives for what you want to achieve. Are you looking to improve communication, enhance collaboration, or identify knowledge gaps? Clear goals will guide your analysis and help you focus on relevant metrics.

2. Regularly Review Analytics:

- Schedule regular reviews of Teams Analytics reports to identify trends and insights. Monthly or quarterly reviews can help assess progress toward goals and identify areas that need attention. Use these reviews to adjust strategies and set new objectives as needed.

3. Engage Your Team in the Process:

- Share insights from Teams Analytics with your team members. Encourage them to participate in discussions about the data and provide input on how to improve collaboration. Engaging the team can foster a culture of transparency and accountability.

4. Train Team Members on Best Practices:

- Use analytics insights to inform training sessions on best practices for using Teams. For example, if you notice low file-sharing activity, consider providing training on how to effectively collaborate on documents within Teams.

5. Utilize Feedback Mechanisms:

- Implement feedback mechanisms, such as surveys or polls, to gather input from team members about their experiences with Teams. Combine qualitative feedback with quantitative analytics to get a comprehensive view of team dynamics and collaboration.

6. Identify Champions and Advocates:

- Identify team members who are effectively using Teams and can serve as champions for the platform. Encourage them to share their best practices with others, helping to raise the overall usage and effectiveness of Teams across the organization.

7. Monitor Changes Over Time:

- Keep track of how metrics change over time, especially after implementing new strategies or tools. Monitoring the impact of changes allows you to assess their effectiveness and make necessary adjustments.

Real-World Example: Improving Engagement with Analytics

Consider a remote team at a software development company that was struggling with communication and collaboration. After reviewing Teams Analytics, the team leader noticed a decline in active users and a significant drop in messages sent.

Actions Taken:

- The team leader set up regular virtual coffee breaks to encourage informal interactions.

- They also implemented bi-weekly stand-up meetings to foster collaboration and discuss ongoing projects.

- The team started using Microsoft Planner to manage tasks and track progress, which encouraged team members to engage more actively with each other.

Results:

After implementing these changes, the team leader monitored the analytics again. Over the next few months, they observed a substantial increase in active users, a rise in messages sent, and improved collaboration on files. Team members reported feeling more connected and engaged in their work.

Conclusion

Leveraging Teams Analytics is essential for optimizing remote work experiences and enhancing team productivity. By understanding key metrics, accessing analytics tools, and implementing data-driven strategies, organizations can foster a collaborative culture that drives engagement and performance. The insights gained from Teams Analytics not only empower leaders to make informed decisions but also promote a sense of accountability and ownership among team members. As remote work continues to evolve, utilizing analytics will remain a critical factor in achieving success in Microsoft Teams.

CHAPTER VII
Security and Compliance

7.1 Security Features in Microsoft Teams

7.1.1 Data Encryption and Protection

Data encryption and protection are fundamental components of Microsoft Teams' security framework. Ensuring that data is secure during transmission and while at rest is crucial for protecting sensitive information and maintaining user trust. This section provides an in-depth look at how Microsoft Teams employs data encryption and protection measures to safeguard your data.

Understanding Data Encryption

Data encryption involves converting information into a code to prevent unauthorized access. In the context of Microsoft Teams, encryption ensures that the data exchanged within the platform, whether it is messages, files, or calls, is protected from eavesdropping and tampering. Microsoft Teams employs both in-transit and at-rest encryption to secure data comprehensively.

1. Encryption in Transit

Encryption in transit protects data as it moves between users and the Teams service. Microsoft Teams uses Transport Layer Security (TLS) and Secure Real-time Transport Protocol (SRTP) to encrypt data during transmission.

- Transport Layer Security (TLS): TLS is a cryptographic protocol designed to provide secure communication over a computer network. It ensures that data sent between clients and servers is encrypted and that the integrity and confidentiality of the data are maintained. Microsoft Teams utilizes TLS 1.2, which offers robust security features.

- Secure Real-time Transport Protocol (SRTP): SRTP is used to encrypt audio, video, and desktop sharing streams. It ensures that real-time media data is protected from interception and eavesdropping during transmission. SRTP adds an extra layer of security to the communication channels within Teams.

2. Encryption at Rest

Encryption at rest protects data stored on servers from unauthorized access. Microsoft Teams encrypts data stored in its data centers using strong encryption methods to ensure data confidentiality and integrity.

- Microsoft 365 Encryption Model: Teams data, including chat messages, files, and other shared content, is stored in the Microsoft 365 cloud. Microsoft 365 employs a multi-layered encryption strategy, utilizing both BitLocker and Distributed Key Manager (DKM) to encrypt data at rest.

- BitLocker: BitLocker is a full-disk encryption feature that encrypts the entire disk where Teams data is stored. It ensures that data is protected even if the physical storage device is accessed by unauthorized individuals.

- Distributed Key Manager (DKM): DKM is used to manage encryption keys across Microsoft's distributed data centers. It ensures that encryption keys are securely generated, stored, and managed, providing an additional layer of security for data at rest.

3. End-to-End Encryption (E2EE)

End-to-End Encryption (E2EE) is a security feature that ensures data is encrypted on the sender's device and only decrypted on the recipient's device, with no intermediate nodes being able to decrypt the data. Microsoft Teams offers E2EE for one-on-one VoIP calls, providing an additional level of security for sensitive communications.

- Configuring E2EE: Administrators can enable E2EE for specific users or groups within the organization. Once enabled, users can activate E2EE for individual calls through the Teams settings.

- Using E2EE: When E2EE is enabled for a call, the call data is encrypted end-to-end, ensuring that only the communicating parties can decrypt and access the data. This feature is particularly useful for confidential discussions and sensitive information sharing.

4. Compliance with Industry Standards

Microsoft Teams' encryption methods are designed to comply with various industry standards and regulations. This compliance ensures that organizations using Teams can meet their legal and regulatory requirements for data protection.

- ISO/IEC 27001: Microsoft Teams is certified under ISO/IEC 27001, an international standard for information security management systems. This certification demonstrates Microsoft's commitment to maintaining robust security practices.

- SOC 1, SOC 2, and SOC 3: Teams complies with Service Organization Controls (SOC) 1, 2, and 3 standards, which are designed to ensure that service providers securely manage data to protect the interests of organizations and the privacy of their clients.

- GDPR Compliance: Microsoft Teams complies with the General Data Protection Regulation (GDPR), ensuring that personal data of EU citizens is protected and that data processing activities meet the stringent requirements of the GDPR.

5. Key Management and Security Controls

Effective key management is crucial for maintaining the integrity of encryption processes. Microsoft Teams employs advanced key management techniques to ensure that encryption keys are securely handled.

- Azure Key Vault: Azure Key Vault is used to safeguard encryption keys and secrets. It provides secure key management capabilities, including key generation, storage, and access control.

- Customer Key: For organizations with specific compliance requirements, Microsoft offers the Customer Key feature. This feature allows organizations to provide and control their own encryption keys for Microsoft 365 data, including Teams.

6. Data Loss Prevention (DLP)

Data Loss Prevention (DLP) is a critical aspect of data protection, designed to prevent the accidental or intentional sharing of sensitive information. Microsoft Teams integrates with DLP policies configured in Microsoft 365, allowing organizations to monitor and control the sharing of sensitive data within Teams.

- Creating DLP Policies: Administrators can create DLP policies to detect and block the sharing of sensitive information such as credit card numbers, social security numbers, and other personally identifiable information (PII).

- Policy Enforcement: DLP policies can be enforced in real-time, preventing users from sharing sensitive information in messages, files, and other content shared within Teams. Alerts and notifications can be configured to inform administrators and users of policy violations.

7. Information Protection and Governance

Information protection and governance are essential for maintaining control over organizational data. Microsoft Teams integrates with Microsoft Information Protection (MIP) to provide comprehensive data classification, labeling, and protection capabilities.

- Sensitivity Labels: Sensitivity labels can be applied to Teams, channels, and files to classify and protect sensitive information. Labels can be configured to enforce encryption, access controls, and other protection measures.

- Retention Policies: Retention policies help organizations manage the lifecycle of their data, ensuring that information is retained for the required period and then securely deleted. Teams integrates with Microsoft 365 retention policies to automate data retention and deletion processes.

Conclusion

Data encryption and protection are paramount in ensuring the security of information within Microsoft Teams. By implementing robust encryption methods for data in transit and at rest, and by providing advanced features such as E2EE and DLP, Microsoft Teams offers comprehensive security measures to protect user data. Compliance with industry standards and the integration of key management and information protection tools further enhance the platform's security, making it a reliable choice for organizations seeking secure and efficient collaboration solutions.

7.1.2 Multi-Factor Authentication

Multi-Factor Authentication (MFA) is a critical security feature that significantly enhances the security of Microsoft Teams by requiring users to provide multiple forms of verification before accessing their accounts. This additional layer of security helps protect against unauthorized access, even if a user's password is compromised. In this section, we will explore the importance of MFA, how it works, and provide a detailed guide on setting up and managing MFA in Microsoft Teams.

Understanding Multi-Factor Authentication

MFA requires users to authenticate their identity through two or more verification methods. These methods generally fall into three categories:

1. Something you know: This is typically a password or PIN.

2. Something you have: This could be a mobile device, security token, or smart card.

3. Something you are: This includes biometric verification methods such as fingerprints or facial recognition.

By combining these factors, MFA makes it much harder for malicious actors to gain access to user accounts. Even if one factor is compromised, the chances of all factors being compromised are significantly lower.

Benefits of Multi-Factor Authentication

- Enhanced Security: MFA provides an additional layer of security beyond passwords, which are often susceptible to phishing attacks and other forms of cyber threats.

- Compliance: Many regulatory frameworks and standards require MFA to ensure the security of sensitive data.

- User Trust: By implementing MFA, organizations can assure users that their data is protected, building trust and confidence in the system.

How Multi-Factor Authentication Works in Microsoft Teams

When MFA is enabled for a Microsoft Teams account, users must complete the following steps during the login process:

1. Enter Username and Password: Users start by entering their standard login credentials.

2. Second Verification Step: After successfully entering the correct username and password, users are prompted for a second verification method. This could be a code sent to their mobile device, a push notification, or a biometric verification.

Setting Up Multi-Factor Authentication

1. Enable MFA in Azure Active Directory (AD):

- Sign in to the Azure portal as an administrator.

- Navigate to `Azure Active Directory` > `Security` > `Multi-Factor Authentication`.

- Under `Multi-Factor Authentication`, select `Account Settings` and choose the preferred MFA method (e.g., app notification, SMS, or call).

- Enable MFA for the desired users or groups.

2. Configure User Settings:

- Users need to register for MFA the first time they sign in after MFA is enabled.

- They will be prompted to set up their preferred authentication method, such as downloading and configuring the Microsoft Authenticator app or registering their phone number.

3. Conditional Access Policies:

- To enforce MFA more selectively, administrators can configure conditional access policies in Azure AD.

- Navigate to `Azure Active Directory` > `Security` > `Conditional Access`.

- Create a new policy that requires MFA based on specific conditions, such as user location, device type, or application being accessed.

Managing Multi-Factor Authentication

1. Monitoring and Reporting:

- Use the Azure AD portal to monitor MFA usage and generate reports.

- Navigate to `Azure Active Directory` > `Sign-ins` to view sign-in logs and check for MFA attempts.

- Generate security reports to identify potential issues and ensure compliance with organizational policies.

2. User Support and Troubleshooting:

- Provide users with clear instructions and support for setting up and using MFA.

- Address common issues such as lost devices or difficulties with receiving verification codes.

- Ensure users know how to update their authentication methods, such as adding a new phone number or changing their verification method.

3. Policy Adjustments:

- Regularly review and adjust MFA policies based on emerging threats and organizational needs.

- Ensure policies are flexible enough to balance security with user convenience.

Best Practices for Implementing Multi-Factor Authentication

- Educate Users: Ensure that users understand the importance of MFA and how it works. Provide training sessions and documentation to help them set up and use MFA effectively.

- Test and Rollout Gradually: Start with a pilot group to test the MFA implementation. Gather feedback and address any issues before rolling it out to the entire organization.

- Backup Verification Methods: Encourage users to set up multiple verification methods to ensure they can access their accounts if one method is unavailable.

- Regularly Review Access Logs: Use Azure AD's reporting tools to regularly review access logs and identify any unusual activity or potential security breaches.

- Stay Updated on Security Practices: Keep up with the latest security trends and practices. Update MFA methods and policies as needed to address new threats and vulnerabilities.

Common Challenges and Solutions

1. User Resistance:

- Challenge: Some users may resist the implementation of MFA due to perceived inconvenience.

- Solution: Educate users on the importance of MFA for security. Highlight real-world examples of data breaches that could have been prevented with MFA.

2. Technical Issues:

- Challenge: Users may face technical issues such as not receiving verification codes or problems with biometric verification.

- Solution: Provide detailed troubleshooting guides and support. Ensure users have access to backup verification methods.

3. Device Dependence:

- Challenge: Users may be concerned about losing access if they lose their primary verification device.

- Solution: Encourage users to register multiple devices and verification methods. Provide guidelines on what to do if a device is lost.

Conclusion

Multi-Factor Authentication is a vital security measure for protecting Microsoft Teams accounts and data. By requiring multiple forms of verification, MFA significantly reduces the risk of unauthorized access. Implementing MFA involves enabling it in Azure AD, configuring user settings, and managing policies and user support. Adhering to best practices and addressing common challenges can ensure a smooth and effective MFA implementation. With MFA, organizations can enhance their security posture, comply with regulatory requirements, and build trust with their users.

In the next section, we will delve into Compliance and Governance, exploring how Microsoft Teams helps organizations meet regulatory requirements and manage their data effectively.

7.1.3 Managing Guest Access

Introduction

Managing guest access in Microsoft Teams is a critical aspect of maintaining the balance between collaboration and security. As organizations increasingly rely on external collaboration with partners, vendors, and clients, it is essential to ensure that guests have the appropriate level of access without compromising the security of internal data and resources. This section provides a detailed guide on how to effectively manage guest access in Microsoft Teams, including setting up guest access, configuring permissions, and monitoring guest activities.

Setting Up Guest Access

1. Enable Guest Access:

- To begin with, ensure that guest access is enabled in the Microsoft Teams admin center. Navigate to the Teams settings and toggle the guest access option to 'On'. This setting allows external users to join your teams and channels.

- Office 365 Admin Center: Make sure that guest access is enabled at the Office 365 tenant level. Without this, even if guest access is enabled in Teams, external users will not be able to join.

2. Inviting Guests:

- To invite a guest, go to the desired team, click on 'Manage team', and then 'Add member'. Enter the guest's email address, and an invitation will be sent to them. The guest will need to accept the invitation and set up their account.

- It is important to inform guests that they will need a Microsoft account to join your Teams environment. If they don't have one, they will be prompted to create one during the invitation process.

Configuring Permissions for Guests

1. Team-Level Permissions:

- Once a guest is added to a team, you can configure their permissions at the team level. Navigate to 'Manage team' and then 'Settings'. Under 'Guest permissions', you can set what guests are allowed to do, such as creating and updating channels, deleting messages, and more.

- It is advisable to limit guest permissions to essential activities to minimize security risks. For instance, you might allow guests to create and update channels but restrict their ability to delete messages or add new members.

2. Channel-Level Permissions:

- Permissions can also be configured at the channel level. This is useful for ensuring that guests only have access to specific parts of the team. To do this, create a private channel and add the guest to it. Private channels restrict access to only the members added to them, providing an additional layer of security.

- Be mindful of the information shared in channels where guests are members. Avoid sharing sensitive or confidential information unless absolutely necessary.

Security Measures and Best Practices

1. Conditional Access Policies:

- Implement conditional access policies to control how guests access your Teams environment. These policies can enforce multi-factor authentication (MFA), limit access based on geographic location, and more.

- For instance, you might require guests to authenticate via MFA every time they access Teams, or you could restrict access to certain IP addresses to ensure that only authorized users can join.

2. Data Protection:

- Use data loss prevention (DLP) policies to protect sensitive information. DLP policies can help identify, monitor, and automatically protect sensitive information such as credit card numbers, social security numbers, and more.

- Configure DLP policies in the Security & Compliance Center, and apply them to Teams to prevent guests from sharing sensitive information inadvertently.

3. Guest Access Reviews:

- Regularly review the list of guests who have access to your Teams environment. Remove any guests who no longer need access to ensure that only current, relevant external users have access to your data.

- Use tools such as Azure AD Access Reviews to automate this process. Access Reviews can help you identify inactive accounts and streamline the process of removing unnecessary access.

Monitoring and Auditing Guest Activities

1. Audit Logs:

- Enable and regularly review audit logs to track guest activities within Teams. These logs can provide detailed information about who accessed what information and when, helping you to detect any suspicious activities.

- Access audit logs through the Security & Compliance Center. You can search for specific activities, such as file downloads or message deletions, to ensure that guests are using your Teams environment appropriately.

2. Alerts and Notifications:

- Set up alerts to notify you of specific activities that could indicate a security risk. For example, you might set an alert for when a guest attempts to download a large number of files or tries to access a restricted area.

- Configure these alerts in the Security & Compliance Center. Alerts can be sent via email, SMS, or through the Microsoft 365 admin center, allowing you to respond quickly to potential threats.

3. Usage Reports:

- Utilize usage reports to gain insights into how guests are interacting with your Teams environment. These reports can help you understand trends and identify any unusual activity that might warrant further investigation.

- Access usage reports through the Teams admin center. You can generate reports on user activity, app usage, and more, providing a comprehensive view of guest interactions.

Conclusion

Managing guest access in Microsoft Teams is crucial for maintaining a secure and collaborative environment. By carefully setting up guest access, configuring permissions, implementing security measures, and monitoring activities, you can ensure that external users can collaborate effectively without compromising the security of your organization's data. Regular reviews and audits will help you stay on top of guest access, ensuring that only those who need access have it and that any potential security risks are promptly addressed.

7.2 Compliance and Governance

7.2.1 Compliance Policies and Settings

Introduction to Compliance Policies

Compliance policies in Microsoft Teams are critical to ensure that your organization's data remains secure and adheres to legal and regulatory requirements. These policies help manage and safeguard sensitive information, ensuring that data handling practices align with industry standards and government regulations. Microsoft Teams provides various tools and settings that enable administrators to implement and enforce compliance policies effectively.

Understanding Compliance Policies

Compliance policies in Microsoft Teams involve several key aspects, including data retention, eDiscovery, auditing, and information protection. These policies can be tailored to meet the specific needs of your organization and industry. By understanding and implementing these policies, organizations can mitigate risks associated with data breaches, non-compliance, and other security threats.

Setting Up Compliance Policies

1. Data Retention Policies:

Data retention policies dictate how long data is stored and when it should be deleted. This is crucial for compliance with regulations such as GDPR, HIPAA, and others.

- *Creating a Retention Policy:*

  - Navigate to the Microsoft 365 compliance center.

  - Select "Information governance" and then "Retention."

- Create a new policy by selecting "Create" and following the prompts to define the retention settings, including the duration for which data should be retained and the actions to be taken when the retention period expires.

- Apply the policy to specific Teams, channels, or users.

- Managing Retention Policies:

- Regularly review and update retention policies to ensure they remain aligned with regulatory changes and organizational requirements.

- Monitor policy application and effectiveness through compliance center reports.

2. eDiscovery:

eDiscovery (Electronic Discovery) allows organizations to identify, preserve, and retrieve electronic information for legal cases and investigations.

- Setting Up eDiscovery:

- In the compliance center, navigate to "eDiscovery" and create a new eDiscovery case.

- Define the scope of the case by specifying the users, teams, and channels to be included.

- Use search and export tools to gather relevant data.

- Managing eDiscovery Cases:

- Assign roles and permissions to ensure only authorized personnel can access and manage eDiscovery cases.

- Maintain detailed logs of eDiscovery activities for auditing purposes.

3. Auditing and Reporting:

Auditing and reporting tools in Microsoft Teams help track user activities and detect potential compliance issues.

- Enabling Auditing:

- Go to the compliance center and select "Audit log search."

- Ensure that auditing is turned on and configure audit settings to capture relevant events, such as user logins, file access, and administrative actions.

- *Creating Reports:*

- Use built-in reports to monitor compliance and security activities.

- Schedule regular audits and generate custom reports to meet specific compliance requirements.

Implementing Compliance Policies

1. Define Clear Compliance Objectives:

- Understand the regulatory requirements and standards applicable to your organization.

- Define clear objectives for your compliance policies, such as data protection, legal readiness, and risk management.

2. Develop Comprehensive Policies:

- Develop detailed policies that address all aspects of compliance, including data retention, eDiscovery, and auditing.

- Ensure that policies are documented and accessible to relevant stakeholders.

3. Training and Awareness:

- Conduct regular training sessions to educate employees about compliance policies and their importance.

- Promote awareness of compliance practices and encourage adherence to policies.

4. Monitor and Review:

- Continuously monitor compliance policies and their effectiveness.

- Conduct regular reviews and updates to ensure policies remain aligned with regulatory changes and organizational needs.

5. Leverage Technology:

- Utilize Microsoft Teams' built-in compliance tools and integrate third-party solutions if necessary.

- Automate compliance processes to reduce manual effort and improve accuracy.

Challenges and Best Practices

1. Challenges:

- Keeping up with regulatory changes and ensuring policies are updated accordingly.

- Ensuring consistent policy enforcement across all Teams and users.

- Balancing compliance requirements with user productivity and experience.

2. Best Practices:

- Stay informed about regulatory developments and industry best practices.

- Implement automated tools to enforce compliance policies consistently.

- Foster a culture of compliance within the organization by promoting awareness and training.

Conclusion

Implementing compliance policies and settings in Microsoft Teams is essential for protecting sensitive data, meeting regulatory requirements, and ensuring the integrity of your organization's operations. By understanding the various aspects of compliance, setting up robust policies, and leveraging Microsoft Teams' compliance tools, organizations can achieve a high level of data security and regulatory adherence. Regular monitoring, training, and updates are key to maintaining effective compliance policies and mitigating risks associated with data breaches and non-compliance.

7.2.2 Data Retention and eDiscovery

Data retention and eDiscovery are critical components in maintaining compliance and governance within any organization using Microsoft Teams. These processes ensure that your organization can effectively manage, retain, and discover data as required by legal, regulatory, and business mandates.

1. Understanding Data Retention in Microsoft Teams

Data retention in Microsoft Teams involves policies that control how long data is kept and when it is deleted. These policies help organizations manage their data lifecycle and ensure that data is not kept longer than necessary, reducing the risk of data breaches and minimizing storage costs.

Key Components of Data Retention:

- Retention Policies: Define how long data is retained and when it should be deleted. Policies can be applied to chats, channels, and files.

- Retention Labels: These are tags applied to data to classify and manage retention. They help in identifying data that should be kept for compliance purposes.

- Retention Settings: Settings that specify the duration for which data should be retained and what happens after the retention period ends (e.g., deletion or archival).

Implementing Data Retention Policies:

- Identify Data Types: Determine which types of data need retention policies. In Microsoft Teams, this includes chat messages, channel messages, and files shared within the platform.

- Define Retention Requirements: Establish how long each type of data should be retained based on legal and business requirements.

- Apply Retention Policies: Use the Microsoft 365 compliance center to create and apply retention policies. Policies can be applied to specific users, groups, or the entire organization.

- Monitor and Review: Regularly review retention policies to ensure they meet current compliance requirements and adjust them as necessary.

2. eDiscovery in Microsoft Teams

eDiscovery (electronic discovery) refers to the process of identifying, collecting, and producing electronically stored information (ESI) in response to a request for evidence in legal cases. Microsoft Teams integrates with Microsoft 365's eDiscovery tools to facilitate this process.

Key Features of eDiscovery:

- Content Search: Allows you to search for content across Microsoft Teams, including chat messages, channel messages, and files.

- eDiscovery Cases: Enables you to create cases for managing legal holds, searches, and exports of data relevant to specific legal matters.

- Legal Holds: Ensures that data is preserved and cannot be deleted or altered while on hold, which is crucial for compliance during litigation.

Steps to Use eDiscovery in Microsoft Teams:

- Set Up eDiscovery Manager: Assign the eDiscovery Manager role to users who need access to the eDiscovery tools.

- Create an eDiscovery Case: In the Microsoft 365 compliance center, create a new case and add members who will manage the case.

- Place Legal Holds: Within the case, apply legal holds to specific users, teams, or channels to preserve relevant data.

- Conduct Searches: Use the content search tool to find relevant information based on keywords, dates, and other criteria.

- Review and Export Data: Analyze the search results and export the data for legal review and production.

3. Best Practices for Data Retention and eDiscovery

Implementing effective data retention and eDiscovery practices is crucial for maintaining compliance and minimizing legal risks. Here are some best practices to consider:

Develop a Comprehensive Data Management Policy:

- Establish clear guidelines for data retention and eDiscovery, including roles and responsibilities for managing these processes.

- Ensure that the policy is aligned with legal and regulatory requirements specific to your industry.

Regularly Audit and Review Policies:

- Conduct periodic audits of your data retention and eDiscovery policies to ensure they remain effective and compliant.

- Update policies as needed to reflect changes in regulations, business practices, and technology.

Train Employees:

- Provide regular training for employees on data retention and eDiscovery procedures to ensure compliance and minimize the risk of data mishandling.

- Emphasize the importance of following established policies and the potential legal implications of non-compliance.

Utilize Automation:

- Leverage automation tools within Microsoft 365 to streamline data retention and eDiscovery processes, reducing the risk of human error.

- Automate the application of retention policies and legal holds to ensure consistency and efficiency.

Ensure Proper Documentation:

- Maintain detailed records of all retention policies, eDiscovery cases, and actions taken to ensure transparency and accountability.

- Document the rationale for data retention periods and legal holds to provide a clear justification for these decisions in the event of an audit or legal inquiry.

4. Challenges and Solutions in Data Retention and eDiscovery

While data retention and eDiscovery are essential for compliance, they come with several challenges that organizations must address.

Data Volume and Complexity:

- Challenge: The sheer volume and complexity of data within Microsoft Teams can make retention and eDiscovery efforts overwhelming.

- Solution: Implement robust data classification and management practices to categorize and organize data effectively. Use advanced search and filtering capabilities to narrow down relevant information.

Compliance with Diverse Regulations:

- Challenge: Organizations may need to comply with a variety of regulations, each with different data retention requirements.

- Solution: Develop a flexible and adaptable data retention policy that can accommodate various regulatory requirements. Use retention labels and policies to manage different data types and regions.

Ensuring Data Security and Privacy:

- Challenge: Balancing data retention and eDiscovery with the need to protect sensitive information and maintain privacy.

- Solution: Apply encryption, access controls, and other security measures to safeguard data. Ensure that eDiscovery processes comply with data protection regulations like GDPR.

Resource and Cost Management:

- Challenge: Data retention and eDiscovery can be resource-intensive and costly.

- Solution: Use automation and cloud-based solutions to reduce the burden on IT resources and minimize costs. Regularly review and optimize retention policies to avoid unnecessary data storage.

5. Conclusion

Effective data retention and eDiscovery are essential for maintaining compliance, protecting sensitive information, and minimizing legal risks in Microsoft Teams. By implementing comprehensive policies, leveraging Microsoft 365's robust tools, and following best practices, organizations can ensure that they manage their data efficiently and responsibly.

In summary, data retention involves defining and applying policies to manage the lifecycle of data, while eDiscovery focuses on identifying and preserving relevant information for legal purposes. Both processes are crucial for compliance and require careful planning, regular review, and proper training to be effective. With the right approach, organizations can navigate the complexities of data retention and eDiscovery, ensuring they meet their legal and regulatory obligations while optimizing their use of Microsoft Teams.

7.2.3 Auditing and Reporting

Auditing and reporting are critical components of maintaining compliance and ensuring governance within any organization using Microsoft Teams. These processes help organizations monitor, review, and analyze activities to ensure that they adhere to regulatory requirements, internal policies, and best practices. In this section, we will explore the tools and methodologies available in Microsoft Teams for effective auditing and reporting.

1. Importance of Auditing and Reporting

Auditing and reporting serve multiple purposes in an organizational setting:

- Regulatory Compliance: Ensure adherence to industry regulations such as GDPR, HIPAA, and other legal requirements.

- Security Monitoring: Detect and respond to security breaches or suspicious activities.

- Operational Transparency: Provide insights into user activities and system performance.

- Policy Enforcement: Verify that internal policies and protocols are followed.

- Risk Management: Identify and mitigate potential risks before they escalate into serious issues.

2. Auditing Tools in Microsoft Teams

Microsoft Teams offers a suite of auditing tools that integrate seamlessly with the broader Microsoft 365 environment. These tools provide comprehensive logs and reports that can be used to monitor activities within Teams.

a. Microsoft 365 Compliance Center

The Microsoft 365 Compliance Center is a central hub for managing compliance across all Microsoft 365 services, including Teams. It provides tools for data governance, auditing, and compliance management.

b. Unified Audit Log

The Unified Audit Log allows administrators to search and filter activity logs across Microsoft 365 services. It includes detailed records of user and admin activities in Teams, such as:

- User logins and sign-ins.

- Creation and deletion of Teams and channels.

- Changes to team settings and policies.

- File sharing and collaboration activities.

- Meeting and call logs.

To access the Unified Audit Log:

1. Navigate to the Microsoft 365 Compliance Center.

2. Select "Audit" from the left-hand menu.

3. Use the search and filter options to locate specific activities or events.

c. Advanced Auditing Capabilities

Advanced auditing capabilities in Microsoft 365 provide extended retention of audit logs and enhanced granularity of audit data. These features are particularly useful for organizations with stringent compliance requirements.

3. Generating and Analyzing Reports

Generating and analyzing reports is a key aspect of maintaining compliance and governance. Microsoft Teams offers various reporting tools that help administrators and compliance officers to generate insights and actionable information.

a. Activity Reports

Activity reports in the Microsoft Teams admin center provide detailed information about how Teams is used within the organization. Key reports include:

- Teams Usage Report: Provides metrics on the number of active users, messages sent, meetings held, and other engagement statistics.

- Teams Device Usage Report: Shows the types of devices being used to access Teams, helping to ensure compliance with device policies.

- Teams App Usage Report: Highlights the usage of third-party apps and integrations within Teams, allowing for better management of app permissions and compliance.

b. Security and Compliance Reports

Security and compliance reports focus on activities related to data protection, policy adherence, and security events. Key reports include:

- Data Loss Prevention (DLP) Report: Monitors and reports on incidents where sensitive information is shared or leaked, helping to enforce data protection policies.

- eDiscovery Report: Provides insights into the use of eDiscovery tools for legal and compliance purposes, ensuring that data can be efficiently retrieved and preserved during legal proceedings.

- Security Incident Report: Tracks security incidents and responses, allowing for quick identification and mitigation of potential threats.

c. Custom Reports

For organizations with specific reporting needs, custom reports can be created using Microsoft Power BI. Power BI integrates with Microsoft Teams and the broader Microsoft 365 environment, allowing for the creation of tailored reports that meet unique compliance and governance requirements.

4. Best Practices for Effective Auditing and Reporting

To maximize the effectiveness of auditing and reporting, organizations should follow best practices that ensure comprehensive monitoring and analysis of activities within Microsoft Teams.

a. Establish Clear Policies and Procedures

Develop and document clear policies and procedures for auditing and reporting. Ensure that these policies align with regulatory requirements and internal governance standards.

b. Regularly Review and Update Audit Logs

Regularly review audit logs to identify any unusual or suspicious activities. Establish a routine schedule for auditing activities, and update logs as needed to reflect changes in organizational policies or compliance requirements.

c. Train Staff on Compliance Protocols

Provide training and resources to staff on compliance protocols and the importance of auditing and reporting. Ensure that all team members understand their roles and responsibilities in maintaining compliance.

d. Utilize Automated Tools and Alerts

Leverage automated tools and alerts to monitor activities in real-time. Configure alerts to notify administrators of potential compliance violations or security incidents, allowing for immediate response and mitigation.

e. Conduct Periodic Audits and Assessments

Conduct periodic audits and assessments to evaluate the effectiveness of your auditing and reporting processes. Use the insights gained from these assessments to improve and refine your compliance strategies.

f. Maintain Documentation and Records

Maintain detailed documentation and records of all auditing and reporting activities. Ensure that records are stored securely and can be easily accessed for compliance reviews or legal proceedings.

5. Responding to Audit Findings

Responding to audit findings is a critical aspect of maintaining compliance and governance. Organizations should have a clear process for addressing issues identified during audits.

a. Investigate and Address Issues Promptly

Investigate any issues or anomalies identified during audits promptly. Determine the root cause of the issue and take corrective actions to address it.

b. Implement Corrective Actions

Implement corrective actions to rectify compliance violations or security issues. Ensure that these actions are documented and communicated to relevant stakeholders.

c. Monitor and Follow Up

Monitor the effectiveness of corrective actions and follow up to ensure that the issues have been resolved. Conduct additional audits or assessments if necessary to verify compliance.

d. Report to Stakeholders

Report audit findings and corrective actions to stakeholders, including senior management, compliance officers, and regulatory bodies as required. Ensure that reports are clear, accurate, and comprehensive.

6. Leveraging eDiscovery for Compliance

eDiscovery (electronic discovery) is a vital tool for organizations to manage and retrieve electronic information for legal and compliance purposes. Microsoft Teams integrates with eDiscovery tools in Microsoft 365 to streamline the process of identifying, collecting, and preserving data.

a. Setting Up eDiscovery

To set up eDiscovery in Microsoft Teams:

1. Navigate to the Microsoft 365 Compliance Center.

2. Select "eDiscovery" from the left-hand menu.

3. Create a new eDiscovery case or manage existing cases.

b. Conducting eDiscovery Searches

Use eDiscovery searches to locate relevant data within Microsoft Teams. Searches can be refined using keywords, date ranges, and other filters to narrow down results.

c. Exporting and Preserving Data

Export and preserve data identified during eDiscovery searches. Ensure that data is stored securely and in compliance with regulatory requirements.

d. Managing Legal Holds

Implement legal holds to preserve data that is relevant to ongoing or anticipated legal proceedings. Legal holds ensure that data cannot be altered or deleted, maintaining its integrity for compliance purposes.

Conclusion

Auditing and reporting are fundamental aspects of compliance and governance in Microsoft Teams. By leveraging the tools and best practices outlined in this section, organizations can ensure that they maintain regulatory compliance, monitor security, and enforce internal policies effectively. Regular audits, detailed reports, and a proactive approach to compliance will help organizations mitigate risks and build a secure, transparent, and compliant collaboration environment.

7.3 Best Practices for Secure Collaboration

7.3.1 Establishing Security Protocols

Establishing robust security protocols is crucial for ensuring secure collaboration within Microsoft Teams. Security protocols are sets of rules and guidelines designed to protect the integrity, confidentiality, and availability of data. These protocols help prevent unauthorized access, data breaches, and other security incidents that could compromise the safety of sensitive information. Here is a comprehensive guide on establishing effective security protocols in Microsoft Teams:

1. Define Security Objectives and Policies

Understanding Security Needs:

Before establishing security protocols, it's essential to understand the specific security needs of your organization. This involves identifying the types of data you handle, the level of sensitivity of this data, and the potential risks associated with its exposure.

Developing Security Policies:

Security policies are the foundation of any security protocol. They should be developed based on the organization's security objectives and should cover aspects such as data classification, access control, incident response, and user behavior. Key policies include:

- Data Classification Policy: Defines how data should be classified based on its sensitivity and value.

- Access Control Policy: Establishes rules for granting, modifying, and revoking access to resources.

- Incident Response Policy: Outlines procedures for responding to security incidents.

- User Behavior Policy: Sets guidelines for acceptable use of Microsoft Teams and other IT resources.

2. Implementing Access Controls

Role-Based Access Control (RBAC):

Implementing RBAC ensures that users have access only to the resources they need to perform their job functions. This minimizes the risk of unauthorized access to sensitive data. Define roles based on job functions and assign appropriate permissions to each role.

Multi-Factor Authentication (MFA):

MFA adds an extra layer of security by requiring users to provide two or more verification factors to gain access. This can include something the user knows (password), something the user has (smartphone), and something the user is (fingerprint).

Conditional Access Policies:

These policies restrict access based on specific conditions such as user location, device type, or risk level. For instance, access can be restricted for users attempting to log in from untrusted locations or devices.

3. Securing Communications

Data Encryption:

Ensure that all data in transit and at rest is encrypted. Microsoft Teams uses TLS (Transport Layer Security) for data in transit and encryption for data at rest. Regularly update and manage encryption keys to maintain data security.

Secure Meetings and Calls:

Enable secure meeting options such as lobby settings, which allow meeting organizers to control who can join meetings. Use meeting options to restrict recording, disable anonymous join, and control screen sharing permissions.

Compliance Recording:

For organizations that require meeting and call recordings for compliance purposes, ensure that these recordings are stored securely and access is restricted to authorized personnel.

4. Monitoring and Auditing

Activity Logs:

Enable logging of user activities within Microsoft Teams. Activity logs provide a detailed record of actions taken by users, which can be invaluable for identifying and responding to security incidents.

Auditing and Reporting:

Regularly review audit logs and generate reports to identify unusual or suspicious activities. Use these reports to enforce compliance and detect potential security threats. Microsoft 365 provides a comprehensive audit log search tool to help with this process.

Threat Detection and Response:

Implement threat detection tools such as Microsoft Defender for Office 365. These tools provide real-time alerts and automated responses to potential security threats, helping to mitigate risks quickly.

5. User Training and Awareness

Security Awareness Training:

Regularly conduct security awareness training for all users. This training should cover topics such as recognizing phishing attempts, creating strong passwords, and understanding the importance of MFA.

Regular Updates:

Keep users informed about the latest security threats and best practices. Provide regular updates and reminders about security protocols and the importance of following them.

6. Incident Response and Management

Incident Response Plan:

Develop a detailed incident response plan that outlines the steps to be taken in the event of a security breach. This plan should include procedures for identifying, containing, eradicating, and recovering from incidents.

Incident Response Team:

Establish an incident response team responsible for managing and responding to security incidents. This team should include representatives from IT, security, legal, and communications.

Post-Incident Review:

After resolving a security incident, conduct a post-incident review to identify what went wrong and what improvements can be made to prevent future incidents. Document the findings and update security protocols accordingly.

7. Data Protection and Privacy

Data Loss Prevention (DLP):

Implement DLP policies to prevent the accidental or intentional sharing of sensitive information. These policies can automatically detect and block the sharing of confidential data such as credit card numbers, social security numbers, and other sensitive information.

Privacy Controls:

Ensure that privacy settings are configured to protect user data. Limit the visibility of user information to only those who need it and regularly review privacy settings to maintain compliance with data protection regulations.

Data Retention Policies:

Establish data retention policies that define how long different types of data should be retained. These policies help ensure compliance with legal and regulatory requirements while minimizing the risk of data breaches.

8. Regular Review and Improvement

Periodic Security Assessments:

Conduct regular security assessments to evaluate the effectiveness of your security protocols. These assessments can identify potential vulnerabilities and areas for improvement.

Continuous Improvement:

Security is an ongoing process. Continuously monitor the security landscape, stay informed about new threats, and update your security protocols as needed to address emerging risks.

Feedback and Adaptation:

Encourage feedback from users and IT staff on the effectiveness of security protocols. Use this feedback to make necessary adjustments and ensure that security measures remain effective and user-friendly.

Conclusion

Establishing security protocols in Microsoft Teams is essential for protecting sensitive data and ensuring secure collaboration. By defining clear security policies, implementing robust access controls, securing communications, monitoring activities, training users, managing incidents, protecting data, and continuously reviewing and improving protocols, organizations can create a secure environment for their teams to collaborate effectively. Adhering to these best practices not only helps prevent security breaches but also fosters a culture of security awareness and responsibility within the organization.

7.3.2 Training Teams on Security Practices

Training your team on security practices is a critical component of ensuring the secure use of Microsoft Teams. Proper training helps users understand the importance of security measures and equips them with the knowledge to prevent security breaches. This section will provide a detailed guide on how to effectively train your team on security practices.

Importance of Security Training

Security training is essential for several reasons:

1. Awareness: It raises awareness about potential security threats and the importance of adhering to security protocols.

2. Responsibility: It instills a sense of responsibility among team members for maintaining security.

3. Prevention: It equips users with the knowledge to identify and prevent security incidents.

4. Compliance: It ensures compliance with organizational and legal security requirements.

Developing a Security Training Program

To effectively train your team, it is important to develop a comprehensive security training program. The following steps outline the process:

1. Assess Training Needs

- Conduct a security audit to identify current security practices and potential vulnerabilities.

- Survey team members to understand their current knowledge and identify gaps.

2. Set Clear Objectives

- Define the goals of the training program, such as understanding data encryption, recognizing phishing attempts, and managing access controls.

3. Design the Training Program

- Content Development: Create engaging and informative content that covers essential security topics.

  - Introduction to Security: Explain basic security concepts and their importance.

  - Data Protection: Teach how to handle and protect sensitive data.

  - Access Management: Cover the principles of user access control and the importance of using strong passwords and multi-factor authentication.

- Threat Awareness: Educate on common threats like phishing, malware, and social engineering attacks.

- Training Methods: Use a variety of training methods to cater to different learning styles.

- Workshops: Conduct interactive workshops where team members can ask questions and participate in discussions.

- E-Learning Modules: Provide online courses that team members can complete at their own pace.

- Simulations: Use simulations to mimic real-world security incidents and test team members' responses.

- Regular Updates: Keep the training material up-to-date with the latest security trends and threats.

4. Implement the Training Program

- Schedule training sessions at regular intervals to ensure continuous learning.

- Make training mandatory for all team members, including new hires and existing employees.

- Provide resources such as guides, checklists, and FAQs for reference.

Key Topics for Security Training

1. Understanding Data Encryption and Protection

- What is Data Encryption?: Explain the concept of data encryption and its importance in protecting data.

- Types of Encryption: Describe different types of encryption, such as symmetric and asymmetric encryption.

- Encryption in Microsoft Teams: Demonstrate how Microsoft Teams uses encryption to protect data in transit and at rest.

2. Implementing Multi-Factor Authentication (MFA)

- What is MFA?: Define multi-factor authentication and its role in enhancing security.

- How to Use MFA: Guide team members on setting up and using MFA in Microsoft Teams.

- Benefits of MFA: Highlight the benefits of MFA in preventing unauthorized access.

3. Managing Guest Access

- Understanding Guest Access: Explain what guest access is and how it can be securely managed in Microsoft Teams.

- Setting Permissions: Show how to set appropriate permissions for guests to ensure they only have access to necessary information.

- Monitoring Guest Activity: Teach how to monitor guest activity to detect and respond to any suspicious behavior.

4. Identifying and Responding to Phishing Attempts

- What is Phishing?: Define phishing and its different forms, such as email phishing and spear phishing.

- Recognizing Phishing Attempts: Provide examples of phishing emails and teach team members how to identify them.

- Reporting Phishing: Explain the steps to report phishing attempts to the IT department.

5. Using Strong Passwords and Authentication

- Creating Strong Passwords: Provide guidelines on creating strong passwords, including using a mix of characters and avoiding common phrases.

- Password Management Tools: Recommend tools for managing passwords securely.

- Changing Passwords Regularly: Encourage regular password changes to maintain security.

Engaging Team Members in Security Practices

1. Creating a Security Culture

- Foster a culture where security is prioritized and everyone is responsible for maintaining it.

- Recognize and reward team members who demonstrate good security practices.

2. Encouraging Open Communication

- Create an environment where team members feel comfortable reporting security incidents or concerns.

- Provide clear channels for reporting and ensure timely responses.

3. Regular Security Drills and Simulations

- Conduct regular security drills to test the team's readiness and response to security incidents.

- Use simulations to create realistic scenarios that help team members practice their skills.

4. Providing Ongoing Support and Resources

- Offer continuous support through regular training sessions and updates.

- Provide resources such as security guides, checklists, and FAQs for reference.

Measuring the Effectiveness of Security Training

1. Assessing Knowledge and Skills

- Conduct pre- and post-training assessments to measure knowledge gains.

- Use quizzes and practical exercises to test understanding.

2. Monitoring Security Incidents

- Track the number and types of security incidents before and after training.

- Analyze incident reports to identify areas for improvement.

3. Gathering Feedback

- Collect feedback from team members on the training program to understand its effectiveness and areas for improvement.

- Use surveys and interviews to gather insights.

4. Continuous Improvement

- Regularly update the training program based on feedback and the latest security trends.

- Ensure the program remains relevant and effective in addressing new threats.

Conclusion

Training teams on security practices is an ongoing process that requires commitment and continuous improvement. By developing a comprehensive training program, engaging team members, and regularly assessing its effectiveness, organizations can ensure that their teams are well-equipped to maintain security in Microsoft Teams. A proactive approach to security training not only helps prevent security incidents but also fosters a culture of security awareness and responsibility.

7.3.3 Monitoring and Responding to Threats

Ensuring the security of your Microsoft Teams environment involves continuous monitoring and an efficient response strategy for potential threats. This section provides a detailed guide on how to effectively monitor and respond to threats within Microsoft Teams.

1. Implementing Continuous Monitoring

Continuous monitoring is crucial for identifying and mitigating threats before they escalate. Here are the steps to set up effective monitoring:

- Utilize Microsoft 365 Security Center: Microsoft 365 Security Center provides a centralized view of security alerts and incidents across Microsoft services, including Teams. Regularly review the security dashboard for insights into potential threats.

- Enable Advanced Threat Protection (ATP): Microsoft Defender for Office 365 includes ATP, which helps protect against sophisticated threats. Configure ATP to scan all files shared in Teams and to provide real-time protection against malware and phishing attacks.

- Set Up Security Alerts: Configure security alerts for specific activities, such as unusual sign-in attempts, data exfiltration attempts, and changes in security settings. Alerts can be sent via email, SMS, or integrated into your incident management system.

- Use Threat Analytics: Leverage threat analytics to understand the current threat landscape and how it might affect your organization. Microsoft provides tools like the Threat & Vulnerability Management dashboard to assess and mitigate risks.

2. Identifying and Assessing Threats

Effective threat identification and assessment involve several key steps:

- Analyze Security Logs: Regularly analyze security logs to identify unusual patterns or behaviors that may indicate a threat. Use log management solutions to aggregate and analyze logs from various sources.

- Conduct Threat Intelligence: Utilize threat intelligence feeds to stay updated on the latest threats and vulnerabilities. Integrate these feeds into your security monitoring tools to enhance threat detection capabilities.

- Perform Regular Security Audits: Conduct periodic security audits of your Teams environment. These audits should include a review of user access rights, configuration settings, and compliance with security policies.

3. Responding to Threats

Once a threat is identified, a structured response is essential to mitigate the impact. Here's how to respond effectively:

- Develop an Incident Response Plan: An incident response plan outlines the steps to take when a threat is detected. It should include roles and responsibilities, communication protocols, and escalation procedures.

- Isolate Affected Systems: Immediately isolate affected systems to prevent the spread of the threat. This may involve disconnecting devices from the network, disabling compromised accounts, and blocking malicious IP addresses.

- Investigate the Incident: Conduct a thorough investigation to determine the nature and scope of the incident. This involves identifying the entry point, the affected systems, and the data that may have been compromised.

- Remediate the Threat: Implement remediation measures to remove the threat and restore affected systems. This may include applying patches, updating security configurations, and conducting a full malware scan.

- Communicate with Stakeholders: Keep all relevant stakeholders informed about the incident, including affected users, management, and regulatory bodies if necessary. Transparent communication helps maintain trust and ensures compliance with reporting requirements.

4. Post-Incident Review

After responding to a threat, conduct a post-incident review to evaluate the response and improve future preparedness:

- Analyze the Incident: Review the incident to understand what happened, how it was handled, and what could have been done better. Identify any gaps in your security posture and response plan.

- Update Security Measures: Based on the findings from the post-incident review, update your security measures and response plan. This may involve implementing new technologies, revising policies, and conducting additional training.

- Document the Incident: Document the incident and the response actions taken. This documentation is essential for future reference, compliance reporting, and for improving incident response strategies.

5. Training and Awareness

Regular training and awareness programs are vital for maintaining a secure Teams environment:

- Conduct Security Training: Provide regular security training for all users, focusing on the specific threats and security practices related to Microsoft Teams. Training should cover topics like recognizing phishing attempts, safe file sharing practices, and reporting security incidents.

- Promote Security Awareness: Foster a culture of security awareness within your organization. Use posters, newsletters, and intranet posts to highlight security best practices and the importance of vigilance.

- Simulate Security Incidents: Conduct regular security incident simulations to test the effectiveness of your incident response plan. These simulations help identify weaknesses and improve response times.

6. Leveraging Microsoft Security Tools

Microsoft provides several tools to enhance security monitoring and response:

- Microsoft Cloud App Security (MCAS): MCAS provides comprehensive visibility and control over your cloud applications, including Teams. Use it to monitor user activity, detect anomalies, and enforce security policies.

- Azure Sentinel: Azure Sentinel is a scalable, cloud-native security information and event management (SIEM) solution. It uses AI to analyze large volumes of data and provides actionable insights to detect and respond to threats.

- Microsoft Defender for Endpoint: This tool provides advanced threat protection for endpoints, including devices used to access Teams. It offers real-time detection, investigation, and response capabilities.

7. Integrating Security with DevOps (DevSecOps)

Integrating security into the development and operations process (DevSecOps) ensures that security is considered at every stage of the Teams deployment:

- Embed Security in Development: Incorporate security practices into the development lifecycle of custom Teams apps and integrations. Conduct code reviews, use secure coding practices, and perform regular security testing.

- Automate Security Testing: Use automated tools to test the security of Teams applications and configurations. Automated testing helps identify vulnerabilities early and ensures compliance with security standards.

- Collaborate Across Teams: Foster collaboration between development, operations, and security teams. Regular communication and joint planning sessions help ensure that security is a shared responsibility.

Conclusion

Monitoring and responding to threats in Microsoft Teams is a continuous process that requires vigilance, advanced tools, and a proactive approach. By implementing robust monitoring strategies, conducting regular threat assessments, and developing a comprehensive incident response plan, organizations can effectively protect their Teams environment from potential threats. Continuous training and leveraging Microsoft's security tools further enhance the security posture, ensuring a safe and productive collaboration platform.

CHAPTER VIII Troubleshooting and Support

8.1 Common Issues and Solutions

8.1.1 Connectivity Problems

Microsoft Teams, like any other online tool, can face connectivity issues that disrupt smooth communication and collaboration. Identifying and troubleshooting these problems effectively ensures minimal downtime and a better user experience. This section provides detailed steps to diagnose and resolve common connectivity issues in Microsoft Teams.

1. Checking Internet Connection:

Step 1: Verify Network Connectivity

- Ensure your device is connected to the internet. Check the network icon on your taskbar (Windows) or menu bar (Mac) to confirm a stable connection.

- If connected via Wi-Fi, verify the signal strength. A weak signal can cause intermittent connectivity issues.

- If using a wired connection, ensure the Ethernet cable is securely connected to both your device and the router.

Step 2: Test Internet Speed

- Use online tools such as Speedtest (www.speedtest.net) to measure your internet speed. Microsoft Teams requires a minimum of 1.2 Mbps for video calls and 4 Mbps for group video calls. Insufficient bandwidth can cause connectivity issues.

- If your internet speed is below the required threshold, consider contacting your Internet Service Provider (ISP) to upgrade your plan or resolve connectivity problems.

2. Restarting Network Devices:

Step 1: Power Cycle the Router and Modem

- Unplug your router and modem from the power source.

- Wait for about 30 seconds to 1 minute.

- Plug the modem back in first, wait until it fully reboots, and then plug in the router.

- This process refreshes the network connection and can resolve many connectivity issues.

Step 2: Restart Your Device

- Restart your computer or mobile device to clear any temporary glitches affecting the network connection.

3. Configuring Network Settings:

Step 1: Update Network Drivers

- Outdated network drivers can cause connectivity problems. Ensure your drivers are up-to-date.

- On Windows, go to Device Manager, find Network Adapters, right-click your network adapter, and select 'Update driver.'

- On Mac, use Software Update to ensure your macOS and network drivers are current.

Step 2: Adjust DNS Settings

- Sometimes, changing your DNS settings can improve connectivity. Use reliable DNS servers such as Google's (8.8.8.8 and 8.8.4.4) or OpenDNS (208.67.222.222 and 208.67.220.220).

- On Windows, access Network and Sharing Center > Change adapter settings > right-click your network connection > Properties > Internet Protocol Version 4 (TCP/IPv4) > Properties > Use the following DNS server addresses.

- On Mac, go to System Preferences > Network > Advanced > DNS > click the + button to add new DNS servers.

4. Managing Firewall and Antivirus Settings:

Step 1: Configure Firewall Settings

- Ensure your firewall is not blocking Microsoft Teams. Allow Microsoft Teams through your firewall settings.

- On Windows, go to Control Panel > System and Security > Windows Defender Firewall > Allow an app or feature through Windows Defender Firewall. Ensure both private and public network boxes for Microsoft Teams are checked.

- On Mac, go to System Preferences > Security & Privacy > Firewall > Firewall Options, and add Microsoft Teams to the list of allowed applications.

Step 2: Adjust Antivirus Software

- Some antivirus software can interfere with Microsoft Teams. Temporarily disable your antivirus software to check if it's causing connectivity issues.

- If disabling the antivirus resolves the issue, add Microsoft Teams to the antivirus exception list.

5. Resolving Proxy and VPN Issues:

Step 1: Check Proxy Settings

- Incorrect proxy settings can disrupt connectivity. Ensure your proxy settings are correctly configured.

- On Windows, go to Settings > Network & Internet > Proxy, and ensure 'Use a proxy server' is toggled off unless required by your organization.

- On Mac, go to System Preferences > Network > Advanced > Proxies, and adjust settings as needed.

Step 2: Disable VPN Temporarily

- VPNs can sometimes cause connectivity issues with Microsoft Teams. Temporarily disable your VPN to see if it resolves the problem.

- If disabling the VPN resolves the issue, consider configuring your VPN to work correctly with Microsoft Teams or contact your VPN provider for support.

6. Updating Microsoft Teams:

Step 1: Check for Updates

- Ensure you are using the latest version of Microsoft Teams. Updates often include bug fixes and improvements.

- On Windows and Mac, click on your profile picture in Microsoft Teams, select 'Check for updates,' and follow the prompts to install any available updates.

Step 2: Reinstall Microsoft Teams

- If updating doesn't resolve the issue, consider reinstalling Microsoft Teams.

- Uninstall Microsoft Teams from your device, download the latest version from the official Microsoft website, and reinstall it.

7. Contacting IT Support:

Step 1: Gather Information

- Document the connectivity issues you are experiencing, including error messages, steps taken to troubleshoot, and the results.

- This information will help IT support diagnose and resolve the problem more efficiently.

Step 2: Reach Out to Support

- Contact your organization's IT support team or Microsoft Support for further assistance. Provide them with the documented information for a quicker resolution.

Conclusion

Connectivity issues in Microsoft Teams can disrupt your workflow and communication. By systematically troubleshooting these problems, you can often resolve them quickly and efficiently. Ensuring a stable internet connection, properly configured network settings, and up-to-date software are key steps in maintaining seamless connectivity in Microsoft Teams.

In the following sections, we will explore other common issues and solutions, such as audio and video problems, file sharing and syncing issues, and more. Each section will provide detailed, step-by-step guidance to help you resolve these issues and optimize your experience with Microsoft Teams.

8.1.2 Audio and Video Issues

Microsoft Teams is a powerful tool for virtual collaboration, but users often encounter audio and video issues that can disrupt meetings and impede productivity. In this section, we will explore common audio and video problems and provide detailed solutions to ensure seamless communication.

Identifying Audio and Video Problems

Before diving into solutions, it is essential to accurately identify the type of issue you are facing. Audio and video problems can broadly be categorized into:

1. Audio Issues:

- No sound
- Distorted or choppy sound
- Echo or feedback
- Microphone not working

2. Video Issues:

- No video
- Poor video quality
- Video freezing or lagging
- Camera not recognized

Troubleshooting Audio Issues

1. No Sound

If you can't hear any sound during a Teams call, follow these steps:

- Check Volume Levels: Ensure that the volume on your device and within Teams is not muted or set too low. You can adjust the volume by clicking the speaker icon in the system tray and using the volume slider.

- Select the Correct Audio Device: Sometimes, Teams may select the wrong audio device. Go to your Teams settings by clicking on your profile picture, selecting "Settings," and then "Devices." Choose the correct speaker and microphone from the dropdown menus.

- Update Audio Drivers: Outdated or corrupted audio drivers can cause sound issues. Update your drivers by visiting the device manager, right-clicking your audio device, and selecting "Update driver."

- Restart Teams and Your Device: Restarting Teams or your entire device can resolve temporary glitches. Close Teams completely and restart your computer.

2. Distorted or Choppy Sound

If you experience distorted or choppy sound, consider these solutions:

- Check Your Internet Connection: Poor network connectivity can cause audio disruptions. Ensure you have a stable and high-speed internet connection. Switching to a wired connection instead of Wi-Fi can also help.

- Close Background Applications: Running multiple applications simultaneously can strain system resources and affect audio quality. Close unnecessary applications to free up system resources.

- Adjust Teams Settings: In Teams settings, navigate to "Devices" and check the "Noise suppression" setting. Setting it to "High" can help reduce background noise and improve audio clarity.

3. Echo or Feedback

Echo or feedback can be distracting during calls. Here's how to address it:

- Use Headphones: Using headphones or a headset instead of your device's built-in speakers and microphone can significantly reduce echo and feedback.

- Mute When Not Speaking: Encourage participants to mute themselves when not speaking. This practice minimizes background noise and prevents feedback loops.

- Adjust Microphone Settings: In Teams settings, under "Devices," adjust the microphone sensitivity to reduce the chances of feedback.

4. Microphone Not Working

If your microphone isn't working, follow these steps:

- Check Physical Connections: Ensure that your microphone is properly connected to your device. If using an external microphone, check the cables and ports.

- Select the Correct Microphone: In Teams settings, go to "Devices" and ensure the correct microphone is selected. You can also test the microphone within Teams to verify it is working.

- Check Privacy Settings: On Windows, go to "Settings," then "Privacy," and ensure that microphone access is allowed for Teams. On macOS, go to "System Preferences," then "Security & Privacy," and check the microphone permissions.

Troubleshooting Video Issues

1. No Video

If your video isn't showing, try these solutions:

- Check Camera Connections: Ensure that your camera is properly connected to your device. For external cameras, check the USB connection.

- Select the Correct Camera: In Teams settings, navigate to "Devices" and select the correct camera from the dropdown menu.

- Check Camera Permissions: On Windows, go to "Settings," then "Privacy," and ensure that camera access is allowed for Teams. On macOS, go to "System Preferences," then "Security & Privacy," and check the camera permissions.

- Update Camera Drivers: Outdated drivers can prevent your camera from working correctly. Update your camera drivers through the device manager.

2. Poor Video Quality

To improve video quality, consider the following:

- Check Your Internet Connection: A stable, high-speed internet connection is crucial for good video quality. Switch to a wired connection if possible and ensure no other applications are using excessive bandwidth.

- Adjust Video Settings: In Teams settings, go to "Devices" and check the video quality settings. Lowering the resolution can sometimes help with bandwidth issues but may affect video clarity.

- Improve Lighting: Ensure you have adequate lighting in your environment. Poor lighting can make the video appear grainy. Use natural light or place a light source in front of you.

3. Video Freezing or Lagging

If your video freezes or lags, try these solutions:

- Check System Resources: High CPU or memory usage can cause video issues. Close unnecessary applications to free up system resources.

- Update Teams: Ensure you are using the latest version of Teams. Updates often include bug fixes and performance improvements.

- Check Network Latency: High latency can cause video lag. Use a tool like Ping or Traceroute to check your network latency. Contact your ISP if latency is high.

4. Camera Not Recognized

If Teams does not recognize your camera, follow these steps:

- Restart Teams and Your Device: Close Teams completely and restart your computer.

- Reinstall Camera Drivers: Uninstall and reinstall your camera drivers through the device manager.

- Try a Different USB Port: If using an external camera, try plugging it into a different USB port.

Additional Tips and Best Practices

- Regularly Update Software: Keep your operating system, Teams application, and drivers up to date to avoid compatibility issues.

- Use High-Quality Equipment: Invest in a good quality microphone and camera to enhance your audio and video experience.

- Test Before Meetings: Test your audio and video settings before important meetings to ensure everything is working correctly.

- Seek Professional Help: If you continue to experience issues, consider seeking help from your IT department or a professional technician.

By following these troubleshooting steps and best practices, you can resolve most audio and video issues in Microsoft Teams, ensuring smooth and productive meetings.

8.1.3 File Sharing and Syncing Problems

File sharing and syncing are essential features of Microsoft Teams, allowing users to collaborate seamlessly on documents, presentations, and other files. However, users can encounter various issues that disrupt the flow of work. This section will explore common problems related to file sharing and syncing, along with detailed solutions to address these issues effectively.

Common File Sharing Issues:

1. File Upload Failures:

- Symptom: Users are unable to upload files to Teams channels or chats.

- Possible Causes: Insufficient permissions, file size limitations, network issues, or corrupted files.

- Solutions:

1. Check Permissions: Ensure that the user has the necessary permissions to upload files to the specific channel or chat. Administrators can adjust permissions in the Teams settings or SharePoint site associated with the team.

2. File Size: Verify that the file size does not exceed the maximum allowed limit for uploads in Teams. As of the latest updates, the limit is typically 100 GB per file, but this can vary based on organizational policies.

3. Network Connection: Ensure a stable internet connection. Poor connectivity can cause file uploads to fail. Users can try uploading the file again when the connection is stable.

4. File Integrity: Check if the file is corrupted. Attempt to open the file locally to confirm its integrity. If corrupted, try re-saving or repairing the file before uploading.

2. Slow Upload and Download Speeds:

- Symptom: File uploads and downloads are slower than expected.

- Possible Causes: Network bandwidth issues, server load, or large file sizes.

- Solutions:

1. Network Bandwidth: Ensure that the network has sufficient bandwidth for file transfers. Users can perform a speed test to check their connection speed and contact their IT department if the bandwidth is insufficient.

2. Server Load: High server load can slow down file transfers. Users can try uploading or downloading files during off-peak hours to avoid congestion.

3. File Size: Compress large files before uploading to reduce transfer time. Tools like ZIP can help compress files without losing quality.

3. File Access Denied:

- Symptom: Users receive an "Access Denied" error when attempting to open shared files.

- Possible Causes: Insufficient permissions, file moved or deleted, or syncing issues.

- Solutions:

1. Permissions: Verify that the user has the correct permissions to access the file. Owners can adjust permissions in the SharePoint library or directly within Teams.

2. File Location: Ensure that the file has not been moved or deleted. Check the file path and location in SharePoint or OneDrive.

3. Sync Status: Confirm that the file is fully synced with the cloud. Unsynced changes can cause access issues.

Common File Syncing Issues:

1. Files Not Syncing:

- Symptom: Changes made to files in Teams do not reflect in OneDrive or SharePoint, and vice versa.

- Possible Causes: Sync errors, outdated sync client, or network issues.

- Solutions:

1. Sync Client: Ensure that the OneDrive sync client is up-to-date. Outdated clients can cause syncing issues. Users can check for updates in the client settings.

2. Sync Errors: Resolve any sync errors displayed by the OneDrive client. These errors can often provide specific guidance on what needs to be fixed.

3. Network Issues: Verify that the device has a stable internet connection. Intermittent connectivity can disrupt the sync process.

2. Duplicate Files and Conflict Errors:

- Symptom: Duplicate files or conflict errors appear when syncing.

- Possible Causes: Simultaneous edits by multiple users, sync delays, or improper file handling.

- Solutions:

1. Version Control: Use version control features in Teams and SharePoint to manage simultaneous edits. This ensures that changes are tracked and conflicts are minimized.

2. Edit Notifications: Encourage team members to use the "Check Out" feature before making changes to shared files. This prevents others from editing the file simultaneously.

3. Conflict Resolution: Manually resolve conflicts by comparing the duplicate files and merging changes as necessary. Users can rename or delete duplicate files once conflicts are resolved.

3. OneDrive Sync Issues:

- Symptom: Files stored in OneDrive do not sync with Teams or SharePoint.

- Possible Causes: Sync client problems, file path limitations, or account issues.

- Solutions:

1. Sync Client: Ensure that the OneDrive sync client is properly configured and running. Reinstall the client if necessary to resolve persistent issues.

2. File Path: Avoid long file paths or deeply nested folders, as they can exceed the maximum path length supported by OneDrive. Simplify file structures to prevent sync errors.

3. Account Issues: Verify that the OneDrive account is correctly linked to the Teams account. Users can sign out and sign back in to refresh the account connection.

General Troubleshooting Steps:

1. Restart Applications:

- Restart Microsoft Teams and the OneDrive sync client to resolve temporary glitches or software issues.

2. Check System Updates:

- Ensure that the operating system and Microsoft Teams application are up-to-date. Updates often include bug fixes and performance improvements.

3. Clear Cache:

- Clearing the Teams cache can resolve various issues, including file sharing and syncing problems. Users can clear the cache by deleting the contents of the Teams cache folder located in the user's profile directory.

4. Reinstall Applications:

- If issues persist, reinstall Microsoft Teams and the OneDrive sync client. This can resolve deeper software problems that simple updates cannot fix.

Specific Case Studies and Solutions:

Case Study 1: File Upload Failure Due to Insufficient Permissions

Scenario:

A user, Jane, attempts to upload a project report to her team's General channel but receives an error message indicating insufficient permissions.

Solution:

1. Identify Permissions Issue:

- Jane checks with her team owner and confirms she does not have the required permissions to upload files to the channel.

2. Adjust Permissions:

- The team owner navigates to the Teams settings and grants Jane the necessary permissions to upload files.

3. Upload File:

- Jane attempts to upload the file again, and the upload is successful.

Case Study 2: Slow File Download Speeds During Peak Hours

Scenario:

During a busy workday, employees experience slow file download speeds from Teams, impacting productivity.

Solution:

1. Network Bandwidth Check:

- The IT department performs a network bandwidth test and confirms congestion during peak hours.

2. Server Load Management:

- IT schedules non-critical file transfers during off-peak hours and advises employees to download large files outside of peak times.

3. Improve Bandwidth Allocation:

- The organization upgrades its internet plan to ensure adequate bandwidth is available for critical tasks.

Case Study 3: Sync Conflict Due to Simultaneous Edits

Scenario:

Two team members, John and Mary, edit the same budget file simultaneously, resulting in duplicate files and a sync conflict error.

Solution:

1. Use Version Control:

- The team decides to use the "Check Out" feature in SharePoint for critical documents. John checks out the file before making edits, preventing others from editing it simultaneously.

2. Resolve Conflict:

- John and Mary compare their changes manually, merge the edits, and save the final version of the document.

3. Educate Team Members:

- The team receives training on version control and best practices for collaborative editing to avoid future conflicts.

Advanced Troubleshooting Tools:

1. OneDrive Sync Troubleshooter:

- Microsoft provides a built-in sync troubleshooter for OneDrive. Users can access this tool through the OneDrive client settings to diagnose and fix sync issues.

2. SharePoint Health Analyzer:

- SharePoint's Health Analyzer can identify and report issues with the SharePoint environment, including those affecting file sync and access.

3. Microsoft Support and Diagnostics Tool:

- The Microsoft Support and Recovery Assistant (SaRA) can help troubleshoot and fix problems with Microsoft Teams and related services. Users can download SaRA from the Microsoft website.

Preventive Measures:

1. Regular Training:

- Provide ongoing training for users on best practices for file sharing and syncing in Microsoft Teams. This includes how to properly share files, manage permissions, and use version control.

2. Proactive Monitoring:

- IT departments should proactively monitor network performance, server load, and sync status to identify and resolve issues before they impact users.

3. Clear Communication Protocols:

- Establish clear communication protocols for teams, including guidelines for file naming, folder organization, and document management to prevent confusion and conflicts.

Conclusion:

File sharing and syncing are vital components of Microsoft Teams that facilitate seamless collaboration and productivity. By understanding common issues and implementing the detailed solutions provided in this section, users can overcome challenges related to file sharing and syncing. Regular training, proactive monitoring, and clear communication protocols further enhance the user experience, ensuring that Microsoft Teams remains a powerful tool for collaborative work.

8.2 Getting Help and Support

8.2.1 Accessing Microsoft Teams Support

In any software environment, users will inevitably encounter issues that require external assistance to resolve. Microsoft Teams, despite its robust design and extensive functionalities, is no exception. When faced with challenges, understanding how to access and utilize Microsoft Teams support is crucial for maintaining productivity and minimizing downtime. This section delves into the various avenues available for obtaining support, ensuring users can find the help they need efficiently and effectively.

1. Microsoft Teams Help Center

The Microsoft Teams Help Center is a comprehensive resource that provides a wealth of information on a wide range of topics. This platform is designed to assist users in troubleshooting common issues, learning about new features, and understanding how to use Teams more effectively.

- Navigating the Help Center

The Help Center can be accessed directly from the Teams interface. To reach it, click on your profile picture or the three-dot menu in the upper-right corner of the Teams app, then select "Help." From there, you can choose "Topics" to browse through categories or use the search bar to find specific articles.

- Using Articles and Guides

The Help Center contains numerous articles and step-by-step guides. These resources cover everything from basic setup and navigation to advanced troubleshooting. Articles are categorized by topic, making it easy to find relevant information.

- Interactive Demos and Tutorials

In addition to written content, the Help Center offers interactive demos and video tutorials. These can be particularly helpful for visual learners who prefer to see processes in action rather than read about them.

2. Contacting Microsoft Support

When the Help Center does not provide a solution, contacting Microsoft Support directly may be necessary. There are several ways to get in touch with Microsoft Support, each catering to different types of issues and user preferences.

- Support Through the Teams App

You can contact support directly from within the Teams application. Click on your profile picture or the three-dot menu, select "Help," and then choose "Contact Support." This will guide you through the process of describing your issue and submitting a support request.

- Microsoft Support Website

The Microsoft Support website (support.microsoft.com) is another valuable resource. Here, you can search for solutions, browse through support topics, and initiate contact with support agents via chat or email. The site also offers a "Get Help" app for Windows 10, which can streamline the support process.

- Phone Support

For urgent or complex issues, phone support is often the best option. Microsoft provides phone numbers for different regions, allowing users to speak directly with a support agent. This can be particularly helpful for resolving time-sensitive problems that require immediate attention.

3. Microsoft Teams Community Forums

Community forums are a great place to seek help from fellow Teams users. These forums are frequented by a diverse group of users, including IT professionals, administrators, and everyday users who share their experiences and solutions.

- Microsoft Tech Community

The Microsoft Tech Community is a popular forum where users can ask questions, share solutions, and discuss best practices. It includes specific sections for Microsoft Teams, ensuring that your queries reach the right audience. To participate, visit techcommunity.microsoft.com and navigate to the Microsoft Teams section.

- Reddit and Other Online Communities

In addition to official forums, there are several unofficial communities on platforms like Reddit (reddit.com/r/MicrosoftTeams). These communities can be excellent sources of peer support, offering diverse perspectives and creative solutions.

4. Utilizing Microsoft Teams' Built-in Features

Microsoft Teams includes several built-in features designed to help users troubleshoot issues on their own before reaching out for support.

- Troubleshooting Tools

Within Teams, there are diagnostic tools that can help identify and resolve common issues. For example, the "Call Health" feature provides real-time feedback on call quality, helping users pinpoint connectivity or hardware problems.

- Feedback and Reporting Issues

Teams allows users to send feedback directly to Microsoft. By clicking on your profile picture or the three-dot menu and selecting "Help," then "Give feedback," you can report bugs, suggest features, or share general feedback. This input is valuable for Microsoft's ongoing efforts to improve the platform.

5. Training and Certification

For users looking to deepen their understanding of Teams and improve their troubleshooting skills, Microsoft offers various training and certification programs.

- Microsoft Learn

Microsoft Learn is an online platform offering free, interactive learning paths and modules on Microsoft Teams and other Microsoft products. These courses range from beginner to advanced levels, covering topics such as deployment, administration, and integration.

- Microsoft Certifications

Obtaining a Microsoft certification can validate your expertise and enhance your ability to troubleshoot and support Teams. Certifications like the Microsoft Certified: Teams

Administrator Associate demonstrate proficiency in managing Teams environments, troubleshooting issues, and implementing best practices.

6. Leveraging IT Support

For organizations with dedicated IT support teams, leveraging internal resources can often be the fastest way to resolve issues. IT professionals typically have access to advanced tools and direct support channels with Microsoft, allowing them to diagnose and fix problems more efficiently.

- Internal IT Help Desk

Many organizations have an internal help desk that can assist with Teams-related issues. Submitting a ticket or contacting the help desk directly can provide quick solutions, especially for issues related to network settings, account permissions, and software updates.

- IT Training and Resources

Ensuring that your IT team is well-versed in Teams is crucial for maintaining smooth operations. Providing ongoing training and access to the latest resources can help your IT team stay ahead of potential issues and implement best practices.

Conclusion

Accessing Microsoft Teams support effectively involves utilizing a combination of self-help resources, direct support channels, and community forums. By familiarizing yourself with these options, you can ensure that help is readily available whenever you encounter issues. Whether you prefer to troubleshoot independently using the Help Center, engage with community forums, or contact Microsoft Support directly, understanding these resources is key to maintaining a seamless Teams experience. Moreover, leveraging training and certification programs can enhance your troubleshooting skills, empowering you to resolve issues more efficiently and support your team effectively.

8.2.2 Using the Help Center and Documentation

Microsoft Teams is a powerful collaboration tool that is continuously updated with new features and improvements. As users encounter various challenges or seek to optimize their experience, leveraging the Help Center and official documentation becomes essential. This section provides a comprehensive guide on how to effectively use these resources to resolve issues and enhance your understanding of Microsoft Teams.

Understanding the Help Center

The Microsoft Teams Help Center is a centralized repository of resources designed to assist users in troubleshooting problems, learning new features, and maximizing their use of the platform. Here are the key components of the Help Center:

1. Search Functionality: The Help Center features a robust search bar that allows users to quickly find articles and guides related to their queries. By typing in keywords or phrases, users can access relevant information promptly.

2. Popular Topics: The Help Center highlights popular topics that are frequently accessed by users. This section is useful for finding solutions to common problems or learning about widely used features.

3. How-To Guides: Detailed step-by-step guides cover a wide range of topics, from basic functionality to advanced features. These guides are essential for users looking to deepen their understanding of specific aspects of Microsoft Teams.

4. Video Tutorials: For visual learners, the Help Center offers video tutorials that demonstrate how to perform various tasks. These videos are helpful for grasping complex processes through visual representation.

5. Frequently Asked Questions (FAQs): The FAQ section addresses common queries and concerns. This is a quick way to find answers to standard questions without having to search through multiple articles.

Accessing the Help Center

To access the Help Center, follow these steps:

1. Within Microsoft Teams:

   - Click on your profile picture or initials in the top right corner of the Teams application.

   - Select "Help" from the dropdown menu.

   - Choose "Help" again to open the Help Center in a new window or tab.

2. Through a Web Browser:

   - Open your preferred web browser and navigate to the Microsoft Teams Help Center by visiting [Microsoft Teams Help Center](https://support.microsoft.com/en-us/teams).

Navigating the Help Center

Upon entering the Help Center, you will find several navigation options to help you find the information you need:

1. Search Bar: Use the search bar at the top of the page to enter keywords or phrases related to your query. The search results will display relevant articles and guides.

2. Categories and Topics: The Help Center is organized into categories and topics. Common categories include:

   - Getting Started: Basic setup and initial configuration.

   - Meetings and Calls: Scheduling, joining, and managing meetings.

   - Chat and Collaboration: Messaging, file sharing, and collaboration features.

   - Teams and Channels: Creating and managing teams and channels.

   - Security and Compliance: Information on maintaining security and compliance within Teams.

3. Popular Articles: The homepage of the Help Center often features popular articles that address common user issues. This section is a great starting point for finding quick solutions.

4. Video Tutorials: Look for the section dedicated to video tutorials if you prefer learning through visual aids. These videos cover a range of topics and provide clear, step-by-step instructions.

Utilizing Documentation

In addition to the Help Center, Microsoft Teams offers comprehensive documentation that delves deeper into the platform's features and capabilities. The documentation is especially useful for IT administrators, developers, and power users who need detailed technical information.

1. Official Microsoft Documentation:

- Access the Microsoft Teams documentation by visiting [Microsoft Teams Documentation](https://docs.microsoft.com/en-us/microsoftteams/).

- The documentation is organized into sections such as "Overview," "Get Started," "Plan and Deploy," "Manage," and "Use Teams."

2. Key Sections of the Documentation:

- Overview: Provides a high-level introduction to Microsoft Teams, its features, and benefits.

- Get Started: Guides users through the initial setup and configuration of Microsoft Teams.

- Plan and Deploy: Detailed information for IT professionals on planning and deploying Teams within an organization.

- Manage: Covers administrative tasks, including managing users, policies, and settings.

- Use Teams: User-focused guides on utilizing various features and functionalities of Microsoft Teams.

3. Documentation for Developers:

- For developers, Microsoft Teams documentation includes resources on building apps, bots, and integrations. Visit the "Develop" section to access APIs, SDKs, and sample code.

- The [Microsoft Teams Developer Platform](https://docs.microsoft.com/en-us/microsoftteams/platform/) provides detailed guidance on creating custom solutions and extending the capabilities of Teams.

Best Practices for Using the Help Center and Documentation

To make the most of the Help Center and documentation, consider the following best practices:

1. Stay Current with Updates: Regularly check the Help Center and documentation for updates on new features and improvements. Microsoft frequently updates Teams, and staying informed will help you leverage the latest capabilities.

2. Bookmark Key Resources: Save frequently accessed articles and guides as bookmarks in your browser for quick reference. This is especially useful for troubleshooting common issues or performing routine tasks.

3. Engage with the Community: Participate in community forums and user groups to learn from the experiences of other Teams users. These platforms often provide practical solutions and tips that may not be covered in official documentation.

4. Provide Feedback: If you encounter incomplete or unclear information, use the feedback options available in the Help Center and documentation pages. Your feedback helps improve the quality of the resources for all users.

5. Use Multiple Learning Formats: Take advantage of the various formats available, such as written guides, video tutorials, and interactive content. Different formats can enhance your understanding and retention of information.

Examples of Common Queries and How to Resolve Them Using the Help Center

1. Issue: Unable to Join a Meeting

- Search Query: "Cannot join meeting"

- Solution: An article titled "Troubleshoot meeting join issues in Microsoft Teams" provides step-by-step instructions to resolve common problems, such as checking network connections, verifying meeting links, and updating the Teams app.

2. Issue: File Not Syncing

- Search Query: "File sync issues"

- Solution: The guide "Fix OneDrive sync problems" offers solutions for syncing issues, including checking OneDrive settings, ensuring sufficient storage, and troubleshooting specific error messages.

3. Issue: Audio Problems During Calls

- Search Query: "Audio issues in calls"

- Solution: The article "Troubleshoot audio and video in Microsoft Teams" covers common audio problems, such as checking microphone settings, updating drivers, and configuring audio devices.

Advanced Usage of the Help Center and Documentation

1. Customizing Search Queries: Use advanced search techniques to narrow down results. For example, include specific error codes or phrases in quotes to find more precise information.

2. Exploring Related Articles: At the bottom of many Help Center articles, you will find links to related articles. Explore these links for additional context and solutions.

3. Following Documentation Updates: Subscribe to updates or follow the Microsoft Teams blog to stay informed about changes and new documentation releases.

By effectively utilizing the Microsoft Teams Help Center and documentation, users can resolve issues quickly, stay informed about new features, and optimize their use of the platform. These resources are invaluable tools for both novice and experienced Teams users, providing the support needed to navigate the complexities of modern team collaboration.

8.2.3 Community Forums and User Groups

Introduction to Community Forums and User Groups

Microsoft Teams is a complex platform with a vast array of features designed to enhance productivity and collaboration. Despite its comprehensive documentation and built-in support options, users often encounter unique issues or have specific questions that may not be immediately addressed through official channels. This is where community forums and user groups come into play. These platforms provide a space for users to share experiences, solutions, and tips, fostering a collaborative environment where knowledge is freely exchanged.

Benefits of Participating in Community Forums

Community forums offer several benefits for Microsoft Teams users:

1. Real-Time Solutions: Forums allow users to post questions and receive answers from other users who may have encountered similar issues. This can often result in quicker resolutions than waiting for official support.

2. Diverse Perspectives: Forums bring together users from various industries and backgrounds, providing a wide range of perspectives and solutions. This diversity can lead to innovative approaches to common problems.

3. Learning and Development: By participating in discussions, users can stay updated on the latest features, best practices, and troubleshooting techniques. This continuous learning helps users maximize the potential of Microsoft Teams.

4. Networking: Engaging in community forums allows users to connect with peers, build professional relationships, and expand their network within the industry.

Popular Microsoft Teams Community Forums

Several community forums are popular among Microsoft Teams users. These platforms provide a wealth of information and support, making them invaluable resources for troubleshooting and learning.

1. Microsoft Tech Community:

- The Microsoft Tech Community is one of the most comprehensive platforms for Microsoft product users, including Microsoft Teams. It features discussion boards, blogs, and webinars, providing users with a robust support system.

- How to Use: To get started, create an account on the Microsoft Tech Community website, navigate to the Microsoft Teams section, and start browsing the discussion threads. You can post questions, share insights, and participate in ongoing conversations.

2. Reddit:

- Reddit hosts several communities (subreddits) dedicated to Microsoft Teams, such as r/MicrosoftTeams. These communities are highly active, with users frequently posting questions, tips, and updates.

- How to Use: Visit Reddit, create an account, and subscribe to relevant subreddits. Use the search function to find discussions related to your issue or start a new thread to seek help from the community.

3. Stack Overflow:

- While primarily a platform for developers, Stack Overflow has a wealth of information on Microsoft Teams, especially for technical issues and development-related queries.

- How to Use: Create an account on Stack Overflow, search for existing questions related to your issue, or post a new question. Be sure to provide detailed information to receive accurate responses.

4. Spiceworks Community:

- Spiceworks is a community for IT professionals, featuring discussion boards, articles, and tools. The Microsoft Teams section is particularly useful for IT admins and support staff.

- How to Use: Join the Spiceworks community, browse the Microsoft Teams topics, and engage with other IT professionals. This platform is especially useful for troubleshooting complex IT issues.

Finding the Right User Groups

User groups are another valuable resource for Microsoft Teams users. These groups often host regular meetings, webinars, and events, providing opportunities for in-depth learning and networking.

1. Microsoft User Groups:

- Microsoft hosts official user groups around the world. These groups often meet in person or virtually to discuss Microsoft products, including Teams.

- How to Use: Visit the Microsoft User Groups website to find a group near you. Join the group, participate in meetings, and take advantage of the resources and networking opportunities available.

2. Meetup:

- Meetup is a platform that connects people with similar interests. Many cities have Meetup groups dedicated to Microsoft products and technologies, including Teams.

- How to Use: Search for Microsoft Teams groups on Meetup, join the group, and attend events. These meetings can be a great way to learn from others and share your own experiences.

3. LinkedIn Groups:

- LinkedIn hosts several professional groups focused on Microsoft Teams. These groups are useful for discussing professional use cases, sharing articles, and networking.

- How to Use: Search for Microsoft Teams groups on LinkedIn, request to join, and start participating in discussions. LinkedIn groups often feature industry experts and thought leaders.

Best Practices for Engaging in Community Forums and User Groups

To get the most out of community forums and user groups, consider the following best practices:

1. Be Respectful and Professional: Always maintain a respectful and professional tone in your communications. Remember that you are part of a community, and your behavior reflects on you and your organization.

2. Provide Detailed Information: When seeking help, provide as much detail as possible about your issue. Include screenshots, error messages, and steps to reproduce the problem. This helps others understand your situation and provide accurate advice.

3. Search Before Posting: Before posting a new question, use the search function to see if your issue has already been discussed. This can save time and help you find solutions more quickly.

4. Contribute to the Community: Share your knowledge and experiences with others. If you've solved a problem, consider writing a post about it to help others who might face the same issue.

5. Stay Active and Engaged: Regular participation helps you stay updated on the latest developments and build stronger relationships within the community.

6. Follow Up and Close Threads: If your issue is resolved, follow up with a thank-you message and mark the thread as resolved if the platform allows it. This helps others know that the solution worked.

Case Studies: Success Stories from Community Engagement

1. Resolving a Complex Integration Issue:

- A project manager was struggling with integrating Microsoft Teams with a third-party project management tool. After posting detailed information about the issue on the Microsoft Tech Community forum, several users responded with potential solutions. By combining the advice received, the project manager was able to successfully resolve the integration issue, improving the team's workflow and productivity.

2. Enhancing Remote Work Setup:

- An IT administrator needed to optimize Microsoft Teams for a company transitioning to remote work. By joining a LinkedIn group focused on remote work technologies, the administrator connected with experts who shared best practices and tools for remote team management. Implementing these recommendations led to a smoother transition and better remote collaboration.

3. Learning from Webinars and Meetups:

- A teacher looking to enhance virtual classroom experiences joined a local Microsoft User Group on Meetup. Through regular webinars and meetups, the teacher learned advanced features of Microsoft Teams for Education, such as creating interactive assignments and using breakout rooms. This knowledge significantly improved student engagement and learning outcomes.

Conclusion

Community forums and user groups are indispensable resources for Microsoft Teams users. They provide a platform for sharing knowledge, troubleshooting issues, and staying updated on the latest developments. By actively participating in these communities, users can enhance their understanding of Microsoft Teams, solve problems more efficiently, and connect with peers and experts.

Remember, the value you get from these communities is proportional to the effort you put in. Engage respectfully, share your knowledge, and be open to learning from others. In doing so, you'll not only improve your own skills but also contribute to the collective growth of the Microsoft Teams community.

8.3 Staying Up-to-Date with Microsoft Teams

8.3.1 Tracking Updates and New Features

Staying current with updates and new features in Microsoft Teams is crucial for maximizing its potential and ensuring a seamless user experience. Microsoft regularly releases updates that enhance functionality, improve security, and introduce new tools designed to boost productivity. This section will guide you through the best practices for tracking updates and integrating new features into your workflow.

Understanding the Update Cycle

Microsoft follows a structured update cycle for its Office 365 suite, including Teams. Updates are typically released in two main channels: the Current Channel (Monthly Channel) and the Semi-Annual Enterprise Channel. The Current Channel provides the latest features and updates as soon as they are ready, often on a monthly basis. This is ideal for users who want to stay on the cutting edge. The Semi-Annual Enterprise Channel, on the other hand, offers updates twice a year, in January and July, and is geared towards enterprise environments where stability and extensive testing are paramount.

Enabling Automatic Updates

To ensure you receive updates as soon as they are available, enable automatic updates. This can be done through the Microsoft Teams app settings. Here's how:

1. Open Microsoft Teams.

2. Click on your profile picture in the top-right corner.

3. Select Settings.

4. Navigate to the About section.

5. Ensure that the Auto-update option is enabled.

Enabling automatic updates ensures that you are always using the latest version of Microsoft Teams, with all the new features and security enhancements.

Microsoft 365 Admin Center

For administrators, the Microsoft 365 Admin Center is a powerful tool for managing updates across an organization. The Admin Center provides detailed information on update availability, scheduled deployments, and the status of updates. Here's how administrators can use it:

1. Log in to the Microsoft 365 Admin Center.

2. Navigate to Health and select Service Health.

3. Here, you will find information on the latest updates, including detailed release notes and potential issues.

4. Use the Message Center to receive notifications about upcoming updates and feature releases.

Release Notes and Documentation

Microsoft publishes detailed release notes and documentation for every update. These resources provide comprehensive information on new features, improvements, and bug fixes. Release notes can be accessed through:

1. The official Microsoft Teams Blog.

2. The Microsoft 365 Roadmap website.

3. The Microsoft Docs portal.

Regularly reviewing release notes helps you understand the changes and how they might affect your usage of Teams.

Insider Programs

Participating in Microsoft's Insider programs allows you to access new features before they are released to the general public. The Office Insider program has two levels:

1. Insider Fast: Provides the earliest access to new features and updates, with releases often occurring weekly. This level is ideal for users who want to test and provide feedback on the latest developments.

2. Insider Slow: Offers more stable releases with early access to new features, typically updated on a monthly basis.

To join the Office Insider program:

1. Open any Microsoft 365 app.

2. Click on your profile picture in the top-right corner.

3. Select Office Insider.

4. Choose your preferred level of participation (Insider Fast or Insider Slow).

Webinars and Training Sessions

Microsoft frequently conducts webinars and training sessions to educate users about new features and best practices. These sessions are invaluable for staying informed and getting hands-on experience with the latest tools. You can find upcoming webinars and register for them on the Microsoft Teams Events page or through the Microsoft 365 Training Center.

Utilizing Feedback and User Voice

Providing feedback on new features is crucial for their improvement. Microsoft encourages users to share their experiences and suggestions through the User Voice platform. This platform allows users to:

1. Submit feedback and suggestions.

2. Vote on existing ideas and suggestions submitted by others.

3. Track the status of their feedback and see how Microsoft responds.

By actively participating in the feedback process, you can influence the development of Microsoft Teams and ensure it meets your needs.

Community Engagement

Engaging with the Microsoft Teams community is another effective way to stay updated. Community forums, such as the Microsoft Tech Community, offer a platform for users to share tips, ask questions, and discuss new features. Here are some key benefits of community engagement:

1. Networking: Connect with other users, IT professionals, and Microsoft MVPs (Most Valuable Professionals).
2. Knowledge Sharing: Learn from others' experiences and best practices.
3. Problem Solving: Find solutions to common issues and share your own solutions.

Customizing Notifications

Customizing your notification settings ensures that you receive timely updates about new features and changes. In Microsoft Teams:

1. Click on your profile picture and select Settings.
2. Navigate to the Notifications section.
3. Customize notifications for mentions, replies, likes, and new features.

By tailoring your notifications, you can stay informed without being overwhelmed by alerts.

Continuous Learning

To keep up with the evolving features of Microsoft Teams, adopt a mindset of continuous learning. Resources such as the Microsoft Learn platform, LinkedIn Learning, and Pluralsight offer courses and tutorials on Microsoft Teams. These platforms provide structured learning paths, hands-on labs, and certification programs to enhance your proficiency.

Creating a Culture of Adoption

Encouraging a culture of adoption within your organization is essential for maximizing the benefits of new features. This involves:

1. Training: Regular training sessions and workshops to educate team members about new features.

2. Communication: Clear communication about the benefits of new updates and how they improve workflow.

3. Support: Providing ongoing support and resources to help team members adapt to changes.

By fostering a proactive approach to new features, you can ensure that your team fully utilizes the capabilities of Microsoft Teams.

In summary, staying up-to-date with Microsoft Teams involves a combination of enabling automatic updates, utilizing the Microsoft 365 Admin Center, reviewing release notes, participating in insider programs, attending webinars, engaging with the community, customizing notifications, and adopting a culture of continuous learning. By following these practices, you can ensure that you and your team are always equipped with the latest tools and features to enhance collaboration and productivity.

8.3.2 Participating in Beta Programs

Staying current with the latest features and updates in Microsoft Teams is crucial for maximizing its potential and ensuring a smooth user experience. One of the most proactive ways to stay ahead of the curve is by participating in Microsoft's beta programs. These programs allow users to access new features and improvements before they are officially released to the general public. In this section, we will explore the benefits of participating in beta programs, how to join them, and best practices for making the most out of this early access.

Benefits of Participating in Beta Programs

Participating in beta programs offers several advantages:

1. Early Access to Features: Beta programs provide users with early access to new features and enhancements. This allows you to familiarize yourself with updates and integrate them into your workflows ahead of the official release.

2. Influence Product Development: As a beta tester, your feedback can directly impact the development of Microsoft Teams. By providing feedback on new features, you can help shape the product to better meet your needs and those of the broader user community.

3. Competitive Advantage: Staying ahead of new features can give your team a competitive edge. Early adopters can leverage new tools and capabilities to improve productivity and collaboration.

4. Preparation for Deployment: IT administrators can use beta programs to prepare for upcoming changes, ensuring that their organization is ready for the official release. This preparation can include updating training materials, adjusting configurations, and informing users about new features.

Joining Microsoft Teams Beta Programs

Joining a beta program is a straightforward process, but it requires an understanding of the different types of beta releases and the potential impact on your workflow.

1. Types of Beta Programs:

- Public Preview: This is open to all users and provides access to pre-release features. It's ideal for users who want to experience new features without significant risk.

- Targeted Release: This is intended for organizations that want to provide feedback on new features before they are generally available. It involves a more structured feedback process and may include direct communication with the development team.

- Private Preview: This is an invitation-only program for a select group of users. It involves early access to features still in active development and typically requires a Non-Disclosure Agreement (NDA).

2. Enrolling in the Public Preview:

- Individual Users:

  - Open Microsoft Teams.

  - Click on your profile picture in the upper-right corner.

  - Select Settings.

  - Navigate to the About section.

  - Select Public Preview and then confirm your choice.

- Administrators:

  - Open the Microsoft 365 admin center.

  - Navigate to Settings > Org settings > Services & add-ins.

  - Select Microsoft Teams.

  - Under Update settings, enable Allow users to install Public Preview.

  - Users will then be able to opt-in to the Public Preview through their Teams settings.

3. Joining Targeted Release and Private Preview:

- Targeted Release:

  - IT administrators need to enroll their organization via the Microsoft 365 admin center.

  - Navigate to Settings > Org settings > Services & add-ins.

  - Select Release preferences and choose Targeted release for entire organization or Targeted release for selected users.

  - Follow the prompts to complete the enrollment process.

- Private Preview:

- Invitation to Private Preview is typically extended by Microsoft to selected organizations.

- If invited, follow the instructions provided by Microsoft, which may include signing an NDA and setting up specific accounts for testing.

Best Practices for Participating in Beta Programs

Once you have enrolled in a beta program, it's important to follow best practices to ensure a positive experience and meaningful contribution to the development process.

1. Environment Setup:

- Test Environment: Whenever possible, use a test environment to try out new features. This minimizes the risk of disruptions to your production environment.

- Backup: Ensure that critical data is backed up before testing new features to prevent any potential data loss.

2. Feedback and Reporting:

- Detailed Feedback: Provide detailed feedback on new features, including what works well and what needs improvement. Be specific about your use cases and any issues encountered.

- Bug Reporting: If you encounter bugs, report them through the designated feedback channels. Include detailed steps to reproduce the issue, screenshots, and any relevant logs.

- Feature Requests: Suggest new features or enhancements that could improve your experience with Microsoft Teams.

3. Documentation and Training:

- Update Training Materials: As new features become available, update your training materials and documentation to reflect the changes. This ensures that your team is prepared to use new features effectively.

- User Training: Conduct training sessions for users to familiarize them with new features and how they can be integrated into existing workflows.

4. Communication and Collaboration:

- Internal Communication: Keep your team informed about new features and updates. Use internal communication channels, such as email newsletters or intranet posts, to share information about beta program participation and its benefits.

- External Collaboration: Participate in community forums and user groups to share your experiences and learn from others. Engaging with the broader Microsoft Teams community can provide valuable insights and support.

5. Monitoring and Evaluation:

- Monitor Impact: Continuously monitor the impact of new features on your workflows. Evaluate whether the features are improving productivity and collaboration as expected.

- Adjust as Needed: Be prepared to adjust your configurations or usage based on the feedback and findings from your testing. Flexibility is key to making the most out of beta program participation.

Real-World Examples of Beta Program Benefits

To illustrate the benefits of participating in beta programs, consider the following real-world examples:

1. Enhanced Collaboration with Together Mode:

- A company participating in the Public Preview of Together Mode was able to implement this feature in their virtual meetings ahead of the official release. They found that Together Mode significantly improved engagement and reduced meeting fatigue. By the time the feature was generally available, their team was already proficient in using it, giving them a competitive edge in virtual collaboration.

2. Streamlined Workflow with Power Automate Integration:

- An organization enrolled in the Targeted Release program had early access to the integration of Microsoft Teams with Power Automate. They developed automated workflows for common tasks, such as approval processes and notifications. This early adoption allowed them to streamline operations and provide valuable feedback to Microsoft, which helped refine the integration for other users.

3. Improved Security with Advanced Threat Protection:

- A company in the Private Preview program tested advanced security features, including enhanced threat protection and data loss prevention (DLP) capabilities. Their feedback on usability and performance led to important improvements in the final release. By the time these features were officially launched, the company had already enhanced their security posture and trained their staff on best practices.

Conclusion

Participating in Microsoft Teams beta programs is a proactive approach to staying up-to-date with the latest features and improvements. By enrolling in these programs, providing detailed feedback, and following best practices, you can maximize the benefits of early access and contribute to the continuous improvement of Microsoft Teams. Whether you are an individual user looking to stay ahead of new features or an organization aiming to optimize team collaboration and productivity, beta program participation is a valuable strategy for achieving your goals.

8.3.3 Continuous Learning and Development

Continuous learning and development are crucial for leveraging the full potential of Microsoft Teams. This section will guide you through various methods and resources to stay informed about updates, enhance your skills, and keep your team proficient in using Microsoft Teams effectively.

1. Leveraging Microsoft Learning Paths and Certifications

Microsoft offers a range of learning paths and certifications that can help users at all levels to enhance their knowledge and skills in using Microsoft Teams.

- Microsoft Learn: Microsoft Learn provides interactive, self-paced training for a variety of Microsoft products, including Teams. Courses range from beginner to advanced levels, covering topics such as collaboration, communication, and app integrations within Teams. To get started, visit the [Microsoft Learn website](https://docs.microsoft.com/learn/).

- Certifications: Microsoft certifications validate your expertise in using Microsoft Teams. Some relevant certifications include Microsoft Certified: Teams Administrator Associate and Microsoft Certified: Modern Desktop Administrator Associate. These certifications not only enhance your skills but also increase your value in the job market.

2. Participating in Webinars and Virtual Events

Webinars and virtual events are excellent opportunities to learn from experts and network with other Microsoft Teams users. Microsoft regularly hosts events that cover new features, best practices, and industry-specific use cases.

- Microsoft Ignite: Microsoft Ignite is an annual conference that covers a wide range of Microsoft products and services, including Teams. It features keynotes, breakout sessions, and hands-on labs.

- Teams Tuesdays: This is a series of free webinars focusing on different aspects of Microsoft Teams, from basic usage to advanced configurations.

3. Engaging with Online Communities

Joining online communities allows you to connect with other Microsoft Teams users, share experiences, and learn from each other. Some valuable communities include:

- Microsoft Tech Community: This is a platform where users can ask questions, share insights, and collaborate on Microsoft products. The Microsoft Teams community within this platform is very active.

- Reddit: Subreddits like r/MicrosoftTeams are great places to find discussions, tips, and solutions from a broad user base.

4. Utilizing Online Resources and Blogs

There are numerous online resources and blogs dedicated to Microsoft Teams that provide updates, tutorials, and tips.

- Microsoft Teams Blog: The official Microsoft Teams blog is a reliable source for the latest updates, feature releases, and tips directly from the Microsoft Teams team.

- Third-Party Blogs: Blogs such as Practical 365, Petri, and AvePoint often cover Microsoft Teams in their articles, providing in-depth guides and expert opinions.

5. Enrolling in Online Courses

Online courses from platforms like LinkedIn Learning, Coursera, and Udemy can provide structured learning experiences with expert instructors.

- LinkedIn Learning: Offers courses on Microsoft Teams, ranging from beginner to advanced levels, often taught by industry professionals.

- Coursera: Partners with universities and companies to offer courses on Microsoft Teams and related tools.

6. Encouraging Peer Learning and Internal Training

Within your organization, promoting a culture of peer learning and regular internal training sessions can be highly beneficial.

- Lunch and Learn Sessions: Informal sessions where team members share their knowledge about specific features or best practices in Microsoft Teams.

- Mentorship Programs: Pairing less experienced users with more proficient colleagues to facilitate knowledge transfer and skills development.

7. Staying Informed Through Newsletters and Social Media

Subscribing to newsletters and following relevant social media accounts can keep you informed about the latest developments and tips.

- Microsoft 365 Newsletter: Provides updates on all Microsoft 365 products, including Teams.

- Social Media: Follow official accounts like @MicrosoftTeams on Twitter and join LinkedIn groups focused on Microsoft Teams.

8. Using Microsoft Teams Resources

Microsoft Teams itself has built-in resources that can help users learn and develop their skills.

- Help and Training: Accessible from the Teams app, this section provides tutorials, how-to guides, and videos.

- What's New: Regularly updated within the app, this section highlights new features and improvements.

9. Implementing a Learning Management System (LMS)

An LMS can be used to deliver structured training programs on Microsoft Teams within your organization.

- Integration with Teams: Many LMS platforms can integrate with Microsoft Teams, allowing seamless access to training materials and courses directly within Teams.

10. Promoting Continuous Improvement

Encourage a mindset of continuous improvement by regularly reviewing and updating your Microsoft Teams practices and processes.

- Feedback Mechanisms: Regularly solicit feedback from users on their experience with Teams and areas for improvement.

- Process Audits: Conduct periodic audits of how Teams is being used to identify inefficiencies and opportunities for enhancement.

Conclusion

Staying up-to-date with Microsoft Teams and fostering continuous learning and development are essential for maximizing the tool's potential and ensuring that your team remains productive and engaged. By leveraging the resources and strategies outlined in this section, you can keep your knowledge current, enhance your skills, and maintain an efficient and collaborative work environment. Continuous learning is not just about keeping up with changes but also about anticipating future needs and preparing for them proactively. By doing so, you and your team can fully harness the power of Microsoft Teams to achieve your organizational goals.

CHAPTER IX
Tips and Tricks for Power Users

9.1 Keyboard Shortcuts and Commands

9.1.1 Essential Shortcuts

Mastering keyboard shortcuts in Microsoft Teams can dramatically improve your productivity and efficiency. These shortcuts help you navigate through the application swiftly, access features without fumbling through menus, and streamline your workflow. This section will cover the most essential shortcuts every power user should know.

1. General Navigation Shortcuts

- Open Activity: `Ctrl + 1`

- This shortcut takes you directly to the Activity feed, where you can see all the latest updates and notifications from your teams and channels. It's a great way to stay on top of what's happening across your organization.

- Open Chat: `Ctrl + 2`

- Jump straight to the Chat tab to view your recent conversations and start new ones. This is especially useful for quickly responding to messages and maintaining communication with colleagues.

- Open Teams: `Ctrl + 3`

- Navigate directly to the Teams tab to view all your teams and channels. This is where you manage team interactions, post updates, and access shared files and resources.

- Open Calendar: `Ctrl + 4`

- This shortcut brings up your calendar, allowing you to check your schedule, join meetings, and manage appointments without leaving the Teams interface.

- Open Calls: `Ctrl + 5`

- Access the Calls tab to make or receive voice and video calls. This is particularly useful for quickly setting up impromptu calls.

- Open Files: `Ctrl + 6`

- Go to the Files tab to view and manage all your documents stored in Teams. This shortcut helps you access your files quickly, facilitating seamless collaboration on shared documents.

2. Chat and Messaging Shortcuts

- Start New Chat: `Ctrl + N`

- Initiate a new chat conversation instantly, allowing you to communicate with colleagues without navigating through the interface.

- Reply to a Thread: `R`

- Use this shortcut within a channel to reply to an existing thread. It helps keep conversations organized and ensures your messages are contextual.

- Search: `Ctrl + E`

- Quickly access the search bar to find messages, people, or files across Teams. Efficient searching is crucial for retrieving information promptly.

- Toggle Mute: `Ctrl + Shift + M`

- Mute or unmute your microphone during a call or meeting. This is essential for managing audio inputs during discussions, ensuring you only speak when necessary.

- Toggle Video: `Ctrl + Shift + O`

- Turn your camera on or off during a video call. Managing video feeds can help maintain privacy and control over your presence in meetings.

3. Calendar and Meeting Shortcuts

- Schedule a Meeting: `Ctrl + Shift + N`

- Open the new meeting scheduling window to quickly set up meetings with your team members or clients.

- Join a Meeting: `Ctrl + J`

- Join a scheduled meeting directly from your calendar. This shortcut simplifies the process of entering meetings, ensuring you're always on time.

- Raise or Lower Hand: `Ctrl + Shift + K`

- During a meeting, use this shortcut to raise or lower your hand. This feature helps manage participation in larger meetings, allowing everyone a chance to speak.

4. General Productivity Shortcuts

- Mark as Read: `Ctrl + Shift + E`

- Mark selected messages or notifications as read. This helps manage your Activity feed and ensures you're not distracted by already-seen notifications.

- Mark as Unread: `Ctrl + Shift + U`

- Conversely, mark messages as unread if you need to revisit them later. This is useful for keeping track of important messages you need to address.

- Open Settings: `Ctrl + ,`

- Access the settings menu to customize your Teams experience, manage notifications, and configure your account preferences.

5. Teams and Channels Shortcuts

- Go to Previous Section: `Ctrl + Shift + F6`

- Navigate back to the previous section you were viewing. This is particularly useful when you need to switch between different parts of Teams quickly.

- Go to Next Section: `Ctrl + F6`

- Move to the next section within Teams. This shortcut helps you cycle through different areas of the application efficiently.

6. Message Formatting Shortcuts

- Bold: `Ctrl + B`

- Apply bold formatting to selected text in your messages. Bold text helps emphasize important points.

- Italic: `Ctrl + I`

- Italicize selected text to highlight key information or differentiate parts of your message.

- Underline: `Ctrl + U`

- Underline selected text for additional emphasis.

- Strikethrough: `Ctrl + Shift + X`

- Apply strikethrough formatting to show deletions or changes in your text.

- Code Block: `Ctrl + Shift + ``

- Format selected text as a code block. This is particularly useful for sharing snippets of code or highlighting specific commands.

- Quote Block: `Ctrl + Shift + >`

- Format selected text as a quote block to differentiate quoted content from your main message.

7. Command Box Shortcuts

- Go to Command Box: `Ctrl + /`

- Jump to the command box at the top of the Teams interface. This is a powerful tool for quickly performing actions, searching, and navigating within Teams.

- Search: `/search [term]`

- Use the search command followed by your query to find messages, files, or people quickly.

- Go to a Specific Team or Channel: `/goto [team/channel name]`

- Directly navigate to a specific team or channel using this command.

- Call a Contact: `/call [contact name]`

- Initiate a call to a specific contact directly from the command box.

- Send a Message: `/chat [contact name] [message]`

- Quickly send a message to a contact without navigating to the chat tab.

These essential shortcuts can significantly enhance your efficiency and productivity in Microsoft Teams. By incorporating these shortcuts into your daily workflow, you can navigate the platform more effortlessly, communicate more effectively, and ultimately get more done in less time.

9.1.2 Command Box Tricks

The command box in Microsoft Teams is a powerful tool that can significantly enhance your productivity and streamline your workflows. Located at the top of the app, the command box is more than just a search bar—it allows you to perform a wide variety of tasks quickly and efficiently. In this section, we will delve into the various tricks and tips for using the command box to its full potential.

Understanding the Command Box

The command box is designed to help you find information and perform actions without navigating through multiple menus. You can access the command box by clicking on it or pressing `Ctrl + E` on your keyboard. Once activated, you can type commands to search for people, files, messages, and perform various actions.

Basic Commands

1. Search for People, Files, and Messages

- Simply type the name of a person, file, or keyword related to a message, and Teams will display relevant results.

- Example: Typing "John Doe" will show all conversations, mentions, and files related to John Doe.

2. @ Commands

- Use the `@` symbol to access a range of commands. For instance, typing `@team` will bring up a list of available commands you can use.

- Example: `@Files` allows you to quickly access and open your recent files.

Advanced Command Box Tricks

1. Navigating Quickly

- /goto [team or channel name]: Quickly navigate to a specific team or channel without having to scroll through your list.

- Example: `/goto Marketing Team` takes you directly to the Marketing Team channel.

2. Setting Status

- /available: Set your status to available.

- /busy: Set your status to busy.

- /dnd: Set your status to do not disturb.

- /away: Set your status to away.

- Example: Typing `/dnd` changes your status to Do Not Disturb.

3. Starting a Chat or Call

- /chat [name]: Start a new chat with a specific person.

- /call [name]: Initiate a call with a team member.

- Example: `/chat Jane Doe` opens a new chat window with Jane Doe.

4. Managing Calendar

- /calendar: View your calendar.

- /meeting: Schedule a new meeting.

- Example: Typing `/meeting` will open the schedule meeting window.

5. Finding Files

- /files: Access your recent files.

- /find [file name or keyword]: Search for a specific file.

- Example: `/find budget report` searches for any files related to the budget report.

Using Command Shortcuts Efficiently

1. Combining Commands

- Combine multiple commands for faster workflows.

- Example: `/goto Sales Team` followed by `/files` will quickly take you to the Sales Team channel and open the files tab.

2. Custom Commands

- Create custom commands to suit your workflow needs. For example, if you frequently need to check your mentions, you can set a custom command for it.

- Example: Create a custom command like `/mentions` to quickly view all your mentions.

3. Shortcut Keys

- Use keyboard shortcuts in conjunction with command box commands to enhance efficiency.

- Example: Press `Ctrl + E` to focus on the command box, then type `/call [name]` to initiate a call.

Enhancing Collaboration with Command Box

1. Team Announcements

   - Use the command box to quickly make team-wide announcements.

   - Example: `/goto General` followed by a message can be used to announce important updates.

2. Managing Tasks

   - /tasks: View and manage your tasks.

   - /planner: Access Microsoft Planner to manage your tasks.

   - Example: `/planner` opens the Planner tab where you can organize tasks.

3. Checking Activity

   - /activity: View your activity feed.

   - /unread: See all your unread messages.

   - Example: `/unread` displays all the messages you haven't read yet.

Streamlining Daily Operations

1. Daily Stand-Ups

   - Use the command box to set up daily stand-up meetings.

   - Example: `/meeting` followed by details can schedule a recurring daily stand-up.

2. Project Updates

   - /update [project name]: Send quick updates about specific projects.

   - Example: `/update Project Phoenix` sends an update to the Project Phoenix team channel.

3. Team Polls

- /poll [question] [options]: Create quick polls to get team input.

- Example: `/poll "Which project should we prioritize?" "Project A" "Project B" "Project C"`.

Productivity Enhancements

1. Customizing Notifications

- /settings: Access and customize your notification settings.

- Example: `/settings notifications` allows you to adjust how you receive notifications.

2. Using Bots and Apps

- /bots: List and interact with bots available in Teams.

- /app [app name]: Access specific apps within Teams.

- Example: `/app Trello` opens the Trello app where you can manage your Trello boards.

3. Automating Routine Tasks

- Integrate with Power Automate to automate routine tasks.

- Example: Use `/goto Power Automate` to create flows that automate repetitive tasks like sending reminders or updating spreadsheets.

Optimizing Team Interactions

1. Effective Communication

- /mention [team member]: Use @mentions effectively to get someone's attention.

- Example: `/mention John Doe` highlights John Doe in a message.

2. Organizing Teams

- Use the command box to quickly create and organize teams and channels.

- Example: `/create team "New Project Team"` followed by `/goto "New Project Team"` to start organizing.

3. Tagging and Filtering

- Use tags to categorize and filter messages.

- Example: `/tag @Important` to quickly access all important messages.

Command Box Best Practices

1. Regular Practice

- Regularly practice using the command box to become proficient.

- Example: Spend a few minutes each day exploring new commands.

2. Staying Updated

- Keep up with updates and new commands added to Teams.

- Example: Follow Microsoft Teams updates to learn about new command features.

3. Sharing Knowledge

- Share useful commands and tricks with your team to enhance overall productivity.

- Example: Conduct a short training session on using the command box effectively.

Conclusion

The command box in Microsoft Teams is a versatile tool that, when used effectively, can greatly enhance your efficiency and streamline your workflows. By mastering the various commands and integrating them into your daily operations, you can optimize team collaboration, manage tasks more effectively, and enhance overall productivity. Whether you are navigating quickly, setting your status, starting chats, managing files, or integrating third-party apps, the command box is your go-to feature for a seamless Teams experience. Regular practice, staying updated with new features, and sharing knowledge with your team will ensure that you harness the full potential of this powerful tool.

9.1.3 Customizing Shortcuts

Customizing keyboard shortcuts in Microsoft Teams can significantly enhance your productivity by allowing you to perform actions quickly and efficiently. While Microsoft Teams offers a comprehensive set of predefined keyboard shortcuts, customizing them to fit your workflow can make navigating the platform even smoother. This section provides a detailed guide on how to customize keyboard shortcuts in Microsoft Teams.

1. Understanding the Importance of Customization

Customizing keyboard shortcuts can be crucial for several reasons:

- Efficiency: Custom shortcuts can streamline your workflow by reducing the number of steps required to perform a task.

- Comfort: Personalized shortcuts can reduce the strain of using default combinations that might be awkward or hard to remember.

- Productivity: Tailoring shortcuts to your specific needs can speed up repetitive tasks and free up time for more critical activities.

2. Accessing the Keyboard Shortcuts Menu

To begin customizing keyboard shortcuts in Microsoft Teams:

- Open Microsoft Teams and sign in with your credentials.

- Click on your profile picture in the top-right corner to open the menu.

- Select "Settings" from the dropdown list.

- Navigate to the "Keyboard Shortcuts" tab.

3. Customizing Common Shortcuts

Here are some common shortcuts that you might want to customize:

- Navigating to Teams: The default shortcut is `Ctrl + 3`. You can change it to something more intuitive for you, such as `Ctrl + T`.

- Starting a New Chat: The default shortcut is `Ctrl + N`. If this conflicts with another application you frequently use, you might change it to `Ctrl + Shift + N`.

- Opening the Command Box: The default shortcut is `Ctrl + /`. If you use the command box frequently, you might prefer a simpler combination, like `Ctrl + B`.

To customize a shortcut:

- Click on the action you want to change.

- Press the new key combination you want to assign.

- Confirm the change.

4. Creating New Shortcuts

In addition to modifying existing shortcuts, you can also create new shortcuts for actions that do not have predefined combinations. Here's how:

- In the "Keyboard Shortcuts" menu, click on the "Add New Shortcut" button.

- Select the action you want to create a shortcut for from the dropdown menu.

- Enter your desired key combination.

- Save your new shortcut.

Some useful actions to consider adding shortcuts for include:

- Mute/Unmute Microphone: Useful during meetings to quickly toggle your microphone.

- Toggle Camera: Quickly turn your camera on or off during video calls.

- Open Files: Directly access your files tab with a shortcut.

5. Managing Conflicts

Sometimes, your customized shortcuts might conflict with existing ones or other applications. When a conflict occurs:

- Teams will notify you of the conflict and suggest resolving it.

- You can either change your new shortcut or reassign the conflicting one.

- Ensure that the new combination does not interfere with other essential shortcuts you use regularly.

6. Best Practices for Customizing Shortcuts

- Consistency: Use similar key combinations for related actions to make them easier to remember. For instance, use `Ctrl + Shift + [key]` for all actions related to chat.

- Avoid Overcomplication: While it might be tempting to create shortcuts for every possible action, focus on the ones you use most frequently.

- Test Thoroughly: After customizing your shortcuts, spend some time using them to ensure they feel intuitive and do not interfere with your workflow.

7. Example Custom Shortcuts Setup

Here's an example of a custom shortcuts setup that enhances productivity:

- Ctrl + T: Navigate to Teams

- Ctrl + Shift + C: Start a new Chat

- Ctrl + Alt + F: Open Files

- Ctrl + M: Mute/Unmute Microphone

- Ctrl + Shift + V: Toggle Camera

- Ctrl + B: Open the Command Box

8. Customizing Shortcuts for Accessibility

For users with accessibility needs, customizing shortcuts can make using Teams more manageable. Consider these tips:

- Simplify Combinations: Use fewer keys to minimize strain.

- Voice Commands: Combine custom shortcuts with voice command software for an even smoother experience.

- Test Different Setups: Experiment with various configurations to find the most comfortable setup.

9. Exporting and Sharing Custom Shortcuts

If you find a setup that works exceptionally well, you might want to share it with colleagues or use it on multiple devices:

- Currently, Teams does not have a built-in feature for exporting shortcuts. However, you can manually document your custom shortcuts.

- Create a reference guide or a text document listing your shortcuts.

- Share this document with your team or save it for future reference.

10. Staying Updated with New Features

Microsoft Teams regularly updates its features, including keyboard shortcuts. To ensure you're making the most of new functionality:

- Regularly check the "What's New" section in Teams.

- Subscribe to Microsoft Teams blogs or forums for updates.

- Revisit your shortcuts periodically to incorporate any new actions or features.

Conclusion

Customizing keyboard shortcuts in Microsoft Teams is a powerful way to enhance your productivity and streamline your workflow. By understanding the importance of customization, accessing the keyboard shortcuts menu, managing conflicts, and following best practices, you can create a set of shortcuts that significantly improves your efficiency. Whether you're navigating teams, starting chats, or managing calls, tailored shortcuts can make your experience with Microsoft Teams smoother and more enjoyable. Keep experimenting and adjusting your shortcuts as your needs evolve, and stay updated with new features to continually optimize your setup.

9.2 Enhancing Team Collaboration

9.2.1 Using @Mentions Effectively

Microsoft Teams provides various features that enhance team collaboration, one of the most effective being the use of @mentions. This feature allows you to grab the attention of specific team members or entire teams within a conversation, ensuring that the right people are notified about important messages. Mastering @mentions can significantly boost communication efficiency and ensure that important information does not get overlooked.

1. Understanding @Mentions

@Mentions in Microsoft Teams can be used in chats, channels, and even in meeting chats. When you type "@" followed by a person's name, Teams will suggest matches from your organization, including team members, groups, and even whole teams. Once you select a name, it will highlight that person in the message and send them a notification.

2. Types of @Mentions

There are several types of @mentions you can use in Teams:

- Individual Mentions: To get the attention of a specific person. Example: `@John Doe`

- Channel Mentions: To notify everyone in a specific channel. Example: `@General`

- Team Mentions: To notify all members of a team. Example: `@Marketing Team`

3. Best Practices for Using @Mentions

To make the most out of @mentions without overwhelming your colleagues, it's important to follow best practices.

a. Be Selective

Use @mentions selectively to avoid overwhelming your colleagues with notifications. Overuse can lead to notification fatigue, where important messages get lost in a sea of alerts. Reserve @mentions for genuinely important updates, urgent questions, or when a response is required from specific individuals or groups.

b. Be Specific

When mentioning individuals, make sure the context of the message is clear. Rather than a vague "@Jane, please handle this," provide specifics: "@Jane, can you please update the sales report with the latest figures by EOD?" This clarity helps the mentioned person understand what is required and why they are being tagged.

c. Mentioning Channels vs. Teams

Use channel mentions when you need the attention of all members within a specific channel, and team mentions when the information is relevant to the entire team. Channel mentions help keep the communication focused and relevant to the topic of the channel, while team mentions are useful for broader announcements.

4. Advanced Tips for Effective @Mentions

To enhance the effectiveness of your @mentions, consider these advanced tips:

a. Combining Mentions with Actions

Combine @mentions with clear action items to enhance productivity. For instance, instead of just tagging someone, provide a clear action: "@John, can you approve the budget report by 3 PM?" This approach ensures that the mentioned person knows exactly what is expected.

b. Highlighting Important Messages

Use @mentions to highlight important messages in threads. In busy channels, important information can get buried. By @mentioning relevant individuals or groups, you ensure that critical messages stand out and receive the attention they deserve.

c. Using Mentions in Announcements

When making announcements, especially in larger teams, use @mentions to ensure everyone is aware. For instance, in a team-wide announcement about an upcoming meeting, you could say: "@Marketing Team, please note that our next meeting is scheduled for Monday at 10 AM. Agenda items should be submitted by Friday."

5. Managing Notifications

To avoid being overwhelmed by notifications from @mentions, you can customize your notification settings in Teams. Go to your profile picture, select "Settings," and then "Notifications." Here, you can manage how and when you get notified about mentions, ensuring you stay focused without missing important updates.

a. Notification Settings

Teams offers granular notification settings where you can choose how you want to be notified about @mentions – via banner (pop-up notification), email, or both. You can also mute notifications for specific channels or set priority notifications for critical channels and individuals.

b. Quiet Hours

Set quiet hours to ensure you are not disturbed during non-working hours. This can be particularly useful to maintain a healthy work-life balance, ensuring you only receive @mention notifications during your working hours.

6. Encouraging Effective Use Among Team Members

Promote best practices within your team for using @mentions effectively. Conduct training sessions or share guidelines on how to use @mentions appropriately to enhance communication and collaboration.

a. Training Sessions

Organize short training sessions to educate team members on the effective use of @mentions. Demonstrate different scenarios where @mentions can be beneficial and explain the potential downsides of overusing them.

b. Creating Guidelines

Draft a simple set of guidelines on using @mentions and share it with your team. Include best practices, examples of when to use individual, channel, and team mentions, and tips on managing notifications to avoid disruption.

7. Case Studies and Examples

Let's look at a few real-world examples to understand the impact of using @mentions effectively:

a. Example 1: Project Management

In a project management context, @mentions can streamline communication. For instance, a project manager could say: "@Team, please review the project timeline and provide your feedback by tomorrow EOD." This ensures that all team members are aware of the task and the deadline.

b. Example 2: Issue Resolution

When resolving issues, direct @mentions can expedite the process. If there's a technical problem, an IT manager might say: "@IT Support, we are experiencing network issues. Can someone check and resolve this ASAP?" This direct approach ensures the issue is addressed promptly.

c. Example 3: Collaborative Work

In collaborative document editing, @mentions can guide contributions. For example, in a shared document review, a team member might comment: "@John, can you update the sales figures in section 2.3?" This specificity ensures that the right person addresses the right section.

Conclusion

Mastering the use of @mentions in Microsoft Teams can dramatically improve your team's communication and collaboration efficiency. By being selective and specific, combining mentions with clear actions, and managing notifications effectively, you can leverage this powerful feature to keep everyone informed and engaged without overwhelming them with unnecessary alerts. Encourage your team to adopt these practices, and you will notice a significant improvement in how information flows and how quickly tasks get accomplished in your organization.

9.2.2 Organizing Teams and Channels

Organizing teams and channels effectively in Microsoft Teams is crucial for maintaining clarity, improving communication, and ensuring that your team's collaboration is as efficient as possible. Proper organization can help streamline workflows, minimize confusion, and make it easier for team members to find the information they need. This section will guide you through best practices and tips for organizing teams and channels in Microsoft Teams.

Understanding Teams and Channels

In Microsoft Teams, a "Team" is a group of people working together on a project or a department. Each team contains "Channels," which are dedicated sections for specific topics, projects, or departments. Channels help segment conversations and content, making it easier to focus on relevant information without getting overwhelmed by unrelated discussions.

1. Structuring Your Teams

The first step in organizing Teams is to structure your teams based on your organization's needs. Here are some common approaches:

- Functional Teams: Create teams based on different functions or departments within your organization (e.g., Marketing, Sales, HR).

- Project-Based Teams: Create teams for specific projects where members from various departments collaborate (e.g., Product Launch, Website Redesign).

- Client-Based Teams: If you work with multiple clients, create separate teams for each client to keep their information and communication isolated.

2. Creating and Naming Channels

Once you have structured your teams, the next step is to create channels within each team. Channels should be created based on specific topics or projects to ensure discussions remain focused. Here are some tips for creating and naming channels:

- Use Clear and Descriptive Names: Channel names should clearly indicate their purpose (e.g., "Marketing Campaigns," "Weekly Reports," "Client Feedback").

- Avoid Overlapping Topics: Ensure that each channel covers a distinct topic to prevent confusion and overlap.

- Standardize Naming Conventions: Use a consistent naming convention across your organization (e.g., prefixing project channels with "Proj-" or department channels with "Dept-").

3. Utilizing Standard Channels vs. Private Channels

Microsoft Teams offers two types of channels: Standard and Private. Understanding when to use each type is essential for effective organization.

- Standard Channels: These channels are open to all team members and are ideal for general discussions and content sharing.

- Private Channels: These channels are accessible only to specific members within the team and are suitable for sensitive discussions or confidential projects.

4. Pinning Important Channels

To ensure that critical channels are easily accessible, you can pin them to the top of your channel list. This is especially useful for frequently accessed channels or those that contain important information.

- How to Pin a Channel: Right-click on the channel name and select "Pin." Pinned channels will appear at the top of your channel list for quick access.

5. Using Channel Descriptions and Tabs

Enhance the functionality of your channels by utilizing channel descriptions and tabs.

- Channel Descriptions: Provide a brief description of the channel's purpose in the channel settings. This helps new members understand the channel's context.

- Tabs: Add tabs to channels to link directly to important files, websites, or applications. Common tabs include "Files," "OneNote," "Planner," and "Power BI."

6. Managing Channel Notifications

Channel notifications help team members stay informed about relevant discussions without being overwhelmed by constant alerts.

- Customizing Notifications: Members can customize their notification settings for each channel by clicking on the channel name, selecting "Channel Notifications," and choosing their preferences (e.g., all new posts, only mentions).

- Using Mentions: Encourage the use of @mentions to notify specific members or the entire team about important messages. This ensures that notifications are targeted and relevant.

7. Archiving Inactive Channels

As projects conclude or topics become less relevant, it's important to archive inactive channels to keep your workspace organized.

- Archiving Channels: While Microsoft Teams doesn't have a direct archive feature for channels, you can achieve this by creating a separate team for archived content or by moving old discussions to a designated "Archive" channel within the team.

8. Implementing Governance Policies

To maintain long-term organization and consistency, implement governance policies for creating, managing, and archiving teams and channels.

- Team and Channel Creation: Define who has the authority to create new teams and channels. Consider restricting this ability to team owners or specific roles.

- Naming Conventions: Establish and enforce standardized naming conventions for teams and channels.

- Review and Cleanup: Periodically review and clean up teams and channels to ensure they remain relevant and organized.

9. Training and Onboarding

Ensure that all team members understand the best practices for organizing teams and channels by providing training and onboarding resources.

- Training Sessions: Conduct regular training sessions to educate team members on how to effectively use and organize Teams.

- Documentation: Create and share documentation or guides that outline your organization's standards and practices for Teams.

10. Leveraging External Collaboration

If your team frequently collaborates with external partners or clients, ensure that your organization practices support seamless external collaboration while maintaining security.

- Guest Access: Use the guest access feature to allow external users to join specific teams and channels. Configure appropriate permissions to safeguard sensitive information.

- Channel Policies: Define and enforce policies for external collaboration to ensure consistent practices and security measures are followed.

11. Using Tags for Enhanced Collaboration

Tags in Microsoft Teams allow you to group users and easily mention them in conversations. This is especially useful for large teams or cross-functional projects.

- Creating Tags: Team owners can create tags by going to the team settings and selecting "Tags." Tags can represent roles, departments, or project groups (e.g., @Developers, @Marketing).

- Using Tags in Conversations: Use tags in your messages to notify all members associated with that tag. For example, typing @Developers in a message will notify all users tagged as developers.

12. Regular Audits and Feedback

Regularly audit your teams and channels to ensure they remain well-organized and solicit feedback from team members to continuously improve collaboration.

- Audit Schedule: Set a regular schedule for auditing teams and channels, such as quarterly reviews.

- Feedback Mechanism: Create a feedback mechanism, such as surveys or suggestion boxes, to gather input from team members on how to improve organization and collaboration.

Conclusion

Organizing teams and channels effectively in Microsoft Teams is vital for efficient collaboration and communication. By following these best practices and tips, you can create a well-structured environment that supports your team's needs and enhances productivity. Regularly review and refine your organization strategies to ensure they continue to meet your team's evolving requirements. With a well-organized Teams setup, you can leverage the full potential of Microsoft Teams to drive success in your projects and daily operations.

9.2.3 Leveraging Tags and Filters

In Microsoft Teams, tags and filters are powerful tools that enhance team collaboration by organizing conversations, streamlining communication, and ensuring that important information is easily accessible. This section will explore the benefits and best practices for using tags and filters effectively in your Teams environment.

Understanding Tags in Microsoft Teams

Tags in Microsoft Teams allow you to group users based on certain criteria or roles, making it easier to communicate with specific subsets of your team. For example, you can create tags for departments like "Marketing," "Sales," or "HR," or for roles such as "Managers" or "Project Leads." Once tags are created, you can use them to quickly reach out to all members associated with a tag.

Creating and Managing Tags

1. Creating Tags:

- To create a tag, go to the team you want to add the tag to.

- Click on the three dots (ellipsis) next to the team name and select "Manage tags."

- Click "Create tag" and enter a name for the tag.

- Add members to the tag by searching for their names and selecting them from the list.

- Click "Create" to save the tag.

2. Managing Tags:

- You can manage tags by going to the "Manage tags" option within your team.

- Here, you can edit the tag name, add or remove members, and delete tags that are no longer needed.

- Regularly review and update tags to ensure they reflect the current team structure and communication needs.

Using Tags for Communication

1. Tagging Users in Conversations:

- To use a tag in a conversation, type "@" followed by the tag name.

- For example, typing "@Marketing" will notify all users assigned to the "Marketing" tag.

- This ensures that everyone in the tagged group receives the message, reducing the chances of important information being missed.

2. Tagging Users in Meetings:

- When scheduling a meeting, you can use tags to invite specific groups.

- In the "Add required attendees" field, type the tag name, and Teams will automatically populate the list with users assigned to that tag.

- This makes it easier to schedule meetings with specific departments or roles without manually adding each participant.

Benefits of Using Tags

1. Streamlined Communication:

- Tags allow you to quickly reach out to specific groups, reducing the time spent on individually addressing team members.

- This is especially useful for large teams where communicating with the entire team might not be necessary.

2. Improved Organization:

- Tags help keep conversations organized by grouping users based on relevant criteria.

- This makes it easier to manage and follow up on discussions related to specific topics or projects.

3. Enhanced Engagement:

- By targeting messages to specific groups, you can ensure that the right people are engaged in relevant conversations.

- This leads to more meaningful interactions and better collaboration.

Understanding Filters in Microsoft Teams

Filters in Microsoft Teams help you sort and find information quickly. Whether you're looking for a specific message, file, or conversation, filters can save you time and improve your overall efficiency.

Using Filters to Find Information

1. Filtering Messages:

- To filter messages, go to the "Activity" feed or a specific channel.

- Click on the funnel icon (filter) in the top-right corner.

- You can filter messages by various criteria such as unread messages, mentions, replies, and more.

- This helps you quickly locate important conversations and ensure nothing is overlooked.

2. Filtering Files:

- In the "Files" tab, use the search bar and filter options to find specific documents.

- You can filter files by type (e.g., Word, Excel, PDF), date modified, and more.

- This is particularly useful for teams that share a large number of files, making it easier to find what you need without scrolling through endless lists.

3. Filtering Tasks and Assignments:

- If your team uses the Planner or Tasks app, you can filter tasks by criteria such as due date, priority, and assigned user.

- This helps you stay on top of your to-do list and manage tasks more effectively.

Advanced Filtering Techniques

1. Combining Filters:

- You can combine multiple filters to narrow down your search results.

- For example, you can filter messages to show only unread mentions from a specific date range.

- This level of granularity helps you find exactly what you're looking for, even in the busiest of channels.

2. Using Keywords and Phrases:

- When filtering messages or files, you can use specific keywords or phrases to refine your search.

- This is particularly useful for finding information related to specific projects, clients, or topics.

3. Saving Filtered Views:

- Some filtering options allow you to save your filtered views for quick access later.

- For example, in the Planner app, you can save a filtered view of tasks assigned to you, making it easier to track your responsibilities.

Best Practices for Using Tags and Filters

1. Consistency is Key:

- Ensure that tags are created and used consistently across your team.

- Establish guidelines for tag names and usage to avoid confusion and duplication.

2. Regular Maintenance:

- Periodically review and update tags to ensure they remain relevant.

- Remove or rename tags that are no longer in use or have become redundant.

3. Training and Awareness:

- Provide training to team members on how to use tags and filters effectively.

- Encourage the use of these features to enhance communication and collaboration.

4. Leverage Automation:

- Consider using automation tools to manage tags and filters more efficiently.

- For example, Power Automate can be used to automatically assign tags based on specific criteria or events.

5. Monitor Usage and Feedback:

- Regularly monitor how tags and filters are being used within your team.

- Gather feedback from team members to identify areas for improvement and ensure that these features are meeting their needs.

By leveraging tags and filters in Microsoft Teams, you can significantly enhance your team's collaboration and productivity. These tools help organize communication, streamline workflows, and ensure that important information is easily accessible to those who need it. Implementing best practices and maintaining a consistent approach to using tags and filters will maximize their effectiveness and contribute to a more efficient and engaged team.

9.3 Productivity Hacks

9.3.1 Streamlining Workflows

Streamlining workflows in Microsoft Teams can significantly enhance productivity and efficiency, making team collaboration smoother and more effective. This section will explore various strategies and best practices for optimizing workflows within Microsoft Teams.

Understanding Workflows in Microsoft Teams

A workflow is a sequence of tasks that processes a set of data. In the context of Microsoft Teams, workflows can range from simple task assignments to complex project management processes. By streamlining these workflows, you can reduce redundancy, minimize errors, and ensure that tasks are completed in a timely and efficient manner.

Leveraging Built-in Tools

Microsoft Teams offers several built-in tools that can help streamline workflows. These tools are designed to facilitate collaboration, task management, and communication.

1. Planner

- Creating and Assigning Tasks: Use Planner to create tasks, assign them to team members, and set deadlines. This helps ensure that everyone knows what they need to do and when.

- Tracking Progress: Visualize task progress using boards and charts. This allows team members to see at a glance what tasks are pending, in progress, or completed.

- Integrating with Teams: Add Planner tabs to your Teams channels to keep task management integrated within your collaboration space.

2. To-Do

- Personal Task Management: Use Microsoft To-Do for managing your personal tasks and deadlines. This can help you stay on top of your work and ensure that you don't miss important tasks.

- Syncing with Planner: Sync tasks between To-Do and Planner for a seamless experience. This integration ensures that you have a consolidated view of all your tasks, whether they are personal or team-related.

3. OneNote

- Centralized Note-Taking: Use OneNote for taking meeting notes, documenting processes, and keeping track of important information. OneNote's integration with Teams allows you to easily access and share notes within your channels.

- Organizing Information: Organize notes into sections and pages, making it easy to find and reference information when needed.

Automating Workflows with Power Automate

Power Automate (formerly known as Microsoft Flow) is a powerful tool that allows you to automate workflows and integrate different applications. By setting up automated workflows, you can save time and reduce the likelihood of errors.

1. Creating Flows

- Templates: Use pre-built templates to quickly set up common workflows, such as sending notifications, creating tasks, or syncing data between applications.

- Custom Flows: Build custom flows tailored to your specific needs. Define triggers, actions, and conditions to automate complex processes.

2. Common Use Cases

- Automated Notifications: Set up flows to send automated notifications in Teams when certain events occur, such as a new task being assigned or a deadline approaching.

- Data Syncing: Use flows to sync data between Teams and other applications, such as SharePoint, OneDrive, or external databases. This ensures that everyone has access to the latest information.

- Approval Workflows: Create approval workflows that route documents or requests to the appropriate individuals for review and approval. This helps streamline decision-making processes and ensures that approvals are documented and tracked.

Integrating Third-Party Apps

Microsoft Teams supports integration with a wide range of third-party apps, which can further enhance your workflows and productivity.

1. Project Management Tools

- Trello: Integrate Trello boards with Teams to manage tasks and projects. This allows you to access Trello boards directly within Teams and collaborate with your team more effectively.

- Asana: Use Asana's integration to manage tasks and projects without leaving Teams. This helps ensure that your project management processes are centralized and easily accessible.

2. Communication Tools

- Zoom: Integrate Zoom with Teams to schedule and join Zoom meetings directly from Teams. This can be particularly useful if your organization uses Zoom for video conferencing.

- Slack: Use Slack integration to bridge communication between Teams and Slack. This ensures that messages and updates are shared across both platforms, reducing communication silos.

3. File Management Tools

- Dropbox: Integrate Dropbox with Teams to access and share files stored in Dropbox. This allows you to collaborate on files without switching between applications.

- Google Drive: Use Google Drive integration to access and share files stored in Google Drive. This can be particularly useful if your team uses Google Workspace.

Best Practices for Streamlining Workflows

To effectively streamline workflows in Microsoft Teams, it's important to follow best practices and continuously evaluate and optimize your processes.

1. Standardize Processes

- Document Workflows: Document your workflows and processes to ensure that everyone on your team follows the same procedures. This helps maintain consistency and reduces confusion.

- Create Templates: Use templates for common tasks and processes, such as project plans, meeting agendas, and reports. This saves time and ensures that important information is not overlooked.

2. Encourage Collaboration

- Use Channels Effectively: Organize your Teams channels based on projects, departments, or topics. This helps keep discussions focused and makes it easier to find relevant information.

- Foster Open Communication: Encourage team members to communicate openly and share updates regularly. This helps ensure that everyone is on the same page and can collaborate effectively.

3. Monitor and Adjust Workflows

- Collect Feedback: Regularly collect feedback from team members on the effectiveness of your workflows. Use this feedback to make improvements and address any pain points.

- Analyze Performance: Use Teams analytics and reporting tools to monitor the performance of your workflows. Identify areas where you can improve efficiency and make data-driven decisions.

4. Train Your Team

- Provide Training Resources: Ensure that your team has access to training resources and documentation on how to use Teams and its features. This helps team members become more proficient and self-sufficient.

- Offer Ongoing Support: Provide ongoing support and assistance to help team members with any issues or questions they may have. This helps ensure that everyone can use Teams effectively.

Case Study: Streamlining Workflows in a Marketing Team

To illustrate the concepts discussed in this section, let's consider a case study of a marketing team using Microsoft Teams to streamline their workflows.

1. Setting Up the Team

- The marketing team creates a Team in Microsoft Teams, with channels for different projects, such as "Campaigns," "Content Creation," and "Analytics."

- They use Planner to create tasks for each project, assign them to team members, and set deadlines. This helps ensure that everyone knows what they need to do and when.

2. Automating Notifications

- The team sets up a Power Automate flow to send notifications in the "Campaigns" channel whenever a new task is created or updated in Planner. This keeps everyone informed of task progress without needing to manually check Planner.

3. Integrating Tools

- The team integrates Trello with Teams to manage their content calendar. They use a Trello board to plan and schedule content, and the integration allows them to access the board directly within Teams.

- They also integrate Dropbox with Teams to store and share large media files. This allows team members to collaborate on files without switching between applications.

4. Monitoring Performance

- The team uses Teams analytics to monitor the performance of their workflows. They track task completion rates, project timelines, and communication patterns to identify areas for improvement.

- They regularly review their processes and make adjustments based on feedback and performance data. This helps ensure that their workflows remain efficient and effective.

Conclusion

Streamlining workflows in Microsoft Teams is essential for maximizing productivity and efficiency. By leveraging built-in tools, automating processes with Power Automate, integrating third-party apps, and following best practices, you can optimize your team's workflows and enhance collaboration. Regularly evaluate and adjust your workflows to ensure they continue to meet your team's needs, and provide ongoing training and support to help your team make the most of Microsoft Teams.

9.3.2 Automating Repetitive Tasks

Automating repetitive tasks in Microsoft Teams can greatly enhance productivity, reduce errors, and save time. This section provides detailed guidance on how to automate various tasks using built-in tools and integrations.

Understanding the Need for Automation

In a busy work environment, many tasks are repetitive and time-consuming. These tasks include sending routine updates, scheduling meetings, managing tasks, and handling customer queries. Automating these processes helps streamline workflows, allowing you and your team to focus on more strategic activities. Automation in Microsoft Teams can be achieved through built-in features, Power Automate integrations, and third-party applications.

Getting Started with Power Automate

Power Automate, formerly known as Microsoft Flow, is a service that allows you to create automated workflows between your favorite apps and services to synchronize files, get notifications, collect data, and more. Here's how to get started with automating tasks in Microsoft Teams using Power Automate:

1. Access Power Automate: Navigate to [Power Automate](https://flow.microsoft.com) and sign in with your Microsoft account. If you don't have an account, you can create one.

2. Explore Templates: Power Automate offers numerous templates to help you get started quickly. These templates cover common scenarios such as sending notifications, creating tasks, and managing approvals.

3. Create a Flow:

- From a Template: Select a template that fits your need, such as "Post a message to Teams for a selected item."

- From Scratch: If no template fits your need, you can create a flow from scratch by selecting "Create" from the menu and choosing "Automated flow" or "Instant flow."

Automating Common Tasks in Microsoft Teams

1. Automating Notifications:

- Scenario: You want to receive a notification in Teams whenever a new email arrives in your inbox from a specific sender.

- Solution: Use the template "When a new email arrives in Office 365, post a message to Microsoft Teams."

  - Steps:

    1. Select the template and connect your Office 365 and Teams accounts.

    2. Specify the email address of the sender in the filter condition.

    3. Customize the message that will be posted to the Teams channel.

2. Scheduling and Reminders:

- Scenario: You need to set reminders for upcoming meetings and deadlines.

- Solution: Create a flow that sends reminder messages to Teams channels.

  - Steps:

    1. Create a new flow and select "Scheduled flow."

    2. Set the schedule for reminders, e.g., daily at 9 AM.

3. Add an action to "Post a message in a chat or channel" and customize the reminder message.

3. Task Management:

- Scenario: You want to automate the creation of tasks in Microsoft Planner from messages in Teams.

- Solution: Use the "Create a task in Planner from Microsoft Teams" template.

- Steps:

1. Select the template and connect your Teams and Planner accounts.

2. Define the trigger, such as a new message in a specific channel.

3. Customize the task details, including title, due date, and assignee.

4. Approvals:

- Scenario: You need to streamline the approval process for documents or requests.

- Solution: Use the "Start an approval when a new item is added" template.

- Steps:

1. Select the template and connect to your SharePoint and Teams accounts.

2. Define the trigger, such as a new document added to a SharePoint library.

3. Configure the approval process and specify the approvers.

Using Bots for Automation

Bots can interact with users naturally in Microsoft Teams and automate various tasks. Some popular bots include:

1. T-Bot: Provides help and answers questions about using Microsoft Teams.

2. WhoBot: Helps you find information about people within your organization.

3. Workbot: Connects with various apps to automate workflows directly from Teams.

Creating Custom Bots

For advanced automation, you might consider creating custom bots using the Microsoft Bot Framework. Here's how to get started:

1. Set Up a Bot Framework Account: Register at [Azure Bot Service](https://azure.microsoft.com/en-us/services/bot-services/).

2. Develop Your Bot: Use the Bot Framework SDK to create your bot. You can use languages such as C, JavaScript, or Python.

3. Deploy Your Bot: Host your bot on Azure or another hosting service.

4. Integrate with Teams: Add your bot to Teams and configure it to respond to specific commands or messages.

Leveraging Third-Party Applications

Many third-party applications can be integrated with Microsoft Teams to automate tasks. Some popular ones include:

1. Trello: Automate task management by linking Trello boards to Teams channels.

2. Asana: Integrate Asana to automate project tracking and task assignments.

3. Zapier: Connect Teams with over 2000 apps to automate workflows.

Best Practices for Automation

1. Identify Repetitive Tasks: Start by identifying tasks that are repetitive and time-consuming. Prioritize those that will have the most significant impact when automated.

2. Test and Monitor: Before fully deploying automated workflows, test them to ensure they work as expected. Monitor their performance and make adjustments as needed.

3. Keep Security in Mind: Ensure that automated processes comply with your organization's security policies. Protect sensitive information and manage permissions carefully.

4. Document Workflows: Document your automated workflows so that others in your organization can understand and manage them.

5. Regularly Update and Maintain: Automation tools and processes should be regularly reviewed and updated to ensure they remain effective and relevant.

Conclusion

Automating repetitive tasks in Microsoft Teams can transform how you work, making your team more efficient and productive. By leveraging tools like Power Automate, integrating bots, and using third-party applications, you can automate a wide range of tasks, from notifications and reminders to complex approval processes. Follow best practices to ensure your automation efforts are secure, effective, and well-documented.

9.3.3 Using Templates and Pre-Sets

In the dynamic environment of modern workplaces, efficiency and productivity are paramount. One of the most effective ways to streamline tasks and processes in Microsoft Teams is through the use of templates and pre-sets. By creating reusable frameworks, users can save time, ensure consistency, and improve overall team coordination. This section provides a detailed guide on how to utilize templates and pre-sets in Microsoft Teams to maximize productivity.

Understanding Templates and Pre-Sets

Templates in Microsoft Teams are pre-designed layouts and structures for teams, channels, and tasks that can be reused across different projects and teams. They include pre-configured settings, apps, tabs, and files that provide a standardized way of setting up a new team or channel. Pre-sets refer to predefined settings and configurations for specific functionalities, such as meeting options, messaging policies, and task management.

Benefits of Using Templates and Pre-Sets

1. Time-Saving: By using templates, you eliminate the need to set up the same structure repeatedly for each new project or team, thus saving valuable time.

2. Consistency: Templates ensure that all teams and channels follow a standardized structure, which helps in maintaining uniformity across the organization.

3. Efficiency: Pre-sets streamline workflows by providing ready-made configurations for common tasks, reducing the need for manual adjustments.

4. Error Reduction: Using templates and pre-sets minimizes the chances of errors and omissions, as the predefined structures and settings are based on best practices.

Creating and Using Templates in Microsoft Teams

Step 1: Define the Template Structure

Before creating a template, outline the structure you want to replicate. Consider the following elements:

- Team and channel names

- Channel tabs (e.g., Files, Wiki, Planner)

- Pre-installed apps (e.g., OneNote, SharePoint)

- Default settings (e.g., permissions, privacy settings)

Step 2: Create a New Team as a Template

1. Open Microsoft Teams and go to the "Teams" tab.

2. Click on "Join or create a team" at the bottom of the teams list.

3. Select "Create team."

4. Choose "From scratch" or "From an existing team" if you want to replicate an existing structure.

5. Select the privacy settings for the team (private or public).

6. Add team members if necessary, though this step is optional for a template.

Step 3: Customize the Team

1. Add Channels: Create channels based on the structure you defined. To add a channel, click on the ellipsis (...) next to the team name and select "Add channel."

2. Configure Tabs: Add necessary tabs like Files, Planner, OneNote, etc., to each channel. This can be done by clicking on the "+" sign next to the existing tabs.

3. Install Apps: Integrate apps that will be used frequently. Go to "Apps" on the left sidebar and search for the required apps to install.

Step 4: Save the Team as a Template

1. Currently, Microsoft Teams does not provide a direct feature to save a team as a template. However, you can use the "Team cloning" feature.

2. To clone a team, click on the ellipsis (...) next to the team name, select "Manage team," then click on "Settings," and choose "Team code."

3. Share the team code with members who need to create a new team based on this template, or use it yourself to replicate the team structure.

Using Templates for Meetings and Tasks

Meeting Templates

1. Pre-Set Meeting Options: Configure default meeting options such as lobby settings, presenter permissions, and recording options.

2. Recurring Meetings: Set up recurring meetings with predefined agendas and participant lists to save time in scheduling regular team syncs or project updates.

3. Agenda Templates: Create templates for meeting agendas that can be reused for different meetings. Include sections for introductions, updates, discussions, and action items.

Task Management Templates

1. Planner Templates: Use Microsoft Planner to create task boards with predefined tasks and buckets. Once a planner board is set up, it can be used as a template for future projects.

2. Task Pre-Sets: Define standard tasks that need to be completed for specific types of projects. These tasks can be pre-set with deadlines, priorities, and assigned team members.

Automating Processes with Templates

Using Power Automate with Templates

Microsoft Power Automate (formerly Flow) can be used to automate repetitive tasks by leveraging templates and pre-sets. For example:

1. Automated Team Creation: Set up a flow that automatically creates a new team based on a template when a new project is initiated.

2. Task Automation: Automate task assignment and follow-ups by creating flows that trigger based on certain conditions, such as project milestones or deadlines.

Example Flow for Team Creation

1. Open Power Automate and create a new flow.

2. Choose a trigger, such as "When a new item is created" in a SharePoint list.

3. Add an action to "Create a team" in Microsoft Teams using the pre-defined template structure.

4. Configure additional actions, such as sending a welcome message to the new team members or setting up initial tasks in Planner.

Best Practices for Using Templates and Pre-Sets

1. Regularly Update Templates: Ensure that your templates are regularly updated to reflect changes in processes, tools, and organizational needs.

2. Document Template Usage: Provide documentation on how to use templates effectively. This can include guidelines on when to use which template and how to customize it for specific needs.

3. Feedback and Improvement: Gather feedback from team members on the templates and pre-sets. Use this feedback to make improvements and ensure that they meet the users' needs.

4. Training and Support: Offer training sessions and support to help team members understand how to utilize templates and pre-sets effectively.

Conclusion

Using templates and pre-sets in Microsoft Teams is a powerful way to enhance productivity and streamline workflows. By investing time in creating and maintaining these reusable structures, you can ensure consistency, save time, and reduce errors in your team's operations. Whether you are setting up new teams, organizing meetings, or managing tasks, leveraging templates and pre-sets will help you and your team work more efficiently and effectively.

CHAPTER X
Future of Microsoft Teams

10.1 Upcoming Features and Roadmap

10.1.1 Anticipated Updates

Microsoft Teams is an ever-evolving platform that continues to adapt to the needs of its users by regularly releasing updates and new features. As the digital workplace becomes more dynamic, Microsoft is committed to enhancing Teams to support better collaboration, communication, and productivity. This section will delve into the anticipated updates that are set to shape the future of Microsoft Teams, providing users with advanced tools and capabilities to stay ahead in the rapidly changing work environment.

AI-Powered Enhancements

Artificial Intelligence (AI) is at the forefront of technological advancements, and Microsoft Teams is set to incorporate more AI-powered features. These enhancements aim to make collaboration smarter and more efficient. One such anticipated update is the integration of advanced AI-based meeting assistants. These assistants will not only help schedule meetings but also provide real-time transcription and translation services, making meetings more inclusive and accessible to a global workforce.

Additionally, AI will play a significant role in improving task management within Teams. For instance, AI-driven task suggestions based on meeting discussions and chat conversations can help streamline workflows and ensure that important action items are not overlooked. This will be particularly beneficial in large teams where keeping track of tasks can be challenging.

Enhanced Video Conferencing Capabilities

As remote work continues to be a norm, video conferencing remains a critical component of Microsoft Teams. Microsoft is investing heavily in enhancing the video conferencing experience. Future updates will focus on improving video quality and reducing latency, ensuring smooth and uninterrupted meetings regardless of participants' locations.

One anticipated feature is the introduction of more immersive meeting environments. Virtual reality (VR) and augmented reality (AR) integrations are on the horizon, allowing for more engaging and interactive meetings. These technologies will enable users to create virtual meeting spaces, where they can collaborate on projects and documents as if they were in the same room. This will revolutionize the way remote teams work together.

Improved Integration with Microsoft 365 and Third-Party Apps

Microsoft Teams is a central hub for collaboration within the Microsoft 365 ecosystem. Future updates will see deeper integration with other Microsoft 365 applications such as Outlook, SharePoint, and OneDrive. This will provide a more seamless experience for users, allowing them to access and share information across different platforms without leaving Teams.

Moreover, Microsoft is working on expanding its app store with more third-party applications. The goal is to make Teams a one-stop solution for all business needs. Users can expect to see more industry-specific apps and tools that cater to their unique requirements. For example, there could be new integrations for project management, customer relationship management (CRM), and enterprise resource planning (ERP) systems.

Advanced Security and Compliance Features

As cyber threats become more sophisticated, ensuring the security and compliance of digital collaboration tools is paramount. Microsoft Teams will continue to enhance its security features to protect sensitive data and maintain compliance with industry standards and regulations. Future updates will include more robust encryption methods, advanced threat detection, and automated compliance reporting.

One anticipated update is the introduction of granular access controls. This feature will allow administrators to define specific permissions for different roles within the organization, ensuring that users only have access to the information they need. Additionally, Microsoft is working on improving data loss prevention (DLP) capabilities to prevent accidental sharing of sensitive information.

Personalization and Customization

To cater to the diverse needs of its user base, Microsoft Teams will introduce more personalization and customization options. Users will be able to tailor their Teams experience to match their preferences and work styles. This includes customizable dashboards, themes, and notification settings.

Moreover, Microsoft is exploring ways to make Teams more intuitive and user-friendly. Anticipated updates include the introduction of a more streamlined user interface, with easier navigation and better organization of features. This will help reduce the learning curve for new users and improve overall user satisfaction.

Enhanced Collaboration Tools

Collaboration is at the heart of Microsoft Teams, and future updates will focus on enhancing collaborative features. This includes improvements to shared document editing, making it easier for teams to work together on projects in real-time. Microsoft is also working on expanding the capabilities of its whiteboard feature, allowing for more interactive brainstorming sessions and visual collaboration.

Another exciting update is the introduction of collaborative apps within Teams. These apps will enable users to co-create content, such as presentations and reports, directly within the platform. This will eliminate the need to switch between different applications, making the collaboration process more efficient.

Analytics and Insights

To help organizations make data-driven decisions, Microsoft Teams will introduce more advanced analytics and insights. These tools will provide administrators and team leaders with detailed reports on team activity, meeting attendance, and collaboration patterns. This data can be used to identify areas for improvement and optimize team performance.

One anticipated feature is the integration of AI-driven insights. These insights will analyze user behavior and suggest ways to enhance productivity and collaboration. For example, if the system detects that meetings are frequently running over time, it might suggest strategies for more effective time management.

Support for Hybrid Work Environments

As hybrid work models become more prevalent, Microsoft Teams is adapting to support this new way of working. Future updates will include features specifically designed for hybrid work environments, where employees split their time between working remotely and in the office.

One such feature is the introduction of dynamic workspaces. These workspaces will allow teams to set up virtual offices that mimic physical office layouts. Employees can choose where they want to "sit" in the virtual office, fostering a sense of presence and camaraderie even when working remotely.

Enhanced Mobile Experience

Recognizing the importance of mobile accessibility, Microsoft is committed to improving the mobile experience of Teams. Future updates will focus on optimizing the mobile app for better performance and usability. This includes faster load times, improved navigation, and access to all essential features available on the desktop version.

Additionally, Microsoft is exploring ways to make mobile collaboration more effective. Anticipated updates include enhanced support for mobile document editing and integration with mobile productivity tools. This will ensure that users can stay productive even when they are away from their desks.

User Feedback and Continuous Improvement

Microsoft places a strong emphasis on user feedback and continuous improvement. Future updates to Microsoft Teams will be heavily influenced by user input, ensuring that the platform evolves to meet the needs of its users. Microsoft regularly gathers feedback through user surveys, focus groups, and the Teams UserVoice forum.

Users can expect to see a more transparent development process, with regular updates on new features and improvements. Microsoft is committed to keeping users informed and engaged, providing them with the tools and resources they need to make the most of Microsoft Teams.

10.1.2 Integration with Other Microsoft Products

Introduction

Integration with other Microsoft products is one of the most powerful aspects of Microsoft Teams. The seamless interoperability among various tools within the Microsoft ecosystem can significantly enhance productivity, streamline workflows, and create a more cohesive user experience. In this section, we will explore how Microsoft Teams integrates with other Microsoft products, the benefits of these integrations, and the anticipated updates that will further enhance these capabilities.

Microsoft 365 Suite

Microsoft Teams is a part of the larger Microsoft 365 suite, and its integration with other Microsoft 365 applications is foundational. This integration ensures that users can access and leverage a wide array of tools directly within Teams, making it a central hub for collaboration and productivity.

1. Outlook Integration

- Email and Calendar: Microsoft Teams integrates closely with Outlook, allowing users to schedule and manage meetings, access emails, and sync calendars. This integration means that any meeting scheduled in Teams will automatically appear in the Outlook calendar, and vice versa.

- Emails to Teams: Users can forward important emails directly to a Teams channel. This feature is particularly useful for keeping team members informed and ensuring that all relevant information is stored in one place.

2. SharePoint Integration

- Document Management: SharePoint serves as the backend for file storage in Microsoft Teams. When files are shared in a Teams channel, they are actually stored in SharePoint. This integration allows for robust document management capabilities, including version control, metadata tagging, and advanced search functionalities.

- Intranet Sites: SharePoint sites can be added as tabs within Teams channels, providing easy access to intranet resources, document libraries, and other SharePoint content.

3. OneDrive Integration

- Personal File Storage: OneDrive is integrated with Teams for personal file storage. Users can access their OneDrive files directly from Teams, making it easy to share personal documents with team members or collaborate on files in real-time.

- File Sharing: OneDrive files can be shared in chats and channels, and any changes made to these files are synced across all devices.

4. Microsoft Planner Integration

- Task Management: Microsoft Planner integrates with Teams to provide task management capabilities. Users can create and manage Planner tasks directly within Teams channels. These tasks can be assigned to team members, tracked for progress, and organized using buckets and labels.

- Task Visibility: Teams and Planner integration ensures that all tasks are visible to the relevant team members, fostering transparency and accountability.

5. Power BI Integration

- Data Visualization: Power BI reports and dashboards can be embedded in Teams channels, providing team members with access to critical data and insights without leaving the Teams environment.

- Interactive Reports: Users can interact with Power BI reports within Teams, drilling down into data, applying filters, and generating insights in real-time.

6. Microsoft Forms Integration

- Surveys and Polls: Microsoft Forms can be used to create surveys, quizzes, and polls within Teams. This integration is useful for gathering feedback, conducting assessments, and engaging team members in decision-making processes.

- Form Responses: Responses to forms are collected in real-time and can be analyzed within Teams or exported for further analysis.

7. Power Automate Integration

- Workflow Automation: Power Automate (formerly Microsoft Flow) integrates with Teams to automate repetitive tasks and workflows. Users can create automated flows that trigger actions based on specific events, such as new messages, file uploads, or task completions.

- Custom Workflows: Teams and Power Automate integration allows users to design custom workflows that connect Teams with other Microsoft 365 applications and third-party services, enhancing productivity and efficiency.

Benefits of Integration

1. Centralized Workspace

The integration of Microsoft Teams with other Microsoft products creates a centralized workspace where users can access all the tools they need without switching between applications. This centralization enhances productivity by reducing the time spent navigating between different platforms and streamlining workflows.

2. Enhanced Collaboration

By integrating with tools like SharePoint, OneDrive, and Planner, Microsoft Teams fosters enhanced collaboration among team members. Documents can be co-authored in real-time, tasks can be managed collectively, and critical data can be shared seamlessly, leading to more efficient teamwork.

3. Improved Communication

Integrations with Outlook and Microsoft Forms improve communication within teams. Users can schedule meetings, send emails, and gather feedback directly within Teams, ensuring that all communication is consolidated and easily accessible.

4. Data-Driven Decision Making

Power BI integration empowers teams to make data-driven decisions by providing access to interactive reports and dashboards. Teams can analyze data in real-time, track performance metrics, and generate insights that inform strategic decisions.

5. Workflow Automation

Power Automate integration allows users to automate repetitive tasks and workflows, reducing manual effort and increasing efficiency. Custom workflows can be designed to suit specific business needs, connecting Teams with various Microsoft and third-party applications.

Anticipated Updates and Enhancements

Microsoft continuously evolves its products, and several updates are anticipated to enhance the integration capabilities of Teams with other Microsoft products.

1. Deeper Integration with Microsoft Viva

- Employee Experience: Microsoft Viva is an employee experience platform that integrates with Teams to provide insights, learning opportunities, and well-being resources. Future updates are expected to deepen this integration, making it easier for employees to access Viva features within Teams.

- Viva Insights: Personalized insights from Viva can help employees manage their time better, prioritize tasks, and maintain a healthy work-life balance.

2. Enhanced AI Capabilities

- Microsoft 365 Copilot: Integration with AI-powered tools like Microsoft 365 Copilot can enhance productivity by providing intelligent suggestions, automating routine tasks, and offering data-driven insights.

- AI in Meetings: AI enhancements in Teams meetings, such as real-time transcription, language translation, and sentiment analysis, can improve communication and collaboration.

3. Expanded Integration with Dynamics 365

- CRM and ERP Integration: Deeper integration with Dynamics 365 will enable Teams to be used for customer relationship management (CRM) and enterprise resource planning (ERP) activities. This integration can streamline sales, marketing, and customer service workflows.

- Data Connectivity: Enhanced data connectivity between Teams and Dynamics 365 will allow users to access and analyze business data more effectively.

4. Improved Security and Compliance Features

- Data Governance: Future updates are expected to improve data governance features, ensuring that data shared within Teams complies with organizational policies and regulatory requirements.

- Security Enhancements: Enhanced security features, such as advanced threat protection and information barriers, will further protect sensitive information and maintain data integrity.

Conclusion

The integration of Microsoft Teams with other Microsoft products is a key factor in its success as a collaboration and productivity tool. These integrations create a unified workspace that enhances collaboration, communication, and workflow efficiency. With continuous updates and enhancements, Microsoft Teams is poised to become an even more powerful platform, enabling organizations to adapt to the evolving demands of the modern workplace. By leveraging these integrations, users can maximize the potential of Microsoft Teams and drive their teams towards greater productivity and success.

10.1.3 Innovations in Collaboration Technology

As the landscape of work continues to evolve, so too does the technology that supports it. Microsoft Teams is at the forefront of these innovations, continually integrating cutting-edge features and tools to enhance collaboration and productivity. This section explores the exciting innovations in collaboration technology that Microsoft Teams is incorporating and the potential impact these advancements may have on how teams work together.

1. Artificial Intelligence (AI) and Machine Learning Integration

Artificial Intelligence (AI) and machine learning are transforming the way we work, and Microsoft Teams is leveraging these technologies to provide smarter, more efficient collaboration tools. Some of the key AI-driven features include:

- Meeting Insights and Transcriptions: AI can transcribe meetings in real-time, providing searchable transcripts that make it easier to revisit key points and decisions. This feature enhances accessibility and ensures that important information is not lost.

- Automated Meeting Notes and Action Items: AI can identify and highlight key discussion points and action items during meetings, automatically generating summaries and follow-up tasks. This reduces the administrative burden on team members and ensures that follow-up actions are clearly defined.

- Personalized Assistance: AI-driven personal assistants within Teams can help schedule meetings, find files, and provide reminders about upcoming deadlines. These virtual assistants can learn user preferences and habits, providing increasingly relevant support over time.

2. Enhanced Virtual and Augmented Reality (VR/AR) Experiences

Virtual and augmented reality technologies are making their way into mainstream collaboration tools. Microsoft Teams is exploring the integration of VR and AR to create more immersive and interactive meeting experiences:

- Virtual Meeting Spaces: Teams can use VR to create virtual meeting rooms where participants can interact in a 3D environment. This can enhance the sense of presence and engagement, particularly for remote teams.

- AR Collaboration Tools: AR can be used to overlay digital information onto the physical world. For example, team members can use AR glasses to view and interact with 3D models during product development meetings.

3. Advanced Analytics and Reporting

Data-driven decision-making is becoming increasingly important in the workplace. Microsoft Teams is incorporating advanced analytics and reporting tools to help organizations gain deeper insights into their collaboration patterns and productivity:

- Usage Analytics: Detailed reports on how teams are using Microsoft Teams, including data on meeting frequency, chat activity, and file sharing, can help organizations understand collaboration trends and identify areas for improvement.

- Employee Well-being Metrics: Analytics can also provide insights into employee well-being by tracking metrics such as meeting overload, response times, and work-life balance indicators. These insights can inform policies and practices that promote healthier work environments.

4. Improved Security and Compliance Features

As collaboration platforms become central to business operations, the need for robust security and compliance features grows. Microsoft Teams is continually enhancing its security and compliance capabilities to protect sensitive information and ensure regulatory compliance:

- Advanced Threat Protection: Enhanced threat detection and response tools can identify and mitigate potential security risks, such as phishing attacks and data breaches, in real-time.

- Data Loss Prevention (DLP): Advanced DLP features can prevent sensitive information from being shared outside the organization. This includes the ability to detect and block the sharing of sensitive data in messages and files.

- Compliance Enhancements: Tools for auditing, eDiscovery, and legal hold are being improved to help organizations meet their regulatory obligations. This includes more granular control over data retention and the ability to quickly respond to compliance requests.

5. Seamless Integration with Other Microsoft Products

Microsoft Teams is designed to work seamlessly with other Microsoft products, and this integration is continually being enhanced to provide a more cohesive and efficient user experience:

- Microsoft 365 Integration: Deeper integration with Microsoft 365 tools such as Outlook, OneDrive, and SharePoint ensures that users can access and collaborate on documents, emails, and calendars without leaving Teams.

- Power Platform Integration: Integration with Microsoft Power Platform (Power BI, PowerApps, and Power Automate) allows users to create custom applications, automate workflows, and generate detailed reports directly within Teams.

- Dynamics 365 Integration: For organizations using Dynamics 365, Teams offers enhanced collaboration features that allow users to work on customer relationship management (CRM) and enterprise resource planning (ERP) tasks directly within the Teams environment.

6. Enhanced User Experience and Accessibility

Microsoft is committed to creating an inclusive and user-friendly experience for all Teams users. Ongoing improvements focus on making the platform more intuitive and accessible:

- User Interface Improvements: Continuous refinements to the user interface make Teams easier to navigate and use. This includes simplifying menus, enhancing search functionality, and providing more customization options.

- Accessibility Features: New accessibility features, such as improved screen reader support, keyboard shortcuts, and high-contrast modes, ensure that Teams is usable by individuals with diverse abilities.

7. Integration with Emerging Technologies

Microsoft Teams is also exploring the integration of emerging technologies to stay ahead of the curve and provide cutting-edge collaboration tools:

- Blockchain for Secure Transactions: Blockchain technology can be used to enhance the security and transparency of transactions and communications within Teams. This is particularly useful for industries that require high levels of data integrity and auditability.

- Internet of Things (IoT): Integration with IoT devices can enable new collaboration possibilities, such as real-time data sharing from connected devices and sensors. For example, manufacturing teams can monitor production equipment and collaborate on maintenance tasks directly within Teams.

8. Customization and Extensibility

Recognizing that every organization has unique needs, Microsoft Teams is becoming increasingly customizable and extensible:

- Custom App Development: Organizations can develop custom apps and extensions tailored to their specific workflows and processes. This includes using Teams' development tools and APIs to create bespoke solutions.

- Third-Party App Integration: The Teams App Store continues to expand, offering a growing library of third-party apps that can be integrated into Teams to enhance functionality and streamline workflows.

Conclusion

The future of Microsoft Teams is bright, with a focus on integrating innovative technologies to create a more efficient, secure, and user-friendly collaboration platform. As AI, VR/AR, advanced analytics, and other emerging technologies continue to evolve, Microsoft Teams is poised to lead the way in transforming how teams work together. By staying ahead of these trends and continually enhancing its features, Microsoft Teams is not only adapting to the changing needs of the modern workplace but also driving the future of collaboration technology.

10.3 Final Thoughts

10.3.1 The Impact of Microsoft Teams

Introduction

Microsoft Teams has rapidly evolved into one of the most crucial tools for modern collaboration and communication. Since its launch, it has revolutionized how teams work together, breaking down geographical barriers and creating a seamless platform for sharing information, ideas, and resources. This section explores the profound impact Microsoft Teams has had on various aspects of organizational operations, from enhancing productivity to fostering a collaborative culture.

Transforming Communication

Microsoft Teams has significantly transformed how organizations communicate. By integrating chat, video conferencing, and voice calls into one platform, it has streamlined communication processes. This integration ensures that team members can choose the most appropriate communication method for their needs, whether it's a quick chat for a brief question, a voice call for a more in-depth discussion, or a video conference for a face-to-face meeting.

The introduction of these diverse communication methods within a single platform has reduced the reliance on emails, which can often be time-consuming and less immediate. Teams' real-time messaging capabilities facilitate instant responses and quick decision-making, which are crucial for maintaining momentum in fast-paced work environments. Additionally, the ability to create group chats and channels dedicated to specific projects or topics ensures that conversations are organized and easily accessible.

Enhancing Collaboration

One of the most significant impacts of Microsoft Teams is its ability to enhance collaboration. Teams brings together various Microsoft 365 tools, such as Word, Excel, PowerPoint, and OneNote, into a single interface. This integration allows team members to collaborate on documents in real-time, ensuring that everyone is on the same page and can contribute simultaneously.

Collaboration is further enhanced by Teams' ability to integrate with numerous third-party apps and services. These integrations enable teams to customize their workspace to suit their specific needs, incorporating tools that streamline workflows and increase efficiency. For instance, project management tools like Trello or Asana can be integrated into Teams, allowing users to manage tasks and deadlines without leaving the platform.

The collaborative features of Teams are not limited to internal use. Organizations can invite external partners, clients, and vendors to join Teams meetings and channels, facilitating seamless collaboration across organizational boundaries. This capability is particularly valuable in today's interconnected business environment, where collaboration with external stakeholders is often essential.

Boosting Productivity

Microsoft Teams has been a game-changer in boosting productivity. By centralizing communication and collaboration tools, Teams minimizes the time spent switching between different applications. This centralization not only saves time but also reduces the cognitive load on users, allowing them to focus more on their tasks.

The platform's task management capabilities, such as Planner and To-Do, help users keep track of their responsibilities and deadlines. These tools integrate seamlessly with the rest of the Teams ecosystem, providing a holistic view of all tasks and ensuring that nothing falls through the cracks. Moreover, the ability to set reminders and notifications ensures that users stay on top of their work.

Teams' integration with Microsoft's suite of productivity tools also means that data and documents are easily accessible. Users can quickly search for files, conversations, and other resources, reducing the time spent looking for information. This ease of access is further enhanced by Teams' robust search functionality, which allows users to find information across all channels and conversations quickly.

Fostering a Collaborative Culture

Beyond the technical benefits, Microsoft Teams has played a crucial role in fostering a collaborative culture within organizations. By providing a platform where team members can easily share ideas, feedback, and resources, Teams encourages a more open and inclusive work environment. This cultural shift is essential for driving innovation and ensuring that all voices are heard.

The use of channels dedicated to specific projects or interests helps create communities within the organization. These communities foster a sense of belonging and encourage team members to collaborate and support each other. Additionally, the use of @mentions and threaded conversations ensures that everyone involved in a discussion is kept in the loop, promoting transparency and accountability.

Teams' ability to facilitate virtual social interactions, such as virtual coffee breaks or team-building activities, is also significant. These interactions are vital for maintaining team cohesion, especially in remote work environments where face-to-face interactions are limited. By providing a space for informal conversations, Teams helps maintain the social fabric of the organization.

Supporting Remote and Hybrid Work

The COVID-19 pandemic has accelerated the adoption of remote and hybrid work models, and Microsoft Teams has been at the forefront of this shift. The platform's robust remote work capabilities have enabled organizations to transition smoothly to remote work, ensuring business continuity and productivity.

Teams' video conferencing features have been particularly valuable in maintaining communication and collaboration during the pandemic. The ability to conduct virtual meetings with features such as screen sharing, virtual backgrounds, and breakout rooms has ensured that remote teams can stay connected and collaborate effectively. Additionally, the platform's integration with Microsoft's security and compliance tools ensures that remote work is conducted securely.

Hybrid work, which combines remote and in-office work, has also been supported by Teams. The platform's flexibility allows team members to work from anywhere, ensuring that they can stay productive regardless of their location. Features such as mobile access and offline mode further enhance the platform's suitability for hybrid work environments.

Driving Innovation

Microsoft Teams has been instrumental in driving innovation within organizations. By providing a platform that facilitates seamless collaboration and communication, Teams enables teams to brainstorm, share ideas, and develop innovative solutions more effectively. The integration of tools such as Whiteboard and OneNote allows for creative brainstorming sessions and the capture of ideas in real-time.

The platform's ability to integrate with various third-party apps and services also supports innovation. Teams can be customized to include tools and workflows that align with an organization's specific needs, fostering an environment where new ideas can flourish. This customization capability ensures that Teams can evolve with the organization, supporting continuous improvement and innovation.

Improving Employee Engagement and Satisfaction

Employee engagement and satisfaction are critical for organizational success, and Microsoft Teams has had a positive impact on both. By providing a platform that supports seamless communication and collaboration, Teams helps employees feel more connected and engaged with their work and colleagues.

The platform's ability to facilitate virtual social interactions and team-building activities also contributes to employee satisfaction. These interactions help maintain a sense of community and support, which is especially important in remote and hybrid work environments. Additionally, the ability to easily access information and collaborate with colleagues helps reduce stress and frustration, contributing to overall job satisfaction.

Conclusion

In conclusion, Microsoft Teams has had a profound impact on modern organizations. Its ability to transform communication, enhance collaboration, boost productivity, and foster a collaborative culture has made it an indispensable tool for businesses of all sizes. The platform's support for remote and hybrid work, along with its role in driving innovation and improving employee engagement, further underscores its significance.

As organizations continue to navigate the evolving work landscape, Microsoft Teams will remain a critical component of their toolkit. By embracing the platform's features and capabilities, organizations can unlock new levels of productivity, collaboration, and innovation, ensuring their success in the digital age.

10.3.2 Conclusion

As we conclude our journey through ***"Mastering Microsoft Teams: A Comprehensive Guide,"*** *we hope you have gained valuable insights into the powerful capabilities of Microsoft Teams. This tool is more than just a platform for communication; it's a robust solution for collaboration, project management, remote work, education, and much more. By leveraging the features and best practices outlined in this guide, you can enhance productivity, streamline workflows, and foster a collaborative environment in your organization.*

Remember, the true power of Microsoft Teams lies in its ability to bring people together, no matter where they are, and to provide a seamless, integrated experience for all your communication and collaboration needs. As you continue to explore and use Microsoft Teams, stay curious and open to learning new ways to maximize its potential.

We encourage you to revisit this guide as needed, whether you're troubleshooting an issue, exploring advanced features, or looking for tips to improve your team's efficiency. The world of technology is always evolving, and so is Microsoft Teams. Keep an eye out for updates and new features that can further enhance your experience.

Thank you for embarking on this journey with us. We wish you success in all your collaborative endeavors.

Acknowledgements

We extend our heartfelt gratitude to all our readers for choosing "Mastering Microsoft Teams: A Comprehensive Guide." Your support and trust mean the world to us. This book was crafted with the aim of helping you unlock the full potential of Microsoft Teams, and we hope it has served as a valuable resource in your professional or personal journey.

We would also like to thank the dedicated team of professionals who contributed to the creation of this guide. Their expertise and hard work have been instrumental in bringing this project to life.

Finally, to the Microsoft Teams community and the developers behind this remarkable tool, thank you for your continuous innovation and commitment to improving how we communicate and collaborate.

We appreciate your feedback and would love to hear about your experiences with Microsoft Teams. Feel free to share your thoughts and suggestions with us. Together, we can continue to grow and make the most of the collaborative opportunities that lie ahead.

Thank you once again, and happy teaming!

www.ingramcontent.com/pod-product-compliance
Lightning Source LLC
LaVergne TN
LVHW081329050326
832903LV00024B/1080

* 9 7 9 8 3 3 4 3 4 6 8 4 0 *